Fighting for Immortality

Chris Strange

The opinions expressed in this book are mainly the opinion of the author(s). Boxing like all sport is full of opinions. The intention is to bring out different opinions and raise discussion about the great sport of boxing.

Every effort has been made to trace copyright holders and obtain their permission for the use of any material which may be copyrighted. The author/publisher would be grateful if notified of anything that may be protected by copyright so that it may be corrected in future editions of this book.

ISBN: 9798821338563

Book Cover Design by Emily Rowley

Published by Chris Strange

To Daniel and boxing fans everywhere.

ACKNOWLEDGEMENTS

Thanks to Neil Franks and Barry Cheeseman for their assistance in producing this book.

Thanks to Emily Rowley for the amazing cover artwork.

Fighting for Immortality uncovers the action and back-stories of four huge boxing matches spanning the first two decades of the millennium. Four British boxers cross 'the pond' to fight four top Americans in their own backyard.

The outcome was even. Two British victories, two American victories, including one amazing upset.

CONTENTS

Chapter One

Being a Big, Natural Athlete is Sometimes Not Enough

The Story of Lennox Lewis vs Michael Grant
29th April 2000. Madison Square Garden
New York, New York, USA.

At the start of the new millennium, according to The Ring magazine*, the top five heavyweights on the planet were Lennox Lewis, Evander Holyfield, Michael Grant, Ike Ibeabuchi and David Tua. British born Lennox Lewis held all the major belts and was the lineal heavyweight champion. He had already drawn with and beaten the number 2 ranked Holyfield (many thought Lewis won both fights) and would cross paths with New Zealander, Tua, in the near future. Meanwhile, Ike Ibeabuchi had been arrested and was on remand for charges that would later see him sent to prison for a considerable length of time.

That left the number three ranked contender, the big, undefeated American, Michael Grant.

Lewis would meet Grant at Madison Square Garden on April 29th, 2000, in the first meaningful heavyweight fight of the century. The first of the new millennium.

The fight itself would last less than two rounds. But its significance is in the back story of the two fighters and the preceding decade in which the fight was forged. It is a tale of great expectations and harsh realities. Of misguided optimism and misjudged analysis. It is also an account of cementing a legacy and continually having to disprove the doubters.

How one man became the best of his generation and an all-time great. Taking the long and often bumpy road littered with potential pitfalls, both fistic and political.

While the other man, having finally found his sporting niche, was driven by the hopes of a nation on a fast track to the top. Only to realise that being a big natural athlete is sometimes not enough in the brutal sport of boxing.

* **Footnote:** The number 6 and 7 ranked fighters were Mike Tyson and Vitali Klitschko. Lewis would face these men in his final two fights, but that was still a few years away.

When a boxer has fought professionally for 11 years and spent half of that time at the top of their trade it can be difficult to find the motivation needed for certain fights. It happens all the time. Great fighters suddenly struggle against lesser opposition. It seems that when a boxer has beaten all of their main challengers there is nothing left to prove. This was the case for Lennox Lewis at the dawn of the new millennium.

Lewis had ended the previous decade on a high. In his final fight of the 1990s Lewis beat Evander Holyfield to become the undisputed king of the heavyweights, winning the WBC, WBA and IBF titles. He was also the lineal heavyweight champion of the world.

Arguably the best heavyweight of the 1990s and certainly the top man in the latter half of that decade, Lewis seemingly had nowhere else to go. Nobody left to fight. Apart, maybe, from one man; 'Iron' Mike Tyson. Lewis was almost 36 years of age and a calm, intelligent boxer. Looking at his record it could be argued that the self-proclaimed 'pugilist specialist' was at a crossroads. An avid chess player, he was the thinking man's pugilist. He knew all too well what can happen to boxers who make the mistake of hanging on too long. History is full of ageing champions taking on the younger, up and coming generation, only to get hurt in the process. Should he continue in the dangerous sport of boxing in the hope of securing that elusive big finale or should he retire?

On the other hand, Lewis was the undisputed champion of the world who had beaten that old warrior Evander Holyfield. Maybe he was still hungry. Hungry to prove he could defend that undisputed status and swat the challenge from any young upstart.

Michael Grant was at a different stage in his career. Younger at 27 year of age and relatively new to the sport. He was going to be the 'Next Big Thing', the man tasked with bringing the heavyweight crown back to the USA. With Riddick Bowe retired, Mike Tyson seemingly suspended as much as he was active and an ageing Holyfield (38 at the time), American boxing fans needed a new name to pin their flag on. That name was Michael Anthony Grant and unfortunately for Grant, he was seen as "The Great American Hope".

The 1990s – Backdrop to the rise of Lennox Lewis

When comparing the heavyweight boxing scene from different decades, the 1990s stands up to any other. It had it all. Great boxers, amazing fights and shocks to rival any era in the history of the sport. We can all debate which was the best decade but the 1990s would be near the top of any boxing enthusiast's list. And it wasn't just the sport. There were also some incredible characters, old and new.

At the start of the 90s the undisputed heavyweight champion was 'Iron' Mike Tyson. At the end of the 90s the undisputed champion would be Lennox Lewis. Yet, due to a combination of outlandish behaviour (on Tyson's part) and boxing politics, the two never met in the ring during that decade.

The first big fight of the decade saw 'Iron' Mike Tyson losing in spectacular style to James 'Buster' Douglas in what has been widely referred to as the biggest upset in boxing history. That label is a little harsh on James Douglas who was at an emotional peak just a few weeks after his mother's death. Douglas had accumulated a decent résumé and was ranked 7th best heavyweight by Ring magazine. He was also in great shape when he met Tyson in Tokyo, Japan. It is fair to say that particular version of James Douglas, in that exact snapshot in time, would have been competitive against any heavyweight champion from any era.

Despite possessing a full range of powerful shots, the biggest weapon in Mike Tyson's arsenal was fear. Many opponents had lost before stepping through the ropes. But because of recent events in his life James Douglas didn't care and feared nothing, thereby neutralising Tyson's primary weapon. To put it simply, Douglas, galvanised and fully focussed by the loss of his mother, fought the fight of his life.

4

Although Tyson had his moments, even flooring Douglas in round 8, it was the underdog who controlled the action. When Tyson was knocked down in the 10th round the images of him fumbling to find his gumshield while being counted out sent shockwaves through the boxing world.

The fight was supposed to be a warm-up for a much-hyped clash with Evander Holyfield. 'The Real Deal' Holyfield had risen to be the number 2 ranked heavyweight after being undisputed cruiserweight champion. The two fighters would not meet for a number of years for a variety of bizarre reasons. Only two years later Tyson would be sentenced to six years in prison for rape. (He would be released in 1995 after serving 3 years.)

Meanwhile, Holyfield would become the first fighter to unify both cruiser and heavyweight divisions when he took the belts from Douglas. Visibly not the same fighter who had dominated Tyson, it was Douglas' first and only defence. James Douglas didn't fight again for almost six years (1996). Then in 1997 he had five fights in seven months. Douglas won all six bouts against average opposition. He fought twice in 1998 winning one and losing to Lou Savarese via a first-round knockout.

The man who had started the decade with the shock KO victory over Mike Tyson, ended the nineties (and his career) with another KO win against the American Andre Crowder. While the Tyson victory came against a ferocious fighter unbeaten in 37 bouts, the finale in February 1999, was against a man (Crowder) who had lost six times as many fights as he had won.

To make matters more compelling, the affable 'Big' George Foreman made an unbelievable comeback in the 1990s to regain the title at the age of 45 years of age becoming the oldest ever heavyweight champion. Foreman had been steadily rebuilding his resumé through the late 1980s. He suffered two losses in the early 90s to Evander Holyfield and later to Tommy Morrison. Following the Morrison defeat Foreman knocked out the WBA and IBF champion Michael Moorer. This victory also made Foreman the lineal heavyweight champion, an honorary title he would hold until his last ever fight. Foreman's stunning victory was also about to set the division on the path to disarray.

At the end of 1994 the 45-year-old Foreman was the lineal champion and held the WBA and IBF belts. The unfancied Oliver McCall had risen almost from nowhere to become the WBC champion. The division was wide open. Add to this the fact that Evander Holyfield was coming out of his temporary retirement, with Mike Tyson due to be released from prison early 1995; things were about to get interesting.

Characters...

Evander Holyfield's victory over James Douglas was not a surprise. Holyfield was a revered Cruiserweight and had put together an impressive run of six wins at heavyweight stopping all six opponents. Some of whom were well established names on the heavyweight scene such as Pinklon Thomas, James Tillis and Michael Dokes. After beating Douglas to become the unified champion Holyfield made three defences against much older but still capable warriors; stopping Bert Cooper and unanimous decisions over Larry Holmes and 'Big' George Foreman.

The expectation was that Holyfield would fight Tyson but when life outside of the ring took over Tyson's life and he was being sent to prison, Holyfield took on Riddick 'Big Daddy' Bowe. Much smaller than Bowe, Holyfield still gave a good account of himself but lost on points.

At the same time Lennox Lewis fought and defeated Donavon 'Razor' Ruddock in London, England. This had all been organised as a four-man tournament. The winners of each bout would meet to find out who really was the number one heavyweight. Bowe was now the unified champion and was expected to face the WBC number one contender in Lewis, but instead relinquished the belt. The WBC declared Lewis their champion and awarded him the belt.

After two successful defences of the WBA and IBF versions of the heavyweight title, Bowe fought Holyfield again and this time 'The Real Deal' won the judges' decision.

Holyfield lost the WBA and IBF titles less than six months after regaining them. He lost to Michael Moorer in his next fight in April 1994, paving the way for 'Big' George Foreman to make another unlikely appearance in a world title fight. After the Moorer fight Holyfield went to hospital where he was diagnosed with a heart condition. This forced him into a temporary retirement for almost a year before he passed a medical and was cleared to box again. He made his comeback against the (always) tough Ray Mercer in May

1995. Holyfield not only beat Mercer, on points, but also became the first man to knock him down.

Through the first half of the decade Holyfield and Bowe went on to produce what was one of the best heavyweight trilogies of all time.

Michael Moorer was yet another boxer unable to hold on to the titles for very long. Just over six months after defeating Holyfield, Moorer lost in his first defence to 'Big' George Foreman in an upset to rival the Douglas-Tyson fight. When the well-liked Foreman knocked out Moorer in the 10th round the result was as popular as it was shocking. It also led to another fragmentation of the "world" titles.

Tommy 'The Duke' Morrison was already a known fighter at the start of the decade. But after recording 19 straight wins with no defeats, Morrison attracted the attention of Sylvester Stallone who picked Morrison to appear as fictional fighter 'Tommy Gunn' in his latest instalment in the Rocky film franchise.

In his 20th professional outing Morrison fought Lorenzo Canady in a Bob Arum promotion in West Orange, New Jersey. Morrison was accompanied to the ring by actors Sylvester Stallone and Burt Young, with the intention being to use some of this real-life footage to put into the film Rocky V. Unfortunately, instead of the big knockout they were all expecting, Morrison felt the pressure and fought a nervous and sloppy fight. Canady on the other hand seemed content to grapple and spoil rather than risk being knocked out. Morrison suffered a small cut under his right eye, and there were boos from some of the crowd as a result was read out.

Morrison even wore the trunks that Apollo Creed gave Rocky for his rematch against Clubber Lang (in Rocky III) and Morrison's cornermen even wore "Tommy Gunn" shirts during the fight which are clearly seen in between rounds. During the fight Stallone and Bert Young, playing their characters Rocky and Paulie, made good footage standing in a corner of the ring shouting encouragement and instructions to Tommy as he fought a real heavyweight fight throwing and receiving real heavyweight punches. Stallone even jumps into the ring at the end of the fight as if he was Morrison's real trainer and helped him into a robe with the name "Tommy Gunn" on the back. All very surreal.

On November 8th, 1990, Morrison recorded his 24th win, and was still undefeated. Despite his already noteworthy record Morrison would become a household name after the Rocky V film was released less than a week later.

'The Duke' alias was in honour of his great uncle, John Wayne (real name Marion Morrison). Tommy had a fan-friendly, gung-ho style and began to make inroads in the division, making the Ring magazine top ten rankings. Morrison was always in exciting fights, going toe to toe with the likes of Ray Mercer, George Foreman and Lennox Lewis. The Foreman fight was for the then lightly regarded, vacant WBO heavyweight title. For once Morrison kept his composure and was far more cautious than usual, aware of Foreman's phenomenal punching power. He outpointed 'Big' George and briefly became a heavyweight champion. Following that win Morrison had several fights against lower ranked heavyweights before beating Donavon Ruddock in a sensational slugfest in June 1995. That victory set up the match with Lennox Lewis, in which Lewis knocked Morrison out in round 6.

Shortly after that KO loss to Lewis, Morrison fought once more in 1996 then tested positive for HIV. He was no longer allowed to box, but in 2007 he tested negative for HIV four times and made two more appearances. It remains a mystery whether or not Morrison was infected with HIV or not, but the doubts and suspicions meant that he could not get a licence to fight and that meant that his boxing career was effectively over.

Morrison was regularly in trouble with the law due to his drug and alcohol abuse and spent a couple of years in prison. His record stands at a very respectable 48 wins (42 by KO), 3 losses and one draw. He died in 2013 due to multi organ failure at the age of only 44.

The extremely durable Ray 'Merciless' Mercer was one of Lennox Lewis's toughest opponents and deserves a mention here.

At the time he fought Lewis, Mercer had lost only three fights, two of which were points defeats to all-time great fighters in Larry Holmes and Evander Holyfield. The other loss was to Jesse Ferguson in February of 1993, which Mercer avenged nine months later, after winning another fight only one month earlier. The fight with Holyfield, although a unanimous decision, was a close contest with Holyfield winning by only one round on one of the scorecards. Meanwhile the loss to Lewis was by majority decision – one judge scoring it a draw while the other two had Lewis only one round ahead at the final bell. Indeed, there were some boxing aficionados who thought Mercer beat Lewis. While Lennox Lewis was the super-heavyweight 1988 Olympic champion, Ray Mercer won the heavyweight gold at the same games.

After back-to-back losses to Holyfield and Lewis, Mercer won a unanimous points decision over the perennial 1980s contender Tim Witherspoon. He then amassed six quick KO victories against average opposition before facing Wladimir Klitschko in June 2002. Mercer still possessed that solid chin.

Klitschko knocked Mercer down in round one, only the second knockdown in Mercer's career (at that point) and threatened to finish the fight extremely early. Mercer somehow hung on and managed to reach round 6 despite being hit regularly and solidly by the big Ukrainian. The referee saved Mercer from what was becoming a severe beating in the 6th round. It was the first stoppage loss on his record. Wladimir Klitschko deserves a lot of credit for halting Mercer; something Holmes, Holyfield and Lewis could not do. Perhaps the key to this fight was the age difference. At 41 years of age Mercer was 15 years Klitschko's senior. Not dissimilar to the age gap between the Ukrainian and Anthony Joshua when they met 10 years later. (See Chapter 4)

Ray Mercer fought the best in two eras and still goes largely unrecognised for his boxing achievements. He did, however, manage to win the WBO version of the heavyweight title in 1991, beating Italian Francesco Damiani by ninth round KO when the

WBO title was in its infancy. Mercer defended the WBO title once only in a fantastic fight with Tommy Morrison in October 1991. Both men were unbeaten with 45 wins between them and a combined knockout ratio of 80%. Morrison started fast and for the first three rounds caught Mercer with some huge shots. But Morrison slowed in the fourth round and Mercer began the fifth as the aggressor. After only a few seconds of the round Morrison was in trouble. With the ropes holding him up he was utterly defenceless as Mercer hit him with about ten clean shots. Boxing fans love to see knockouts but fully understand the dangers. It was a brutal knockout that left many fans wondering why the referee took so long to step in between the two fighters.

Rather than defend the WBO title for a second time against Michael Moorer, the then mandatory challenger, Mercer vacated the WBO title for what was probably a more lucrative, and certainly higher profile, fight with Larry Holmes.

Another interesting character in the mix was Oliver McCall. He had a record of 24-5 when he was given the chance to fight Lennox Lewis for the WBC title in 1994. Three of his losses were to good boxers in Orlin Norris, Tony Tucker and one James Douglas. It seemed whenever he faced an above average opponent, he came up short. Maybe that was what Lennox Lewis' handlers thought. After three successful defences of his crown, Lewis was set to get the recognition he deserved. Not only was he emerging from the shadows of Holyfield and Bowe, but the elusive Bowe fight looked set for the following year. Three months before the McCall bout the press was reporting that the Bowe fight had been agreed. While his training should have been fully focussed on Oliver McCall, Lewis clearly had one eye on his nemesis, Riddick Bowe.

It seemed that Lewis was committing the cardinal sin: Looking past his next opponent. That is not to take any credit away from McCall. He did what many an underdog has done and will continue to do. He seized his chance. In this case he saw the opening that his trainer Emanuel Steward told him would be there.

In between losing his title to McCall and regaining the belt in their rematch, Lewis fought four times. Three of those bouts took place in 1995. First, he took on American Lionel Butler in Sacramento, USA in what was supposed to be a WBC title eliminator. Then he fought Australian Justin Fortune in Ireland. Lewis won both inside the distance in 5 and 4 rounds respectively. Then came a 6-round war with the exciting Tommy Morrison in Atlantic City, New Jersey.

Lewis fought only once in 1996 in May, when he faced the tough Ray Mercer in Madison Square Garden. Lewis managed to grind out a majority decision over the durable Mercer. On the undercard of that fight was the young Michael Grant winning his eighteenth straight victory against fellow American and relatively unknown Olian Alexander. Grant won by 4th round TKO.

When McCall met Lewis in their return match for the vacant WBC title in February 1997, he was clearly having some kind of mental health problems. After refusing to fight and turning his back on Lewis for several rounds, the referee stopped the fight. McCall had also refused to sit between rounds pacing around the ring and even breaking into tears. After the fight, in a bizarre interview with the press, McCall tried to claim that he was trying a kind of 'rope-a-dope' technique – a reference to that famous Ali-Foreman fight in 1974. Trying to lull Lewis into some kind of trap. He also explained that he wanted to get as emotional as possible and that is why he had cried. After the fight McCall was suspended from boxing and his purse – a substantial $3 million - was withheld. More importantly, shortly afterwards, he was committed to a mental hospital where he stayed until September 1997.

In a strange twist of fate, Oliver McCall would fight on the undercard when Lennox Lewis regained the heavyweight title for a second time. (Lewis thrashing the only other man to beat him, Hasim Rahman.) The year was 2004 and McCall beat Henry Akinwande by KO to bring him right back into the world heavyweight rankings. It wasn't to be however, and although McCall boxed until as late as 2019, several drug busts and violence against the police saw him spend more than one stint behind bars.

It is impossible to say how good he could have been if drugs and mental issues had not clouded his best fighting years.

At the end of the millennium The Ring magazine heavyweight rankings had a Nigerian born boxer at number 4. Ike Ibeabuchi, standing at 6 foot 2 inches (188cm), was a muscular specimen of a man. He had amassed a record of 20 wins (15 by KO) with no defeats. In 1997 he had knocked out the tough David Tua. Something Lennox Lewis did not manage, despite dominating Tua in their encounter a few years later.

Ibeabuchi was a vicious, hard-hitting slugger in the style of a latter-day Sonny Liston. He had risen up the ranks since the Tua victory but the fight that gave him the number 4 spot in the rankings was a convincing victory over Chris Byrd in March 1999. Byrd was a competent and quick boxer who was climbing the rankings with an impressive 26-0 record. Byrd would go on to beat several big names including Vitali Klitschko to win the then lesser regarded WBO version of the heavyweight title. A title he would hold for only six months when he was beaten by Vitali's younger brother Wladimir. Byrd would also score big career wins against David Tua and Evander Holyfield.

That victory against Byrd was to be Ibeabuchi's last fight. Boxing fans were about to discover what many boxing insiders already knew. Ike Ibeabuchi had a much darker side.

Just three months after his 20th straight win in the ring Ibeabuchi was staying at the Mirage Hotel and Casino in Las Vegas. He phoned an escort service and had a woman sent to his room. The woman said she was only there to strip and demanded to be paid up front. She claimed Ibeabuchi then attacked her. He then barricaded himself in the bathroom when police were called. They reportedly had to discharge pepper spray under the door in order to force him to surrender.

Several similar charges soon emerged. The District Attorney raised similar allegations from eight months earlier, this time in the Treasure Island Hotel and Casino. Then two more similar allegations emerged from Arizona state. Ibeabuchi was judged to have a bipolar disorder. He was treated with medication and eight months later was deemed capable of making a plea. Ibeabuchi entered an 'Alford plea', - pleading guilty without admitting guilt. This meant that he would avoid going to trial but was instead sentenced directly. He was charged with two separate crimes which led to a total sentence of between 3 to 20 years.

While in prison Ibeabuchi gained several college qualifications including business and management as well as a paralegal certificate.

There were many rumours of erratic behaviour as he rose through the ranks, including the time he supposedly turned down a million-dollar contract to fight Michael Grant in a proposed title eliminator (to fight Lewis). He was reported to believe that his alias 'The President' was in fact his true status. He believed he was worth much more than the one-million-dollar purse. He subsequently lost out on that fight when Grant instead went on to fight Golota. If he had taken the Grant fight deal, he (Ibeabuchi) not Grant, could have gone on to fight Lennox Lewis. Many believe he could have been a world champion and even future hall of famer. But his mental issues dictated a different path for his tragic career.

Ibeabuchi was released in 2015 but was arrested again in 2016 due to a parole violation for crimes going back as far as 2003 in Arizona. The situation was further confused as he had applied for a green card and citizenship papers while his native Nigeria refused to give him papers to travel. He was effectively stuck in limbo and was detained. He had even planned a comeback even though he was now in his mid-forties.

Ike Ibeabuchi's boxing career was well and truly finished but he remained unbeaten.

An interesting statistic emerged from the Ike Ibeabuchi vs David Tua fight. By the final bell, Ibeabuchi and Tua had combined to throw 1,730 punches, breaking the heavyweight record set by Muhammad Ali and Joe Frazier in their third fight ('The Thriller in Manilla'), when they totalled 1,591 punches — in 14 rounds, two rounds more than Ibeabuchi and Tua had fought. Ike threw 975 punches, the most ever by a single heavyweight in a 12-round fight.

The heavyweight landscape was relatively straight forward for the first half of the 90s. It was in the latter half of the decade that the scene became rather disjointed. Since James Douglas shocked the sporting world in February 1990 up to 1995, the WBA and IBF titles changed hands five times. Twice passing through the capable fists of 'The Real Deal' Evander Holyfield. When 'Big' George shocked the boxing world in November of 1994, then refused to fight either of the two sanctioning bodies' mandatory challengers, it led to the crowning of two of the most unlikely heavyweight champions in Bruce Seldon (WBA) and Francois Botha (IBF).

Sheldon had crept into the reckoning very much under the radar having had 34 fights including only three losses to top names in Bowe, McCall and the fast handed but large girthed Tony Tubbs. Sheldon took the vacant WBA title beating Tony Tucker; when the fight was stopped in the 7th round due to Tucker's eye being swollen shut. That WBA title fight was on the undercard of Oliver McCall's first WBC title defence (since taking the title from Lewis) against the much older – but still game - Larry Holmes.

In December of 1995 the IBF title was contested in Germany between the mandatory number one contender Axel Schultz and Francois Botha. Schultz had already been beaten by Foreman eight months earlier, but the majority decision was so controversial that the IBF wanted them to fight again. 'Big' George declined and so the IBF stripped him of their title. Botha won a close points decision, but it was later found that he had tested positive for a banned substance. The result was later ruled a "No Contest" and six months later Axel Schultz would fight for the third time in a row for the IBF title, losing yet again. This time to a more highly rated fighter in Michael Moorer.

Interestingly, only a month before Shultz fought Botha for a world title, the conclusion of the Bowe-Holyfield trilogy took place in Las Vegas with no titles on the line.

The WBC title also changed hands five times in the same period. However, this line involved Riddick Bowe giving up the WBC belt to avoid facing Lennox Lewis. Lewis was actually declared WBC champion based on his October 1992 win over Donavon 'Razor' Ruddock. Lewis successfully defended the WBC title three times (including a KO win over Frank Bruno in an all-British affair in Cardiff, Wales) before losing it to Oliver McCall in another huge boxing upset. McCall defended the title once, beating another comeback oldie, 'The Easton Assassin' himself Larry Holmes. McCall then promptly lost the belt to Frank Bruno.

In March 1995 Mike Tyson was released from prison and was fighting again by August. With Lewis, Bowe and Moorer all still active plus Evander Holyfield returning from a temporary retirement, at the close of 1995 the list of heavyweight champions looked just as unlikely as 'Buster' Douglas taking all three belts from Tyson at the start of the decade. Frank Bruno (WBC), Bruce Seldon (WBA) and Francois Botha (IBF). Meanwhile, 46-year-old George Foreman was still the lineal champion.

To illustrate just how disjointed and confusing it had become, by the end of 1995; the reigning WBA champion (the almost anonymous Bruce Seldon) and the WBC champion Frank Bruno both failed to make the top 5 in Ring magazine's rankings. Meanwhile Tyson had been released from prison and had two very quick KO victories. Iron Mike, Holyfield, Bowe and Lewis all made the top five with Bowe still being considered the best heavyweight even though he did not hold any of the belts.

In March 1996 Tyson beat Frank Bruno in only his 3rd fight since being released from prison and was once again the heavyweight champion (WBC). In September of the same year Tyson began unifying the belts by taking the WBA strap from Seldon. The fight was widely decried as a fix when Seldon appeared to go down when a 'punch' barely grazed over his head. It mattered not as most people, not even boxing fans, can barely remember this fighter. He would go on to fight eleven more times but never again reaching the dizzy heights of world title bouts. Seldon had played his part in the Tyson saga and the titles were once again being unified.

Lennox Lewis was the WBC's mandatory challenger, but business dealings and politics would conspire against him so that Lewis would not meet Tyson until 2002. Promoter Don King had allegedly paid Lewis a $4million "step aside fee" to not challenge Tyson. Instead, Tyson finally met Evander Holyfield in the ring in November 1996. This championship contest had been a long time in the making. It had been pencilled in three times over the past 6 years. First it was derailed when James Douglas unexpectedly KO'd Tyson to take the titles. Then when Holyfield had beaten Douglas, Tyson suffered a rib injury that postponed the fight. Later, at the third attempt, Tyson was jailed.

Tyson relinquished the WBC title, so this bout was only for the WBA belt. It made no difference. This was one the fans wanted to see.

Holyfield weathered the usual early Tyson onslaught before turning the tables and bullying the champion. Finally knocking Tyson out in the 11th round.

In June 1997 the pair would meet for what turned out to be a short and extremely bizarre rematch. Holyfield was already getting the better of Tyson in the first two rounds. In the 3rd round, in a clinch, Tyson bit a chunk out of Holyfield's ear. The doctor ruled he could continue but Tyson did it again, spitting out his gumshield to get a better bite. Tyson was disqualified and a melee ensued in the ring. Tyson received an indefinite suspension. However, boxing politics being what they are he was reinstated a year later. The bout infamously came to be known as 'The Bite Fight'.

Meanwhile Michael Moorer made two successful defences of the IBF title before losing it to Evander Holyfield in November 1997.

Before facing Lewis, Andrew Golota had recently out-boxed Riddick Bowe on his previous two outings. Twice in the space of five months. But the big Chicago-based Pole was disqualified in both encounters due to repeatedly throwing low blows. At the time of the disqualifications in both fights, Golota was ahead on all three judges' scorecards even though he had had points deducted. The second fight in December 1996 was an all-out war with both men exchanging huge shots and both men hitting the canvas. Riddick Bowe would not fight again. A few months into 1997 he announced his retirement. He was 29 years old.

Out-boxing Riddick Bowe was something Lennox Lewis always said he would do if they ever met in the ring.

Despite 'losing' both of those Bowe fights Golota must have gained a lot of confidence from the experience. Surely all he needed to do was keep his punches above the belt and he could go on to bigger things.

Golota, entered the square circle fully robed. He looked nervous as he waited for the champion to enter the arena. He had good reason to be nervous. What would happen within the next few minutes would change him as a fighter forever.

Lennox Lewis left the dressing room ready to fight. No robes, not even a T-shirt or towel. Looking every inch the true gladiator; banging his gloves together to the beat of the music as he strutted confidently towards the ring. Staring straight ahead, totally concentrated on the task in hand.

Lewis stepped through the ropes and danced around the ring. As much to the rhythm of his ring walk music as to loosen up. He was relaxed and ready to go the very second that he stepped into the ring. Those 'ready to go' ring-walks were to become a Lewis trademark.

A fully focused Lewis stood almost in the centre of the ring before the first bell sounded. Waiting to pounce. Surprisingly he did not launch an instant attack. He spent most of the opening minute using the left jab to find his range. Then after only 50 seconds, he let fly with both fists and the challenger was in deep trouble. Left and right power shots rained in and down went the big Pole in a neutral corner. He managed to get up but staggered diagonally across the ring to the opposite neutral corner where the referee Joe Cortez gave him extra seconds to recover. It was never going to be enough. Lewis pounded away with every shot landing until Golota slumped in Lewis's own corner. This time he was unable to get up. The fight was over only half-way through the opening round. Now, surely, everyone in America knew how good Lennox Lewis was. Boxing fans stateside were now definitely sitting up and paying attention.

Lewis never managed to secure that grudge fight with his old Olympic rival Riddick Bowe. He did, however, brutally destroy the man who had effectively forced Bowe into retirement. Lewis demolished Golota in a tremendous display of speed, power, timing and accurate punching. Golota never landed a single punch.

Two weeks after Holyfield had unified the WBA and IBF titles, Shannon Briggs outpointed 'Big' George Foreman to become the lineal heavyweight champion. Many believed that Foreman should have won that fight but the judges didn't agree. It was to be 'Big' George's last fight in a very long and very illustrious career. That victory put Briggs on a collision course with Lewis.

Four months later Briggs would fight Lewis in Atlantic City. Lewis was coming off the back of that quick victory against Andrew Golota. The Briggs fight was far more exciting as Briggs made a real go, wobbling the champion, in a to and fro encounter that Lewis ended in the 5th round after flooring Briggs three times in the fight. Lennox Lewis was now the WBC and the lineal heavyweight champion.

By the end of 1998 the picture was much clearer. Evander Holyfield (WBA and IBF champion) and Lennox Lewis (WBC champion and lineal heavyweight champion) were clearly the top two heavyweight boxers.

The following year – the last of the decade, the century and the millennium – would twice see the two boxers face off against each other to decide who was the number one and undisputed heavyweight on the planet.

Lennox Lewis

Lewis was born in West Ham in the east end of London and spent his formative years in England. In 1977 aged 12 he and his mother moved to Kitchener, Ontario, Canada.

He attended Cameron Heights Collegiate Institute high school, and quickly established himself as a natural athlete excelling at Canadian football, (real) football and basketball.

He also took up boxing at the age of 13 and quickly grew into a standout amateur. Five years later in 1983 Lewis won the gold medal at the World Junior Games held in Santo Domingo, Dominican Republic.

A year later aged 18, Lewis represented Canada in the super heavyweight division at the Los Angeles Olympics. He made it through to the quarter finals but lost to Tyrell Biggs of the USA who went on to win the gold medal.

Lewis decided not to turn professional after the Olympics but instead focused on winning the gold at the next Olympics four years later in Seoul, South Korea. He achieved his objective defeating Riddick Bowe in the final.

Lewis didn't want to move to USA and end up under promoters like Don King who had a stranglehold on heavyweight boxing in the US at that time. Canada was not a place to get a big fan base either, so Lewis decided to move back to the country of his birth, Great Britain, under the management of Frank Maloney. He made his professional debut in 1989, less than a year after winning gold in Seoul, and by early 1991 had built an unbeaten record of 14 wins without loss. Only one of those fights going the distance. For his 15th fight Lewis beat the world ranked Gary Mason for the British heavyweight title. From now on Lewis would be fighting known and ranked fighters only. For his 18th contest – and fourth fight in 1991 - Lewis faced the man who had beaten him in the 1984 Olympics, Tyrell Biggs. Lewis dispatched Biggs inside three rounds in what unexpectedly turned out to be a toe-to-toe slugfest.

(Biggs had been in the ring with Mike Tyson and was just coming off a loss to Riddick Bowe.)

That 18th win was in Atlanta, Georgia on the undercard of Evander Holyfield's WBA and IBF title defence against Bert Cooper (another slugfest of 7 rounds). Lewis already had his eye on the prize.

At that time British boxing fans did not immediately take to Lewis. They were suspicious of him. They had reason to be. Afterall this was the man who had boxed for Canada, against Great Britain, in the Olympics.

Over time however they would come to appreciate just how exceptional a boxer he was. By the end of the decade many of those fans would follow him across the pond to the big fights in the USA.

Emanuel Steward was a highly regarded trainer by the time he took on Evander Holyfield for the second fight with Riddick Bowe. Steward had an eye for spotting that one little chink in a fighter's armour that could make all the difference. Sometimes that was something that could be exploited in a split second with a counterpunch. Other times it could be an adjustment of style. Something that was required to nullify your opponent's advantages. Whatever it was Steward had a knack for seeing it. That was the mark of the great trainer.

Steward told Holyfield that he was simply too small to fight Bowe the way he had in their first match. He also told him that Bowe was a better boxer and that his uppercuts would nullify Holyfield's own work on the inside: they had to come up with an alternative fight plan for the rematch or the result would be the same.

He finally found a formula to beat Bowe and that involved Holyfield's movement. Always moving, in and out to take away Bowe's advantages. It worked. Holyfield used the strategy against Bowe in their second encounter and won a majority decision. That fight will probably be remembered more for the "fan man" paragliding into the arena, then onto the ring apron, than for any coaching from Emanuel Steward. None of that mattered however. With Steward's help Holyfield was once again the heavyweight champion.

Holyfield's first defence was against Michael Moorer. Holyfield offered Steward two hundred and fifty thousand dollars to train him for that fight. From a purse of $12 million. It was a mere 2 percent. Holyfield allegedly told Steward that, as heavyweight champion, he could get anyone he wanted to give him water between rounds. Holyfield also told the press that if Emanuel Steward was such a great trainer, then he could find another fighter to train and make them champion. Steward was clearly not happy with being treated so disrespectfully. So, he took Holyfield's advice and off he went and found another fighter to train. As it turned out that fighter was Lennox Lewis. But only after helping Oliver McCall take the WBC belt off Lewis.

Later that same year Don King, who was promoting Oliver McCall, approached Steward to train McCall for his title challenge against Lennox Lewis. After the Holyfield split Steward had enough time on his hands so he took up the offer. In what was a repeat of the Holyfield-Bowe II approach, the trainer explained to McCall that Lewis was bigger, stronger and a better boxer. Steward also told his new charge that despite all that they would find a way to win.

Steward studied Lewis carefully. He noticed that all Lewis's work was based around launching a right hand. He told McCall that they were going to knock him out while he was throwing that right hand. Bingo! He had found that one weakness in Lewis's armour. In the second round, just as Lewis was throwing a right, McCall threw his own. He caught Lewis on the chin and caused one of the biggest upsets in heavyweight history. Oliver McCall, with Steward's help, had become the WBC heavyweight champion.

In the space of five months Emanuel Steward had successfully trained two different underdogs to upset the odds and take two versions of the heavyweight crown. One of them (WBC) was once again back under the control of promoter Don King.

After the fight Lewis parted ways with old trainer Pepe Correa and immediately wanted Steward to train him. Likewise, Steward, seeing the potential in Lewis, immediately expressed interest in wanting to work with the boxer.

He worked on Lewis's technical flaws and emphasised what would soon become his trademark, authoritative jab. Steward went on to train Lennox Lewis for the remainder of his boxing careeer.

After Lewis retired Steward would guide another heavyweight to glory. A boxer who was struggling after two knockout defeats in 12 months. Under Steward's training regime, that boxer would regain his confidence and go on to dominate the heavyweight scene for a decade. That man was Wladimir Klitschko.

Michael Grant

Just over five months after destroying Andrew Golota, Lewis was back in Atlantic City fighting a young rising star and serious contender in Shannon Briggs. Sat in the audience was Michael Grant. The TV cameras picked up on him while all the commentators acknowledged him as a future title challenger. Their paths were now destined to cross. There would be another three title defences for Lewis before then. Two of those were the unification fights against the man most boxing fans considered to be the ultimate warrior, Evander Holyfield.

Around this time Grant himself was no stranger to Atlantic City. He was becoming a regular attraction in the east coast gambling resort. Yet his professional boxing journey was only four years old. It was also anything but conventional. His rapid rise to world heavyweight title challenger is like an idea for a Sylvester Stallone movie. It was also almost by sheer chance.

Grant came to boxing relatively late at the age of 21. His amateur pedigree was nothing compared to that of Lennox Lewis. The champion had started boxing aged thirteen, soon after moving from England to Canada. He had a stand-out amateur career which culminated in that Olympic gold medal. Michael Grant had a minimalist amateur record of only 12 fights, although he only lost one. Because of his late start he was being fast-tracked into the professional ranks. And the heavyweight professional ranks was where the big money was to earned.

Boxers do not have to fight at the Olympics to become great champions. Consider the case of Mexico. A nation with a proud boxing tradition and countless world champions. While most Mexican fighters start off in the amateur ranks, they quickly move on to paid professional bouts. To those who only know a little about the sport, Mexico's Olympic boxing medal tally comes as something of a surprise; a grand total of just 13 medals, two of which were gold. Even Canada, not regarded as a boxing nation, has won more with a total of 17 including three golds – one of which was Lewis's. But Mexican boxing is different; and Michael Grant was not Mexican.

Being such a late starter to boxing does not necessarily mean that a fighter cannot reach the pinnacle. Others had done it in various weight divisions. Consider Sergio Martínez. A former soccer player who did not start boxing seriously till he was 20 years of age. He went on to be a two-weight world champion. In 2010 he received Fighter of the Year awards from both The Ring and the Boxing Writers Association of America, as well as The Ring's Knockout of the Year for his rematch victory against Paul Williams.

Bernard Hopkins only started boxing at the age of 18 while in prison but went on to box professionally for 28 years. He had an incredibly long and successful career boxing until he was 51 (just shy of his 52nd birthday).

Another legendary boxer who started late was the great Rocky Marciano, who supposedly only started seriously at the age of 20.

Ken Norton, the man who gave the great Mohammed Ali so many problems in their three fights, was 24 years of age when he made his professional debut.

Grant was a giant of a man at 6 feet 7 inches and with a physique to match. He was already an accomplished all-round athlete playing basketball, football and baseball at a college near Los Angeles. Despite his sporting prowess his grades were not good enough to gain a sports scholarship and the college let him go. He did not even have a real interest in boxing until he went to Las Vegas with friends in 1993 to watch the Holyfield-Bowe II fight. Boxing was still only his 4th choice sport.

Grant found his way into the ring by pure chance—via a game of chance. In 1993 Las Vegas referee Richard Steele spotted him at a blackjack table at the Golden Nugget. Struck by the young man's size, Steele, who had seen his fair share of big boxers, asked if he'd ever tried boxing. Grant was soon pounding the bag in the Top Rank gym, and Steel made Grant an offer of $200 per day to move to Vegas and train. Steele put Grant in touch with Don Turner, then Holyfield's trainer. The rest, as they say, is history.

After 12 amateur fights Grant made his professional debut in July 1994. He quickly notched up a 22-0 tally with 16 KO's in his first two years as a professional. At this stage in his career it was clear that Grant had a padded record. He had won 22 bouts without facing an opponent with any real quality or anything resembling an eye-catching record. But as he came late to boxing this was perhaps excusable. The quality of opposition however was about to go up.

1997 was a big year for Grant as he got national exposure by going 4-0 in meaningful fights. Two were KO's, including big knockout wins over Al 'Ice' Cole and Jorge Luis Gonzalez. As important as the quality of the wins, Grant was being nationally televised (on ESPN and ABC). He was being trained by the famous Don Turner who was telling anyone who would listen that Michael Grant had the ability to be the greatest heavyweight champion of all time.

In January 1998 Grant made his HBO debut against tough Nigerian David Izon. Grant did well in his HBO debut, taking out Izon in five rounds. He would follow it up with another KO win four months later against another solid opponent in Obed Sullivan. Grant's career was fast and furious. The sky was now the limit.

Things continued at pace for Grant in 1999. He would begin the year with a 10th round stoppage of Ahmad Abdin and followed it five months later with a decisive unanimous decision win over Lou Savarese at the theatre in Madison Square Garden. After the win over Savarese talk of a possible world title fight began to be taken seriously. All Grant had to do was win one more fight to get a shot at the title. The big one. The final fight for the right to challenge the unified king was always going to be a tough test. It came in the form of the experienced and often dirty, Andrew Golota.

The fight took place on 20th November 1999 at the Trump Taj Mahal in Atlantic City, New Jersey. Exactly one week after Lewis had unified the titles by beating Holyfield in their return bout in Vegas.

Grant seemed comfortable in the first round until Golota landed a big right hand that put him on the canvass. The big Pole followed up with more big shots and again put Grant down near the end of the opening period. Golota showed just how rough it can be at the top table as he continually pressured the young pretender, but Grant somehow survived the early onslaught. There were low blows and point deductions on both sides as the fight developed. For several rounds they exchanged blows, like for like.

By the 10th round, Grant knew he had to produce something special if he was to earn a shot at the heavyweight crown. He duly obliged by landing a huge right hand that stopped Golota in his tracks. Grant sensed victory and hit Golota with a good combination that sent him down. Golota got up, but mysteriously indicated that he did not want to continue. The referee called it off and Grant had won.

Grant's team was emboldened by the victory over Golota. It didn't matter that Lewis had battered the Polish brawler in less than a round. Grant's trainer Don Turner was quoted as saying; "The only time Lewis got knocked down [referring to the McCall fight] he lost the fight. Grant showed a strong mind against Golota."

It was not just a tough, street-brawl victory, it was a great comeback win. Michael Grant had shown that he can take heavy punishment, recover and win. Many in the world of boxing now thought that Grant was ready to face Lewis.

In what was the last big heavyweight contest of the millennium Grant had put himself on a collision course with destiny in the shape of Lennox Lewis.

Training with Don Turner put Grant in contact with some top quality, experienced fighters such as Roy Jones Jr. and Evander Holyfield. Grant had become big friends with Holyfield and when Grant was married in 1998, Holyfield was his best man.

In his two fights in 1999 Lewis would fight the 'best man' while his first outing of the year 2000 Lewis fought the groom.

Riddick Bowe & Mike Tyson...

When people analyse Lennox Lewis's career looking for flaws, you almost always hear the same two things. Probably in this order too.

Firstly, that he never fought Tyson when 'Iron' Mike was in his prime. Second, Riddick Bowe: The fight that never was.

Lewis was arguably also on the decline when he fought Tyson. He only fought once more – beating Vitali Klitchsko - and had nothing left to prove. After losing to Lewis, Vitali Klitchsko went on to dominate the division between 2004 and 2012 (with the help of his brother Wladimir). As Lewis himself said of his last fight, a poor Lennox Lewis still managed to beat a peak Vitali Klischko. He had beaten the man who would go on to reign for eight years.

It is reasonable to suggest that Lewis's best years were between 1992 and the Grant fight in 2000. With one lapse in concentration that led to a loss to Oliver McCall in 1994. Something Lewis put right a year later.

It is often said that great champions can be measured not by the fact that they never lost but by the fact that they always get the better of their opponents. Lewis did this. He avenged his only two losses and no man can say they ever got the better of him.

Tyson on the other hand did not. Once his air of invincibility was gone, he struggled to be a real force in the division. He lost to 5 men (including Lewis). He only tried to avenge one of those losses and failed quite miserably when he was disqualified for trying to eat Evander Holyfield's ear.

Tyson was exceptionally famous. Everybody on the planet knew who he was even if they had never seen a boxing match. So, everyone had an opinion of him. You often hear it said that Tyson was past his best when Lewis beat him. Or even when he fought

Holyfield. But that would be naïve and ignorant of some important facts.

Was Tyson a different fighter once he had been proven to be a mere mortal? He still possessed the same knockout punch. He still had the same chin, only now, other fighters knew that if they could connect with it, then they actually had a chance. Due to his early rise through the division to become the youngest ever heavyweight champion people also forget that Tyson was a year younger than Lewis. (Four years younger than Holyfield.)

Tyson's out of the ring lifestyle was often questionable. Some of it you did not even need to question. You knew it was not good. But if he knuckled down and completed a full training camp why would he be any different than the fighter who tore through the division only a few years earlier? Physically at least. Many fighters seem to live an alternative life between fights and yet manage to get in peak shape during fight camp.

Mentally however, everything was different. In Tyson's own mind, but more importantly in the minds of his opponents across the ring. 'Iron' Mike was just a man like them. He was a mere mortal and he could be beaten. The fear factor, his most potent weapon, was no longer quite the same.

Interestingly Riddick Bowe shares the same distinction as Lewis. Bowe's sole loss, to Evander Holyfield in 1993, was avenged in 1995, meaning that he finished their thrilling trilogy 2-1 ahead. With the exception of a 1994 no-contest with Buster Mathis Jr., Bowe defeated every opponent he faced as a professional. Despite all the criticism he came in for – some of it more than justified – Bowe truly was an excellent boxer. His epic battles with Holyfield remain one of the finest and exciting trilogies in boxing history. At any weight.

Tyson could also be accused of ducking Lewis. When he regained the WBC title beating Frank Bruno, he vacated the WBC belt so he could fight Evander Holyfield instead. At that time Lewis was the WBC number one contender but Tyson-Holyfield had been a long time in coming and was the money fight. It made financial sense and was a bigger draw at the box office than Tyson-Lewis (at that time). If Tyson had not vacated the belt the WBC would have stripped him of it anyway.

If Tyson-Lewis should have happened by now, then Tyson-Holyfield should have happened a lot earlier

While Lewis would fight Tyson (eventually), it is not the fact that their contest happened 'too late' that comes up as the biggest disappointment in Lewis's career. In that era, the biggest regret most ardent boxing fans have is that Lewis v Bowe never happened at all. And that one is as much down to boxing politics as anything else.

Who would have won? That is a debate that still goes on. The two boxers were evenly matched on paper. Both in that same Olympic final as amateurs, they were the same height, at 6 feet five inches (196cm). Bowe was three years younger than Lewis, but Lewis had a three-inch (7cm) reach advantage. They both made their professional debuts in 1989 (three months apart). For all the similarities the two arguably peaked at different times. To most boxing aficionados, the younger Bowe peaked sooner.

The closest we came to seeing Lewis vs Bowe was in 1994 when it was widely reported that the fight had been agreed. Lewis beat Phil Jackson by TKO in May 94 and then went on to lose his next fight with Oliver McCall in one of boxing's greatest upsets. Sadly, Lewis v Bowe remains one of the best heavyweight dream fights never to happen. One thing is certain, however. It would have been one hell of a great fight.

While Lewis was demolishing highly ranked opponents like 'Razor' Ruddock in non-title fights, he was clearly being avoided. The then unified heavyweight champion Riddick Bowe seemed desperate to avoid Lewis who repeatedly called him "Chicken" Bowe. On 14th December 1992 Bowe relinquished the WBC belt rather than fight the mandatory challenger in Lewis. Bowe was famously pictured dropping the WBC belt in the trash.

The WBC immediately declared Lewis its champion. He never won the title in the ring. If you were to ask Lewis to this day if there was one regret in his career; he would probably say it was not beating Bowe in the ring for that belt.

Bowe was the first boxer in any division to hold all four major versions of the world championship (WBA, WBC, IBF, and WBO) during his career, an accomplishment emulated in the heavyweight division (far more recently) only by Tyson Fury.

Bowe is one of only five former heavyweight champions to have never been stopped (KO or TKO) during his career. The others being; Gene Tunney, Rocky Marciano, Sultan Ibragimov and Nikolai Valuev.

In 2017, The Ring magazine ranked Bowe as the 19th best heavyweight of all time in a poll of a panel of 30 trainers, matchmakers and members of the boxing media. The consensus on Bowe, was that he was both a "super talent" and a "super waste", that he ultimately disappointed in squandering his undoubted natural talent due to laziness.

It wasn't just his lazy streak. Bowe had a 'hands and mouth' problem. He simply couldn't stop passing food from one to the other. If there was a big cake in the room Riddick Bowe would eat it!

The Gloves Controversy...

Press conferences are great opportunities for a little mischief. Whether it is psychological mind games or trying to sell the last few rows of tickets. Promoters, trainers and boxers all try a little something to make the fight sell. Usually it's just insults but all too often that spills over into pushing and scuffles, often orchestrated and nothing more than handbags at 5 paces. Occasionally however you see real bare-knuckle fisticuffs. A good example being

Riddick Bowe landing two clean shots (a left-right combination to be exact) on Larry Donald during their final press conference. It turned out that the fight itself was just as easy for Bowe. But it probably sold a few last-minute seats.

If there is anything that is going to trigger pre-fight fireworks or psyche out an opponent, it would normally occur at the final press conference. In the case of this contest there had been some disagreement over Lewis's choice of gloves for the fight. As the champion, he made the call on which gloves to use, but Grant had complained that his left hand was too big to fit in the Reyes brand gloves that Lewis preferred.

Grant and his team had conceded the choice of gloves was not going to stop the fight from happening. "We're going to try to work around the problem," Grant said. "I tried on 16 pairs of gloves. But if they want to bring out bigger gloves or another 16 pair, I'll try them. It's kind of a healthy issue. The right hand fits well, but I can't get any comfort or make a fist with my left hand. I'm sure Lennox wouldn't want to fight without being able to make a fist."

They were clearly trying to play mind games. Trying to gain the psychological high ground.

Lewis wasn't having any of it. During that final press conference before the fight, when the glove issue was raised again, Lewis suddenly stood and put his right hand over his head next to where Grant was seated, beckoning the challenger to a measurement of hands.

After a few seconds, Grant stood and put his left hand up to Lewis's. If there was a difference, nobody noticed it. Lewis turned to the microphone and simply said, "Same size." In other words he was saying; "Let's get it on!"

The attempt by Grant's team to gain some kind of advantage by playing mind games had backfired. Lewis had won that game and now had the psychological edge before the big fight. It was Round One to Lewis and they hadn't even put on the hand wraps.

The Fight

"Grant is like what I call hurry come up. He came up fast so he's gonna go in a split second".

Lennox Lewis.

The fight was billed as "Two Big". The two fighters were huge, towering heavyweights and the promoters even used the twin towers of the world trade centre on one of the promotional posters. At that time this was the biggest combined height and weight match-up in boxing history.

Before the fighters entered the fabled arena, HBO's Larry Merchant described Grant as "The Great American Hope", before pausing and adding; "…Or **hype**."

Lennox Lewis had reached his peak, possibly even passed it. At least he had nothing to prove at this point. He had just beaten the ultimate warrior in 'Real Deal' Evander Holyfield. Many thought he had beaten him twice. At this stage in Lewis's career it is quite possible that the only thing still motivating him was the promise of that final, big, and so far elusive fight. 'Iron' Mike Tyson.

Michael Grant on the other hand still had a number of amateur traits in his game. He was still relatively inexperienced when compared to a fighter like Lewis. The British born Lewis had been an excellent amateur winning Olympic gold in the 1988 games. As if that was not enough consider this fact: Lewis was already champion of the world before Grant had ever laced up a pair of boxing gloves.

This was Lewis's first defence since defeating Evander Holyfield to become undisputed heavyweight king. But it would not be for all the belts. Boxing being boxing – meaning there is always politics as well as the sport - it was never going to be that simple. Lewis had refused to defend his WBA belt against John Ruiz – a Don King fighter. King did his thing. He went to court, and Lewis was stripped of the belt. Not that it bothered most fight fans. Lewis was still regarded as the true and undisputed champion and before the fight he was announced to the crowd as such.

Grant was not only unbeaten at 31-0, but he possessed the size and physique to dominate Lewis in the ring. Such was his physique that Grant had already been displayed on several magazine covers. He was seen by many as having a much better chance against Lewis than John Ruiz.

Meanwhile, Lennox Lewis had other, far more destructive plans.

Grant had been knocked down twice in the opening round of his fight with Andrew Golota. He had showed a big heart in recovering, eventually forcing Golota to quit. But that fight left a burning question. Did Grant have a suspect chin?

As the two touched gloves before the fight Lewis said nothing. Grant, a devout Christian, said just two words. "God bless."

Grant surprised Lewis by taking the fight right to him when the bell sounded. Within the first 15 seconds of the fight it looked like becoming a toe-to-toe slugfest. After the first minute things calmed down as Lewis refused to be drawn into a war and started measuring his range.

Exactly half-way through the first round Lewis threw a big right-hand uppercut, quickly followed by a right cross that landed high on the head. Grant went down and almost looked out. He got up but never looked like he could last much longer. Instead of clinching and trying to hold on Grant took the fight back to Lewis who again caught him coming in. Grant stumbled back into the ropes which kept him upright – just. The referee gave him a standing count. There was still almost a minute of the first round remaining and Grant looked out on his feet. This time he changed tactics. Hold on for dear life. It seemed like one more punch would finish the fight. Then with 13 seconds remaining of the round Lewis launched a right hand to the side of the face and down went Grant for the third time. It looked all over. His legs splayed apart. In the excitement HBO commentator and heavyweight great, George Foreman yelled "He broke his leg".

The rules do not allow a boxer to be saved by the bell. The count would continue. But Grant demonstrated amazing resilience, and he somehow hauled himself up at the count of eight, just in time, right as the bell sounded for the end of what for him was a tortuous round.

There was no way that Grant would be fully recovered in the one-minute interval before round two. He was still shaken, and Lewis knew it. There was plenty of time. Three minutes is a long time to wait for another rest after the beating Grant had taken in the first period.

Lewis pawed at the challenger looking for that one opening that would end the fight. Grant tried to hold when he could and even had to trade punches with Lewis just to stop him teeing up for the big KO punch. Then, with 23 seconds of the round to go, Lewis finished it with a huge right uppercut to the chin that dropped Grant again. This time for keeps. The fight was clearly over but Grant showed tremendous courage trying to get up in what was now a lost cause. The official time for the end of the fight was recorded as 2 minutes and 53 seconds into round number 2.

That final KO shot by Lewis was actually assisted by an illegal move. Lewis had hold of Grant's head with his left arm when he launched that righthand bomb. Grant neither knew nor cared. He was out of it and in no fit state to complain.

It was a ruthless KO by the undisputed champion of the world on the "Great American Hope". The plan to attack Lewis had backfired spectacularly.

When asked if he would be back, Grant smiled and said, "It aint over till the fat lady sings, and everyone here is wearing a size 6 dress."

The fight's punch statistics show that Grant was fairly successful with a 47% success rate in landing 22 of the 47 shots he threw. Lewis landed 47 of 80 punches, a percentage of 58%. The problem for Grant was that most of those 47 punches were hard shots.

The crowd in attendance was 17,324. Lewis reportedly earned $7.5 million and Grant $2.5 million.

Ironically, with regards to Foreman's "he broke his leg" remark, Grant did suffer a broken ankle in his very next fight. Grant's come-back fight (over a year later) was against another huge guy in Jameel McCline. Grant was beaten in just 40 seconds when he could not continue the fight. He was caught by a fast, left hand from McCline in the first seconds of the fight. The very first punch thrown. Grant injured his ankle while falling to the canvas. He never recovered. Neither did his career.

When Foreman yelled "he broke his leg" during the commentary he was referring to the involuntary leg splaying when a boxer takes a big hit. It is an interesting way of looking at it. Big George had done a similar thing to a few fighters in his time. This is one of the most spectacular and frightening sights in boxing. Involuntary leg motion when a fighter is hit in the head. It has a double effect on spectators; first giving them an instant, huge rush of excitement, immediately followed by an injection of pure shock. The realisation that the fighter is in a very bad place.

When Lewis landed his powerful right hand to the head, the communication between brain and legs was completely interfered with. While the boxer knows he is hit and has to try to clear his head his legs are completely doing their own thing. The legs seem to be utterly without control. Completely random.

The head and upper body sent one way due to sheer momentum of force. The legs 'dancing' off in different directions. Lewis was a very powerful puncher and did a similar thing when dropping Donavon Ruddock.

"Mike has to fight very aggressively"

The opinion of Evander Holyfield
during the fight build-up on HBO TV

What about Lewis? It is true that through the early 1990s Lewis remained in the shadow of Riddick Bowe and Evander Holyfield (and to a lesser extent Mike Tyson). But in the latter half of that decade Lewis emerged as the genuine number one.

It is the mark of a true champion when he can dispatch a younger up and coming fighter in such a convincing manner. Grant had the size and ought to have had the confidence coming into the bout. But nothing can really prepare a fighter for being in the ring with such a superior boxer. When that boxer possesses KO power as well as speed and skill it takes a brave and resilient man to withstand it. Durability is the only thing that can keep you in a fight when you are hopelessly outmatched. That kind of toughness is a trait very few fighters possess. Men like Marciano, Jake LaMotta and George Chuvalo all had it. These men were as tough as granite. It is often referred to in boxing circles as "having a chin". Michael Grant simply never had it.

Grant was a huge and talented natural athlete, excelling in several team sports. But that does not necessarily make a boxer, and certainly not the best boxer in the world.

The HBO boxing commentator Larry Merchant famously said: "Boxing isn't a game. You can *play* basketball, you can *play* (American) football, but you can't *play* boxing."

Lennox Lewis was also a good all-round athlete, but he had boxing pedigree backed up by a long amateur career. At that time Lewis really was the best boxer on the planet.

> *"I don't care what they say, I'm still undisputed."*
>
> Lennox Lewis after the fight
> and after the WBA had stripped him of their title.

Aftermath

"His team sent a lamb to the slaughter, Grant isn't ready for me.
It's too soon in his career"

Lennox Lewis

Lewis continued to box after the Grant fight. He had 6 fights, one of them not exactly planned. He still needed that Tyson fight.

Such was Lewis's domination in the Grant fight he was ready to fight again and did so just over two months later. The opponent was Fancois Botha. The venue; London. This was a kind of homecoming for Lewis and his fans.

Botha had won 40 bouts and lost only twice to Michael Moorer and Mike Tyson. He was a decent fighter and a potential 'banana skin'. Lewis dispatched him in 2 rounds in a one-sided affair. It was clear that Lewis still had 'the eye of the tiger'.

Then, only four months had passed when Lewis took an even higher risk fight. This time against the tough and highly rated New Zealander David Tua. Lewis was 35 years of age while Tua was 8 years his junior. Yet amazingly the two had almost identical records going into the fight. Both had won 31 and lost one. Lewis had also fought a draw in his first Holyfield bout. The younger Tua even had a better knockout ratio, with 32 of his wins coming by way of KO while Lewis had 29 KOs to his name. This was another high- risk fight for the champion. Earlier in his career Tua had been compared to a young Tyson. He was the same height and a similar build to Tyson, but he was no Tyson.

Lewis avoided being drawn into a war with the dangerous Tua. This had the makings of an Ali versus Frazier fight. The taller, slick boxer against the squat, crouching brawler. But it turned out to be an exhibition by the taller boxer. He did what he did best. He out-boxed the younger man winning comfortably on all three scorecards.

When HBO's Larry Merchant interviewed Lewis immediately after the fight he asked, "Do you think there was anything wrong with him (Tua) or was it just an easy sparring session?". Lewis responded in typical fashion. "Lennox Lewis was wrong with David Tua".

Lewis had fought three times in the first year of the new millennium against three genuine challengers and won all three fights convincingly.

Following these three successful title defences in 2000, Lennox Lewis turned his sights on a potential superfight with Mike Tyson in the summer of 2001. However, Tyson was suspended for three months early in that year after testing positive for marijuana following his recent fight with Andrew Golota.

Lewis decided to defend his titles against a little-known yet capable fighter. Hasim Rahman had only lost twice to David Tua and Oleg Maskaev and was given his opportunity after winning three fights the previous year (like Lewis).

The fight was billed as "Thunder in Africa" and was set to take place in Brakpan, South Africa. Lewis came into the fight as a 20–1 odds-on favourite. Rahman was a massive underdog, fighting for the world title against a top class, feared boxer in a far-off land. This truly was Rahman's 'Buster' Douglas moment.

Lewis was clearly distracted by negotiation for the long-awaited Tyson fight. There was also the WBA belt now held by John Ruiz and the possibility that Lewis could fight Ruiz and take all the belts into the clash with Tyson.

Such backroom negotiations are common and there is no evidence to suggest that these managerial tasks affected Lewis. The real evidence of Lewis overlooking Rahman was in his fight preparation.

Brakpan, Gauteng, South Africa, is 5,200 feet (1585m), just shy of a mile, above sea level. Rahman arrived on March 27th, almost four weeks before the fight, so he would have time to acclimatise to the high altitude. Lewis didn't arrive until April 10th, giving himself less than two weeks to adjust to the conditions. Lewis trained in Las Vegas, Nevada, which is 2,000 feet (609m) above sea level. He trained in Las Vegas because he was involved in a movie being made in Vegas. He was filming scenes for a cameo appearance in the movie Ocean's Eleven. This was a huge distraction from preparations to contest the top prize in sport. After Lewis was knocked out by Rahman, HBO commentator Larry

Merchant said, "He just drowned in Ocean's Eleven." Everyone watching knew it. So did Lewis.

That shock defeat was reversed only seven months later when Lewis knocked Rahman out in spectacular fashion in Las Vegas.

Lewis then went on to finish his career with highlight reel victories over Mike Tyson in June 2002 and Vitali Klitschko in June 2003 – both described above.

From the other nine boxers in The Ring magazine top ten rated fighters in April 2000 (before the Grant fight), Lewis fought and beat six of them. One match could not be made as Ike Ibeabuchi went to prison. The other two fighters were Derrick Jefferson and Oleg Maskaev. Jefferson's high ranking was short lived when he lost twice in 2000. First to David Izon and then to Maskaev. Both were KO defeats. Meanwhile Maskaev went on to lose his next two bouts after the victory over Jefferson. He managed to turn his career around again and several years later claimed the WBC version of the world heavyweight title by beating former Lewis foe Hasim Rahman. But during the first two years of the new millennium neither Jefferson nor Maskaev were worthy opponents for a dominant Lewis.

At that time Lennox Lewis truly was the undisputed heavyweight champion of the world.

Grant's next fight was even shorter than the Lewis bout. Forty seconds to be exact.

Grant's immediate reaction to losing his unbeaten record was to fight James McCleen. A damaged ankle was to cut that fight short. Grant maintained that after being knocked down several times in his fights with Golota and Lewis he had damaged his ankle.

He explained in an interview to mark the 20th anniversary of the Lennox Lewis fight, that his own trainer did not believe him. Despite the 2nd loss in his career he did not feel too bad. He knew the ankle wasn't right so it made a loss easier to take knowing that he went into the fight with a suspect ankle.

Years later when being interviewed about the then upcoming challenger Deontay Wilder's heavyweight title fight against the WBC holder Berman Stiverne, Grant would admit that getting in the ring with Lennox Lewis was on "a whole different level".

> "Andrew Golota and Lou Savarese* they were good fighters. I was very comfortable developing my skills against fighters like that. But when I fought Lennox for the championship, that was moving up to a whole different level. You fight somebody like that, there is a different kind of pressure put on you. I wasn't ready for it. I admit it."
>
> (* Grant beat both Golota and Savarese)

Ultimately Grant did nothing wrong. He was a very good heavyweight in with an all-time great. If hindsight could have arrived earlier, he would have seen this fight for what it really was. An excellent shot at the title, but ultimately a dream. He lost to a very dominant heavyweight in Lewis. If he had realised this was not such a bad loss (which it wasn't) he could have regrouped and maybe come again. Instead, his career began to unravel.

Grant was never the same fighter after this devastating defeat by Lewis. It often happens that when fighters lose their unbeaten status they are never quite the same. Their own self-belief is seriously broken. To record your first loss in such a dramatic way can have a lasting impact which often shows in a fighter's record afterwards. Grant's record before the Lewis fight was 31-0 but after the loss it was a less impressive 17-8. It was like two separate careers.

Grant fought on for another 17 years, finally retiring in 2017 His last three fights – all defeats – stretched over a four-year period.

In an interview with the UK's Boxing News magazine to mark the 20th anniversary of the Lewis fight, Grant would again admit that fighting Lewis at that stage of his career was a mistake. Deep down he never thought that he could beat Lewis. Grant believed that he needed two or three more fights against big boxers. Someone like Shannon Briggs would have been perfect. Grant's team however had read too much into Lewis's two fights with Holyfield the previous year. Lewis had adopted a cautious approach in those fights and failed to stop Holyfield. While Grant's team thought that Lewis won both bouts, they incorrectly saw this as a long career catching up with him. They presumed that Lewis was on the way down and was no longer letting his big right hands go. Grant summed it up; "We saw that and thought it was a good time to attack."

Of the fight itself Grant said, "I realised straight away how good he was. I wanted to make him fight from the first bell, but that went wrong straight away. It was a miracle I got out of that first round…"

Belt History

The tables below chart the history of the three major governing body's belt holders from the start of the Mike Tyson era up to Lennox Lewis taking over the division.

The World Boxing Organisation (WBO) only became a widely recognised body in the sport (at least in the heavyweight division) towards the end of Lennox Lewis' career. Lewis never fought for the WBO title.

WBC

Name	Date	Defences	Days
Mike Tyson	1986 Nov 22	9	1177
James Douglas	1990 Feb 11	0	256
Evander Holyfield	1990 Oct 25	2	750
Riddick Bowe	1992 Nov 13	0	31
Bowe relinquished the belt rather than face the mandatory challenger Lennox Lewis. WBC awarded their title to Lewis.			
Lennox Lewis	1992 Dec 14	3	649
Oliver McCall	1994 Sep 24	1	343
Frank Bruno	1995 Sep 2	0	196
Mike Tyson	1996 Mar 16	0	328
Tyson relinquished WBC belt to avoid facing mandatory challenger Lewis. Instead fighting Evander Holyfield for the WBA title. Lewis then fought Oliver McCall for the vacant title.			
Lennox Lewis (vs McCall)	1997 Feb 7	9	1535
Lewis lost title to Hasim Rahman on April 22nd, 2001, then regained title on November 17th, 2001.			

43

WBA

Name	Date	Defences	Days
Mike Tyson	Mar 7, 1987	8	1072
James Douglas	Feb 11, 1990	0	256
Evander Holyfield	Oct 25, 1990	3	750
Riddick Bowe	Nov 13, 1992	2	358
Evander Holyfield	Nov 6, 1993	0	167
Michael Moorer	Apr 22, 1994	0	103
George Foreman	Nov 5, 1994	0	120
Foreman was stripped for refusing to fight mandatory.			
Bruce Seldon (vs Tony Tucker)	Apr 8, 1995	1	518
Mike Tyson	7 Sep 1996	0	63
Evander Holyfield	9 Nov 1996	4	1,099
Lennox Lewis	13 Nov 1999	0	166
Lewis was stripped April 29th, 2000, after agreeing to fight WBC challenger Michael Grant instead of John Ruiz			

When Lennox Lewis beat Evander Holyfield on 13th November 1999 in Las Vegas, he became the undisputed champion holding all three major recognised belts at that time. He was also the lineal champion.

IBF

Name	Date	Defences	Days
Mike Tyson	1 Aug 1987	6	925
James Douglas	11 Feb 1990	0	256
Evander Holyfield	25 Oct 1990	3	750
Riddick Bowe	13 Nov 1992	1	358
Evander Holyfield	6 Nov 1993	0	167
Michael Moorer	22 Apr 1994	0	197
George Foreman	5 Nov 1994	1	236
Foreman vacated title 29 June 1995			
Francois Botha (vs. Axel Schulz)	9 Dec 1995	0	109
Botha stripped of title 27th March, 1996, due to positive drug test.			
Michael Moorer (vs. Axel Schulz)	22 Jun 1996	2	504
Evander Holyfield	8 Nov 1997	2	735
Lennox Lewis	13 Nov 1999	3	525
Lewis lost title to Hasim Rahman on April 22nd, 2001, then regained title on November 17th, 2001.			

Lewis was forced to vacate the IBF belt in 2002 when he refused to fight their mandatory challenger Chris Byrd who was rated at number 2 or 3 by Ring Magazine. Lewis was due to fight Kirk Johnson (also rated in the Ring Magazine top ten) but when Johnson picked up an injury Lewis agreed to a fight with the then WBC number one contender, Vitali Klitschko. At that time Vitali's brother, Wladimir, was ranked as the number one contender by Ring Magazine. A new era in heavyweight domination was about to begin.

Don King and Frank Maloney...

There are countless books, websites and even movies dedicated to the life and work of that omnipresent promoter of heavyweight fights in the nineties – the one and only Don King. However, this chapter would not be complete without a small mention of the flamboyant promoter. After all, King did have an impact on key fights that Lewis chased unsuccessfully for many of his peak years. Largely managing his fighters to avoid Lewis. This is believed to have happened on several occasions.

King's financial success started in the 1970s and continued into the 1980s and 1990s. In 1994 (the year Grant started boxing) he promoted 47 world championship bouts. King had a business strategy that resulted in his control over many of the top boxers, especially in the heavyweight division - the most lucrative. King used a contractual clause whereby any boxer who challenged a fighter belonging to King, had to agree to be promoted by King in the future, should they win. Thus, no matter which boxer won, "only in America" King represented the winner. Anyone unwilling to sign a contract with this clause found it very difficult to obtain fights, especially title fights, with boxers who were promoted by King.

Such legal loopholes cost Lennox Lewis not only fights but titles.

Lennox Lewis always intended giving Don King a wide berth. That was one of his reasons for moving back to Great Britain once he had established himself on the heavyweight scene.

Don King was rightly considered the most flamboyant and charismatic character in the sport at that time. That said, the man who managed Lennox Lewis through most of his career also deserves a mention.

Frank Maloney was London born like Lewis. He started boxing at school and later trained amateur boxers. In the 1970s he worked with promoter Frank Warren until he set up his own management business, becoming Lennox Lewis's manager in 1989.

King continually tried to entice Lewis over to his camp. Sometimes going to extreme lengths. Back in 1993 on the day Lewis was fighting Tony Tucker for the WBC title in Las Vegas, King organised a leafleting campaign aimed at getting Lewis to leave Maloney. The leaflet was meant to be an open letter to Lewis and was distributed around all the big hotels, slipped under guest's doors in the hope that as many boxing people saw it as possible. In the leaflet King tried to discredit Lewis' manager Frank Maloney. King hoped that Lewis would see that his future lay in the USA under King's management. It was a surreal publicity stunt that failed miserably. Not least because whenever Maloney's name was mentioned by King it came with a typically comical insult. King called Maloney a mental midget and a pugilistic pygmy. That only generated huge interest from the media who all wanted interviews. Maloney was only too happy to oblige. Maloney and Lewis had never had as much free publicity.

While Don King rarely missed the chance to tout his "only in America" alias, always displaying the American stars and stripes flag, Maloney went one better. He *wore* his flag. The trademark Union Jack suit was a lucky charm that Maloney wore to almost every one of Lewis's big championship fights.

Years after Lewis had retired, Maloney trans-gendered and became Kellie Maloney, claiming "I was born in the wrong body and I have always known I was a woman".

Not even the incomparable Don King, for all his showmanship and all his (often controversial) shenanigans; could beat that one.

"Two Big", the fight's marketing slogan, was more than just a catchphrase. It was in many ways quite prophetic. The sheer size of the two combatants in this historic fight marked an indelible change in the heavyweight scene. Heavyweights had been getting bigger over the previous couple of decades. After this fight the heavyweight division would belong to the **super**-heavyweights.

Even compared to Lennox Lewis' huge frame Michael Grant looked an imposing figure. But those who knew Grant best often said that he lacked a certain something that you need in the sport of boxing. He was described as simply being too nice. He lacked that mean streak to go out and hurt another person in the ring.

Boxing is unlike any other sport. It takes a certain type of mentality not just athleticism. It is also a state of mind, an ability to focus your anger, to intimidate and impose your will on an opponent.

Grant's advisor Craig Hamilton was reported as saying at the time that Michael just wasn't cut out to be a fighter and the fact that he got as far as he did was thanks to his superb athleticism.

Michael Grant had all the attributes to make it big in any other sport. Size, power, speed and stamina. Those were great gifts to have as an athlete, but as a boxer it just wasn't enough.

Meanwhile, years later, the name Lennox Lewis regularly appears in the lists of the top ten heavyweights of all time. People interested in boxing finally came to realise just how good Lennox Lewis really was. One of the best ever.

The Undercard

For a big event at Madison Square Garden the undercard contained surprisingly few bouts with any great boxing significance. The show did however feature some interesting characters each with their own back story and in some cases bizarre and tragic futures.

Chief support – and arguably the best fight of the whole show - was an IBF world featherweight title bout featuring Britain's Paul Ingle and the American Junior Jones, a former two weight world champion. Ingle was the holder and was dropped in the 9th round. He later returned the favour putting Jones down twice in the 11th round before stopping him on TKO. Ingle wore down the challenger over those 11 rounds by sheer work rate and will power.

In a comical moment, after the whole event, Ingle was almost refused entry into the post-fight press conference area*. While two gate-crashing fight fans were being asked to leave, a door was opened for their ejection There stood Paul Ingle with his trainer and manager. The security guard mistook them for more gate-crashers and told them that they could not come in. When one of the real gate-crashers said, "You have to let him in. He's the world champion", the security guard, looking rather embarrassed and a little confused, allowed them into the room. (* The author was one of the gate-crashers.)

Ingle would defend his title one more time, losing it almost 8 months later to South African Mbulelo Botile in what would be his last fight. Paul Ingle was knocked down in the 11th round and again in the 12th round. He failed to get up for several minutes and was stretchered out of the ring. He was diagnosed with a blood clot on the brain and spent four weeks in intensive care before recovering.

In the following years Ingle would suffer huge weight gain and the despair that went with it. Eventually, with a close friend, he opened a boxing gym in Hull, England and even gained his training licence.

Ingle's is a tale straight from boxing's horror vault. But just as he always did in the ring, he has fought through it with grit and determination.

Wladimir Klitschko won the WBO inter-continental title. The big Ukranian stopped David Bostice by TKO early in round two. His next fight would see him win the full WBO version of the heavyweight title. He and his brother Vitali would later hold all the belts between them, ruling the division for years to come.

Arturo 'Thunder' Gatti, a firm crowd favourite in north-eastern United States took on Eric Jakubowski in a non-title mismatch. Despite the level of opponent Gatti did his thing and dispatched Jakubowski early in the second round. One of the best 'value for money' fighters of his time, Gatti was never in a dull fight. Nine years later Gatti would be found dead in a hotel in Brazil at the age of only 37. Initially his Brazilian wife was charged with murder but later the coroner declared it was suicide. For many, Gatti's death remains an unsolved mystery.

British fighter Scott Harrison was a colourful character in and out of the ring. Harrison fought Tracey Harris Patterson winning a unanimous decision over 10 rounds. Harrison would go on to win a world title two years later before being jailed twice. First in the UK in 2008 for drink driving and assault and again in Spain in 2009 following another assault in Málaga.

In attendance that night was the young WBC super-featherweight champion by the name of Floyd Mayweather Jr. Sporting an all-red suit, Mayweather stood ringside after the main event while his small entourage tried to attract the attention of the media – who were already making their way to the post-fight press conference. One stood on the ring apron loudly proclaiming the greatest fighter on the planet was right here, while pointing to Mayweather. The 23-year-old Mayweather had recently won his 5th defence of the super-featherweight title – the first of five weight divisions he would conquer. He was already looking every inch the confident, self-promoting superstar the whole boxing world would soon know all too well. In a few years' time *he* would be the main event.

Chapter Two

Being Very Good and Brave is No Match for Greatness

The Story of Floyd Mayweather vs Ricky Hatton.
8th December 2007, MGM Grand, Las Vegas,
Nevada, USA.

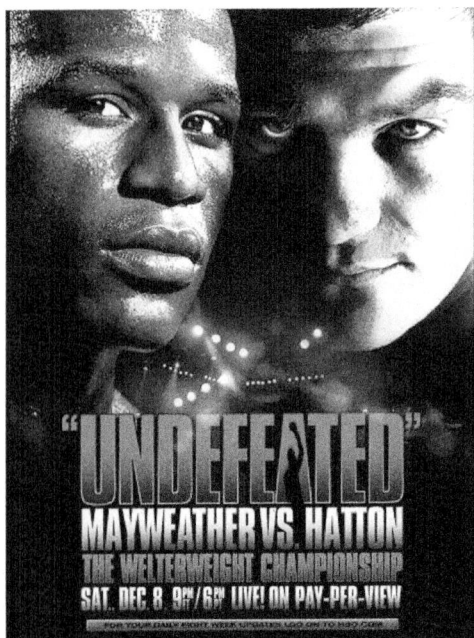

"UNDEFEATED"
MAYWEATHER VS. HATTON
THE WELTERWEIGHT CHAMPIONSHIP
SAT. DEC. 8, 9PM/6PM LIVE! ON PAY-PER-VIEW

FOR YOUR DAILY FIGHT WEEK UPDATES, LOG ON TO HBO.COM

In 2007 a new boxing promotion company was formed. Mayweather Promotions was the inevitable outcome of a fighter rising through the ranks to become the sport's main attraction. More than that, one prize fighter looked set to transcend the sport of boxing.

Floyd Mayweather had established himself as the best 'pound-for-pound' boxer on the planet and was now hand-picking his opponents to appear on his own promotional events. Mayweather Promotions' first main event would feature the flash, brash 'Pretty Boy' Floyd himself, topping the bill at the entertainment and boxing capital of the world; Las Vegas, USA.

His opponent was an affable, down-to-earth, working-class hero from Manchester, UK, who had just beaten the only common opponent the two fighters shared in José Luis Castillo. Ricky 'The Hitman' Hatton had not only beaten Castillo. Hatton had destroyed, in less than four rounds, an opponent that Mayweather could only narrowly beat in two points victories.

In the post-fight interview immediately following his KO win over Castillo, Hatton threw down the gauntlet. Floyd Mayweather immediately acknowledged the challenge and instructed his team to make the fight before the year's end. Mayweather had seen the way Hatton fought and probably knew right then how he wanted to fight Hatton. The stage was set for an epic dual in the desert city.

This is a description of how that fight came about and how it went down. An account of what happens when a good - sometimes very good - brave fighter comes up against a great fighter. One who is simply bigger, faster, better.

This is also the story of how a big fight would be eclipsed by what was happening in the city in the week leading up to the fight. With an incredible invasion of the 'Gambling Capital of the World' by 30,000 British fight fans. Las Vegas had never seen anything like it.

On the face of it, Floyd Mayweather and Ricky Hatton were completely different characters outside of the ring. Opposites even. But inside the ropes they shared that same determination to win by any means necessary. Each prepared to fight the full 12 rounds and then some.

In May 2007 Mayweather had just beaten Oscar De La Hoya to win the WBC world light middleweight title. It was (then) the biggest money grossing fight in history. In the ring interviews immediately after the fight he announced his retirement. He said that he had made enough money and had nothing left to prove to anybody having just won a world title in a fifth weight class. While both of those claims were true nobody believed Floyd was going anywhere, especially after the biggest win in his career. Sure enough, just over a month later, on June 23rd, when Ricky Hatton made his own statements in the ring after cutting Jose Luis Castillo in half with a perfect body shot, Floyd Mayweather quickly brought himself out of retirement.

At this stage in his career Mayweather could sell out a fight just by putting his name on the poster. But that was not Floyd's style. He didn't just perform *inside* the ring. He was theatrical outside of it and definitely dealt with the business side of a big fight like a true entrepreneur. He was well accomplished at doing whatever was needed to hype his fights as well as getting under the skin of his rivals.

But none of his antics seemed to bother the humble, working-class fighter from the north of England - Ricky Hatton.

"*Make the fight fucking happen*"

Floyd Mayweather, to his advisor Leonard Ellerbe
on hearing Hatton 'disrespect' him.

Ricky Hatton was in the mould of Britain's other everyman boxing heroes like Frank Bruno, Henry Cooper and Barry McGuigan. American ego and sporting prowess tends to encourage participants that nothing short of shooting for the stars is acceptable. Meanwhile, the British mentality mocks itself for merely turning up to a sporting event. That British stiff upper lip attitude varies from simply downplaying success all the way up to the doom of gallows humour.

But behind the façade, the joking and the self-effacing, not to mention his lifestyle between fights, Hatton always took training very seriously. Hatton and even his trainer Billy Graham allowed the indulgences between fights. But as soon as training camp began Hatton was as dedicated as any boxer you could name.

By 2007 Ricky Hatton had become the main man in the light welterweight (super lightweight) division. After conquering the Australian based Russian ('The Thunder Downunder') Kostya Tzsyu in dramatic fashion in May of 2005. Hatton had also tested the water at welterweight to become a two-weight world champion. In June of 2007 – a month after Mayweather announced his 'retirement' - Hatton destroyed José Luis Castillo inside 4 rounds with a vicious body hook that dropped the Mexican to the canvas where he failed to beat the count. After the fight the interviewer asked Hatton about Floyd Mayweather. Hatton grinned and mischievously responded; "I think you saw more action in these four rounds than you've seen value for money in Floyd's whole career and I'll just leave it at that."

When Mayweather saw this on TV, he immediately told his people to make the (fucking) fight. Not only would Mayweather have seen that as some kind of insult, but he now had something more to prove than just winning. He not only wanted to beat Hatton. He needed to beat Hatton at his own game and in his (Hatton's) own fighting style. Winning on points and by not engaging his opponent – as Floyd had done capably on many occasions - would not be enough. Mayweather probably already knew his game plan at that point. To meet the 'Hitman' at close range and prove that not only could he (Mayweather) fight that sort of fight but that he could do it effectively. In hindsight it could be said that Hatton had offered up a blueprint for his own downfall.

When Hatton threw down the gauntlet in the ring after the victory over Castillo it not only caught Floyd Mayweather's attention. The wider American boxing public took note. Who was this 'banger' with such a huge following? The cheeky, yet bold manner, in which he challenged Mayweather would have endeared him to many American sports fans (not just fans of boxing) as Mayweather was not particularly liked by everyone. Even though nobody doubted Mayweather's amazing skillset in the boxing ring it did not mean that they liked the man himself. Indeed, just as many sports fans wanted to see him lose as wanted to see him produce another virtuoso performance. Such was Mayweather's polarising effect on followers of the game.

Of course, Floyd Mayweather the businessman knew this as much as anyone and he exploited it to great effect. He knew full well that just as many people would pay good money to see him lose as would pay to see him win. Floyd Mayweather Jr. could sell out arenas to fans of either persuasion. A rare and remarkable ability.

Floyd Mayweather (Jr.)

"A superstar was born"

(On February 24th, 1977)

According to Floyd Mayweather Jr.

So much has been written and spoken about Floyd Mayweather Jr. Books, TV appearances and countless interviews. It goes with the territory, being the best boxer of his generation and the number one box office attraction for over a decade. This write-up cannot offer anything that hasn't already been said (probably numerous times) about Mayweather but merely attempts to scratch the surface. Starting with his family background...

Floyd Mayweather Junior was born into a boxing family. He was born in Grand Rapids, Michigan, USA on the 24th of February 1977. A month later his father Floyd Senior had his 12th professional fight.

Two of Floyd Senior's brothers began their professional careers in the 1980s. Roger Mayweather in 1981 and Jeff in 1988.

'Jazzy' Jeff Mayweather fought professionally from 1988 to 1997 at a reasonably high level but never quite made it to challenge for a world title. Jeff operated mainly at lightweight and finished his career with a respectable 32 wins, 10 defeats and 5 draws. Jeff was only stopped twice in his 10 losses, one of those was at the hands of the new rising star of boxing back in 1993 – Oscar De La Hoya. It was only De La Hoya's fifth fight on his way to becoming the widely acknowledged superstar of the sport. Until that is, he crossed paths with Floyd Jr.

Roger 'The Black Mamba' Mayweather was undoubtedly the best of the three brothers. He fought for and won real world titles in two-divisions, having held the WBA (and lineal) super featherweight title from 1983 to 1984, and the WBC super lightweight title from 1987 to 1989.

Roger fought the best of his era (and in some, arguably among the greatest of all time) in Pernell Whitaker and Julio Cesar Chavez. Late in his career Roger even fought Kostya Tszyu in Australia, losing via unanimous decision. It was Tszyu's first defence of the IBF World super lightweight title and ten years before Tszyu fought Ricky Hatton.

Roger Mayweather would be Floyd Junior's mentor and trainer throughout the peak of his career between 2000 and 2012.

Meanwhile, Floyd Senior fought mostly at welterweight in a career that spanned three decades between 1974 and 1990. Floyd Sr. never made it to boxing's top table, finishing his career with a record of 28 victories, 6 losses and 1 draw. Like his brother Jeff, Floyd Sr. was only stopped twice. One of those technical knockouts was at the hands of the great Sugar Ray Leonard in 1978 when Floyd Jr. was only one year old.

Shortly after the Leonard fight Floyd Sr. was shot in the leg in an altercation over drugs. It is common knowledge that Floyd Junior's mother was a drug addict and that Floyd Senior dabbled in drug dealing. As is often the case with these things Floyd Sr. had a dispute with one of his drug-dealing associates who turned up at the house with a shotgun. In an effort to deter the gunman from shooting him in the face or body, Floyd Sr. used his one-year-old son (Floyd Jr.) as a human shield. The assailant was none other than Floyd Junior's maternal uncle Tony Sinclair. Unable to get a clean body shot, Sinclair lowered the gun and shot Floyd Senior in the leg. The resulting injury kept Floyd Sr. out of the ring for a year.

Fortunately, Floyd Jr. was too young to remember that particular traumatising event, but his upbringing was certainly a complicated one. Despite all of that, with a father and two uncles boxing at such levels, Floyd Jr. was destined to take up boxing at an early age. All three brothers would play a part in teaching the younger Floyd the sweet science. Boxing was in his blood and a big part of his early life. It was both nature and nurture.

In 1993 big Floyd's illegal activities caught up with him and he was sent to prison for five years on drug dealing charges. It was a tricky time for the younger Floyd who was 16 at the time. He lived with his grandmother (in Grand Rapids) before she sent him to live with his uncle Roger in Las Vegas. But Roger was not cut out to raise a teenage kid, plus he didn't have the time as his own boxing career was on an upward trajectory. Roger got in touch with a businessman who he knew back in Grand Rapids. That man was Don Hale, and he provided a stabilising influence for the young Floyd just when he needed it. Hale (who Floyd Jr. calls "my white dad") was also involved in boxing and probably instilled the business acumen in Floyd Jr. When the hungry young boxer saw Hale's house, he knew that he too wanted a nice place like that someday. He also believed that he could reach those goals through boxing.

Floyd became a standout amateur and went on to represent his country in the 1996 Olympic games in Atlanta. The games ended in controversy when Floyd was eliminated in the semi-final stage, leaving him with (only) a bronze medal. Most observers believed Floyd should have been in the Olympic final, but the judges decided otherwise. It was not the first and will not be the last contentious Olympic boxing decision, but it left a bitter taste in Floyd Mayweather's mouth.

After that Olympic Games 'defeat' Mayweather made this bold statement: "Everybody knows Floyd Mayweather is the gold-medal favourite at 57 kilograms. In America, it's known as 125 pounds. You know and I know I wasn't getting hit. They say he's the world champion. Now you all know who the *real* world champion is." Mayweather was already sure of his status at the top of the boxing tree – even in the amateurs. Weeks later he turned professional.

From professional debut to world champion in 18 fights in a little under twenty-four months. Floyd Mayweather stormed through the super-featherweight division winning seventeen fights before facing Genaro Hernandez for the WBC world junior lightweight crown. Thirteen of his wins were via knockout and the other four by winning almost every round on every judge's scorecard. Yet the boxing world was still not overly impressed by Mayweather. The boxing press writers definitely saw that he was highly skilled but failed to recognise him as the superstar that the boxer himself claimed to be.

Mayweather was the first of the 1996 Olympians to fight for a world title. He won that title beating Hernandez via an eighth-round stoppage in his 18th fight. Hernandez had an impressive 38-1-1 record. His only loss at that point was three years earlier losing to boxing's new rising superstar Oscar De La Hoya. But that fight was at lightweight. He had never lost at super-featherweight and had also beaten the legendary Ghanaian super featherweight, Azumah Nelson. The defeat to Mayweather was Hernandez' last fight.

After winning his first world title Mayweather defended it six times over the next two years. The combined record of his opponents in the first five defences was 176 wins, 14 losses and 4 draws. Mayweather won three of those fights by stoppage and the other two via unanimous points decisions. He barely dropped a round on any of the scorecards.

In 2012, before his fight with Miguel Cotto, Mayweather was asked to rate his toughest opponents. During a conference call with reporters, Mayweather had this to say: "...I'm going to rate Emanuel Augustus first compared to all the guys that I've faced. He didn't have the best record in the sport of boxing, he has never won a world title, but he came to fight..."

Emanuel deserves a couple of pages here as one of the most amazing characters and unluckiest of boxers. His record shows 38 wins with 34 losses and 6 draws. But that record does not tell the real story of how good a boxer Augustus was. Many of those defeats were via contentious points decisions. Some were even called out on live TV coverage as blatant robberies.

He wasn't only unlucky in boxing. His luckless streak extended outside of the ring and almost cost him his life. On the night of October 13th, 2014, Augustus was seriously wounded when he was hit in the head by a stray bullet in a random shooting. The incident happened in Baton Rouge, Louisiana. He was in critical condition for some time on life support. Even in crime ridden inner cities getting shot by a stray bullet takes some seriously bad luck. The Baton Rouge police arrested the suspected shooter but subsequently had to drop all charges because there was no witness and no evidence of intent. Incredibly it was claimed that the suspect fired the gun in the air randomly rather than aiming it directly at Augustus (or anyone else). Augustus eventually recovered and continued living in Baton Rouge.

Emanuel Augustus fought half of his pro fights under his birth name, Burton. When his parents married in 2001, he adopted his biological father's surname, Augustus.

Originally, Burton/Augustus went by the boxing alias 'The Outlaw'. However, he became more regularly referred to as 'The Drunken Master' – a nickname taken from the 1978 Jackie Chan martial arts movie of the same name. It was also due to the unusual ring style of Augustus. A combination of shimmying dance moves like a puppet on a string and evasive boxing skills. When he was in top shape, he won fights. When he took fights at short notice, he often lost even though he entertained the crowds with his slick moves. He became a journeyman, but boxing crowds loved him. He was on the wrong end of many bad judges' decisions often due to his dancing and showboating his way through the fight. What entertained the crowds did not necessarily impress the judges. It is widely thought that judges disliked his clowning antics in the ring, mocking his opponent, and this is thought to have cost Augustus a lot of scoring decisions during his career.

When asked about their favourite fights many boxing fans point to the three-round war between Marvellous Marvin Hagler and Thomas Hearns on April 15th, 1985, in Las Vegas. Understandably. That was a truly great fight that has taken on legendary status. But how many of those, who would select that tremendous bout, have seen Floyd Mayweather vs Emanuel Burton? The first three rounds of that Mayweather fight arguably had more action and more talking points than the Hagler-Hearns slugfest.

Mayweather showed incredible balance, speed and skill in this fight and was clearly winning the rounds. But it was Emanuel Augustus (Burton) who was doing all the showboating as he made his own contribution to the fight landing clean punches with surprising regularity. Augustus also managed to smile throughout even when getting nailed by Mayweather. At the end of the fight Mayweather had landed 287 of 669 punches (43%) and Augustus landed 108 of 526 (21%).

It may not have had the war-like ferocity of the Hagler-Hearns battle but from a pure entertainment point of view it was every bit as good. Mayweather teed off with fast combinations throwing many of them with real venom. He had a lot of success. But Augustus (Burton) just kept coming forward, showboating and smiling at Floyd. He even blew a kiss at Mayweather as they parted at the end of the first stanza. It was almost as if he thought his best chance of winning was to wind-up and enrage his more skilful opponent. Augustus even mocked Mayweather in an explosive end to the third session, waving him into a major brawl. The referee had to separate the two fighters as the bell ended the round.

Augustus had relatively low success as he showboated his way through Floyd's punches, but he definitely caught Mayweather a few times, even bloodying Mayweather's nose in the 5th round. Rounds 6 through to 8 were more of the same. Floyd winning the rounds, but never slowing his eager and flamboyant foe. In the end Augustus was denied the chance to go the scheduled 10-round distance with Mayweather. It was not a stoppage by his opponent or the referee but his own corner who threw the towel in at the end of the 9th round.

Nine months and three fights later, Augustus took a fight with renowned brawler 'Irish' Micky Ward with only two weeks' notice. Ward won by unanimous decision, but most rounds were closely contested. The 10-round slugfest was named the 2001 Ring magazine fight of the year.

To appreciate just how well Burton/Augustus did against Mayweather consider the punch statistics provided by CompuBox. In less than 9 rounds Emmanuel Burton managed to land 108 punches in total. Supposedly much more accomplished boxers such as Oscar De La Hoya and Saúl 'Canelo' Álvarez managed to tag Mayweather 123 and 117 times respectively; but those figures were over the full twelve rounds. Several other fighters (undeniably more famous than Emmanuel Augustus) were unable to land as successfully on Floyd Mayweather over the full twelve rounds. These include Manny Pacquiao, Shane Mosley and Miguel Cotto. Ricky Hatton managed to land a mere 63 punches over 10 rounds in a fight where Mayweather, for the most part, stood toe-to-toe with Hatton – the British fighter's preferred battle zone.

Only Jose Luis Castillo and Marcos Maidana in their first encounters with Mayweather managed to land more punches (on average) per round than Emanuel Augustus.

Boxer	Punches Landed on Mayweather	No. of Rounds	Punches Landed Per round
Augustus (Burton)	108	9	12
Miguel Cotto	105	12	8.25
Zab Judah	82	12	6.8
Saúl Álvarez	117	12	9.75
Shane Mosley	92	12	7.66
Manny Pacquiao	81	12	6.75
Oscar De La Hoya	123	12	10.25
Ricky Hatton	63	10	6.3
Jose Luis Castillo 1	203	12	16.9
Jose Luis Castillo 2	101	12	8.4
Marcos Maidana 1	221	12	18.4
Marcos Maidana 2	128	12	10.6

Table 1: Punches landed on Mayweather (by opponent)

It is also worth noting that Castillo 1 and Maidana 1 are widely considered the two closest fights in Mayweather's career. Or to put it another way; the only two times that Mayweather even came close to losing.

Against Emmanuel Augustus, Mayweather threw more punches than he did against almost all of his top opponents. He threw slightly more only against Miguel Cotto over twelve rounds. In punch average per round, Mayweather unleashed more leather against Augustus than against any of his much higher profile opponents. Put simply: He had to! Once again, the punch statistics are worthy of scrutiny – see Table 2 below.

From the punch statistics in Tables 1 & 2 it is clear why Floyd Mayweather has said that his toughest fight was the slugfest against Emanuel Augustus/Burton.

Opponent	No. of Rounds	Total Punches thrown	Average thrown per round
Augustus (Burton)	9	669	74.3
Miguel Cotto	12	687	57.25
Zab Judah	12	404	33.6
Saúl Álvarez	12	505	42
Shane Mosley	12	477	39.75
Manny Pacquiao	12	435	36.25
Oscar De La Hoya	12	481	40
Ricky Hatton	10	329	32.9
Jose Luis Castillo 1	12	506	42.16
Jose Luis Castillo 2	12	399	33.25
Marcos Maidana 1	12	426	35.5
Marcos Maidana 2	12	326	27.16

Table 2: Punches thrown by Floyd Mayweather in key fights.

Mayweather's fight with Augustus was only three months before Floyd's first career defining fight against Diego Corrales for the WBC world super featherweight title.

When his career was over Mayweather would rank three of his rivals very highly. He rated Miguel Cotto for his strength and Manny Pacquiao for his overall boxing ability. Yet Floyd still classed Emanuel Augustus as his toughest opponent.

The victory over Emmanuel Burton took Mayweather's record to 24-0. At this point in time there was another boxer around the same weight carving his way through all before him. Diego 'Chico' Corrales had built up a solid 33-0 record including 27 wins by KO. The fight had been talked about for some time. Many involved in the sport thought that the hard-hitting Corrales would be the fighter who would finally get to Mayweather and possibly hurt him.

Corrales had won the IBF world super featherweight title in October 1999 beating the then undefeated Roberto Garcia (then 32-0) via a seventh round TKO. He fought again in December 1999 before knocking out Derrick Gainer on March 10th, 2000, at the MGM in Las Vegas. That beat-down of the tough Gainer was part one of a two-part Top Rank super featherweight world title event. Corrales fought first followed by Mayweather's unanimous points victory over Gregorio Vargas. While Mayweather won clearly it was Corrales' more exciting stoppage victory that caught the eyes of the boxing press. Once again Mayweather failed to get the media attention that he thought he deserved.

The Corrales fight was mooted to take place sometime in the year 2000 but it would not happen until January 2001. By that time Corrales had taken two more fights including a third round TKO victory against former Mayweather foe Angel Manfredy. On the face of it a confident victory by Corrales but he now had other, bigger problems outside of the ring. He had been arrested and charged weeks earlier for battering his three-month pregnant wife and faced a trial which could see him sent to prison.

In the build-up to the fight Mayweather was quick to capitalise on Corrales' personal problems. "I want Diego because I'm doing it for all the battered women across America", Mayweather said. "Just like he beat that woman, I'm going to beat him."

Both men were undefeated and neither had ever touched the canvas. In a breath-taking performance Mayweather knocked Corrales down five times. After the fifth knockdown, in round 10, Corrales' corner stopped the fight. Corrales barely managed to land nine punches a round (total of 60 out of 205) while Mayweather landed 220 out of 414 punches thrown. An incredibly high 50%+ punch rate against an opponent with height and reach advantage.

This was a true career defining fight for Mayweather. It catapulted him to the number one super featherweight spot. The HBO commentators heralded the arrival of a new pound-for-pound superstar and the whole of the boxing media finally gave Mayweather credit for a great performance. Top Rank promoter Bob Arum claimed that Mayweather was better than Sugar Ray

Leonard. Floyd Mayweather finally had the recognition he had craved.

Diego 'Chico' Corrales was born in Columbia, South Carolina in 1977. His family later moved to Sacramento, California where he became involved in street gangs at aged 13. But it was there that he took up boxing. Corrales compiled an impressive amateur record but reached his peak between Olympic Games. He turned professional in 1995 making his debut in March 1996.

Just over a year after he had become a world champion Corrales was arrested and charged with battering his then three-month pregnant wife in Sacramento, California. It was reported that she suffered a broken collar bone and three broken ribs.

Ironically, after struggling to make the 130-pound limit for the Mayweather fight, Corrales left prison at around 180 pounds. "I ate very well" he was reported as saying. While he was in prison Corrales received a visit from none other than James Prince, the manager of Floyd Mayweather. Prince wanted to manage Corrales on his release and promised to visit him again and look out for him. He kept his promises and Corrales became a Prince managed fighter when he returned to the ring in January 2003.

There were differing opinions on whether Corrales was in the right shape or frame of mind for the Mayweather fight. Some thought it was the impending prison time on his mind – which does not sound unreasonable. Others thought that making the weight was a big problem, again not an unreasonable assumption. Some 'in the know' said that Corrales was not doing the right things in camp. He was out at night drinking smoking and spending time with his future wife. That would fit in with both the issues of making weight for the fight and knowing that prison time loomed large only a matter of weeks after the fight. Whatever the exact truth Corrales was never in the fight, but that was as much to do with a perfectly tuned and ambitious Mayweather as with any problems 'Chico' might have had.

Corrales fought (and won) four times in the first six months of 2003 before facing the American based Cuban, Joel Casamayor, in October. Corrales lost for only the second time in his career. Both men were knocked down during the fight but it was stopped in the seventh round due to a cut inside Corrales' mouth. He trained hard and took a rematch with Casamayor five months later in March 2004, this time for the WBO world super featherweight title. Corrales won a close fight via a split decision. After serving 14 months in prison Corrales had redeemed himself.

In August of 2004 Corrales finally stepped up to lightweight and fought the Brazilian, former super featherweight world titlist and recently crowned WBO world lightweight champion Acelino Freitas. Corrales won the fight and the belt via a 10th round TKO.

In May 2005 Corrales made the first defence of his WBO world lightweight title against Mexican Jose Luis Castillo, who in turn put his own WBC world lightweight title on the line. Corrales won an unbelievable fight with a 10th round TKO after twice being floored himself in the same round. The two fighters would rematch exactly five months later when Castillo overturned the first fight with a fourth-round knockout victory. But it was their first fight everyone remembers.

The first Corrales-Castillo fight was the stuff of legend. It is widely quoted by boxing fans as the most exciting fight they have ever seen. It was 2005 Fight of the Year and also regularly tops lists of top fights of the decade.

After the rematch loss to Castillo, Corrales fought Joel Casamayor for a third time in October 2006 losing a split decision. Six months later in April 2007 Corrales lost by unanimous decision to Ghanaian Joshua Clottey. It was the last fight for 'Chico' Corrales.

On May 7, 2007, one month after his last fight and exactly two years to the day after his legendary first fight with Castillo, Corrales was killed in a road traffic accident near his Las Vegas home. He was riding a new Suzuki 1000cc motorcycle, along a road in the southwest part of the Las Vegas Valley. While attempting to overtake another vehicle at high speed, Corrales struck the back of the car and was thrown more than 100 feet when he was then struck by an oncoming vehicle. Corrales was rushed to a hospital but was pronounced dead on arrival. According to Las Vegas police the accident occurred at approximately 7:30 p.m. but could not say how fast the motorcycle was travelling. Corrales' blood alcohol content was 0.25 at the time of the crash, approximately 3 times the legal limit of 0.08 for the USA and state of Nevada. 'Chico' Corrales had effectively killed himself by riding his motorcycle at speed after consuming a large amount of alcohol. (Note: A blood alcohol content of 0.25 means that every 100 millilitres of blood contains 0.25 grammes of alcohol.)

The coroner checked for further evidence of both legal and illegal drugs but none was found. Corrales had had his motorcycle licence revoked only ten months earlier for driving under the influence of alcohol. He had a history of drinking and it had become problematic. At the time of his death Corrales' girlfriend was pregnant with their fourth child.

Corrales died just two days after Mayweather beat Oscar De La Hoya in the (then) richest prize-fight in history.

Lovemore Ndou was a former IBF Junior Welterweight World champion and long-time title contender who never got to face Ricky Hatton in the ring. Ndou claimed that Hatton considered him too risky a fight. Ndou won the IBF world super lightweight title in February 2007. Hatton had vacated that belt only two weeks earlier – no doubt to chase more lucrative fights in Las Vegas. Ndou did manage to fight a string of top opponents however during his career, including Miguel Cotto, Sharmba Mitchell, Junior Witter and Ricky's brother Matthew (at welterweight). Later in his career Ndou even fought Saúl Álvarez.

In his book (*Tough Love*), Ndou spoke of seeing two very different traits of Floyd Mayweather's character. Ndou was one of Mayweather's sparring partners in the build-up for the Hatton fight.

Ndou witnessed first-hand the brash side of Mayweather throughout fight camp and especially during their tough sparring sessions. But he also witnessed another side to the American fighter's persona. A side that was far more respectful and endearing. A side to his nature that was not shown on the fight build-up documentary series 24/7. At night Mayweather would often go out into the poor neighbourhoods to hand out food to those in need. The cocky 'Pretty Boy', the arrogant 'Money' man, had a caring nature he kept hidden from his stage presence.

Ndou gave as good as he got in sparring Mayweather and was always a tough opponent. Ndou finished his career with a record of 49 wins including 32 by KO, 13 losses and 2 draws. All 13 defeats were on points. No fighter ever stopped Lovemore Ndou.

In another act of kindness in 2011, Mayweather paid for the funeral of former super lightweight world champion and former opponent Genaro Hernandez, who had died of cancer after a three-year battle. It is difficult to know who the real Floyd Mayweather is. The man is a genuine paradox. The strange mix of Mayweather's "bad ass" public persona and the benevolent Floyd is one that remains to this day.

Ricky Hatton on the other hand was always a classic case of 'what you see is what you get'. There were no heirs and graces. No 'on stage' character. No desire to put on a show for the cameras. He didn't need to. He had character of his own and it was all natural. And he was the first to acknowledge that is why the fans loved him.

"I'm Floyd Mayweather and I can fucking fight"

Mayweather, despite all the controversy, prison time and TV persona knew better than anyone how he made all his money.

From his early amateur days Floyd Mayweather wanted to play the bad guy. He was told that with his talent he could be the next Sugar Ray Leonard, but he didn't want that. His reasoning was that people paid to see the bad guys. In many ways he was right.

Afterall, Mike Tyson had set the blueprint for that money-making role. When Mayweather was given his first opportunity for a pay-per-view (PPV) fight against Arturo 'Thunder' Gatti, his (Floyd's) bad guy persona took over and remained for many years.

Gatti was not as talented as Mayweather, but he was big box office. Fans knew he would always be involved in a gruelling do-or-die fight. He would fight anyone and had been involved in so many slugfests that taking this fight with Mayweather was only worth the risk because of the dollars that would be involved.

And a big risk it proved to be for Gatti. Mayweather put on a stunning performance humiliating Gatti from the opening bell and finally winning the bout when Gatti's corner retired their fighter at the end of round 6. Floyd Mayweather Jr. the talented new champion was now Mayweather the superstar. Five months later he had his first fight at welterweight, destroying the classy Sharmba Mitchell inside six rounds. That would be the last time Floyd fought as a non-PPV headliner. Every fight after the Mitchell bout would see Floyd Mayweather's earnings increase exponentially not only from bigger purses but also his share of the PPV revenue.

In 2006 Mayweather fought twice. In April he beat the still relevant and dangerous Zab Judah by unanimous points decision and claim his first "world" welterweight title (IBF). In November he fought the tough Argentinian Carlos Baldomir. Mayweather only dropped a couple of rounds across all three scorecards while (this time) claiming the WBC version of the world welterweight title. After the fight Mayweather proposed a super-fight against the sport's top star, Oscar De La Hoya.

Mayweather had to move up to the super-welterweight (154 lb) division to challenge De La Hoya for his WBC world title.

Oscar De La Hoya (aka 'The Golden Boy' or '*El Chico d'Oro*' in Spanish) also held another, unofficial title. He was universally recognised as the superstar of boxing. Floyd Mayweather wanted that accolade as much as the WBC belt.

Mayweather had just left Top Rank and was now promoting himself under his new company, Mayweather Promotions. He realised that De La Hoya was the A-side fighter and for once allowed his opponent to call all the shots. Mayweather agreed to everything De La Hoya said knowing full well that this fight was going to make him more money than any other (so far). But he also realised that beating 'The Golden Boy' would make himself, Floyd Mayweather, the number one attraction in boxing. He would then be the one calling all the shots and making the deals. This fight was about to put Mayweather exactly where he had wanted to be. Top of the pound for pound rankings and top of the tree in terms of box office earnings.

De La Hoya came out aggressively and won the first few rounds. But Mayweather stuck to his plan and won the latter rounds as De La Hoya slowed. In the end Mayweather won by split decision and most observers agreed. The fight generated a record breaking $165 million (gross) giving both fighters the best payday in their careers.

The promotional roadshow for the De La Hoya fight was a long one and it was said that Oscar found it tough. Mayweather meanwhile, seemed to revel in it as he laid on the trash talk, taking it to new levels. The fight, televised by HBO, was also the first time the channel ran the 24/7 behind the scenes documentary series in the build up to a fight. And it was on this first 24/7 series that 'Pretty Boy' Floyd introduced us to his new alias: Floyd 'Money' Mayweather. He knew that the money angle would cut right across every culture and every type of fan.

Throwing hundred-dollar bills at the camera attracted attention and he didn't care what kind. People would turn up and pay their money even if it was just to see him lose. Mayweather already had the winning formula inside the ring. Now he had found it outside of the ring too.

Ricky 'The Hitman' Hatton

> *"A working-class hero is something to be..."*
> John Lennon

Ricky Hatton never came from a boxing family like Floyd Mayweather. If anything, Hatton's sporting DNA was football related. His father Ray Hatton played for Manchester City football club. His grandfather played for Manchester City's B team. Naturally Ricky supported Manchester City. The young Ricky Hatton also played football and reveals in his books that as a youngster he was chosen by City to train at their school of excellence. But it was fighting that grabbed the attention of a young Ricky Hatton. By age eleven he was a regular on the local amateur scene.

While Hatton never boxed at the Olympics, he did manage to secure several junior ABA titles four years running between 1994 and 1997. He won the ABA title in 1997 at junior welterweight.

In 1996 Hatton represented his country at the AIBA Youth World Boxing Championships in Havana, Cuba. He was controversially eliminated in the semi-final where he fought Russian Timur Nergadze in the 63kg class. Four of the five judges made Hatton the winner, but the fifth judge awarded the bout to the Russian by a massive 16 points. Under the scoring rules (using the combined judges' scores) that meant Hatton lost the bout. Unsurprisingly, that fifth judge was later found to have accepted a bribe. Disillusioned with the amateur game, much as Mayweather had been after his Olympic semi-final loss, Hatton turned professional and would make his debut ten months later.

Ironically, Nergadze went on to convincingly win the gold medal in that world championship final. As the humorous Hatton would say: 'Fighting a Russian in Cuba? What could possibly go wrong?'

Having had a successful amateur career Ricky Hatton made his professional debut only 11 months after Floyd Mayweather Jr.'s first pro fight.

Hatton turned professional, aged 18 and was based at Billy 'The Preacher' Graham's gym in Moss Side in the south side of Manchester close to Manchester City's (now former) football stadium. His pro debut was not so much on the undercard of a boxing show as the *after* card. Hatton boxed *after* the main event – Robin Reid making the first defence of his WBC super-middleweight world title at a leisure centre in his hometown of Widnes, England. Hatton was made to wait even longer than he originally expected when Reid suddenly collapsed in the ring after his fight, due to exhaustion. By the time Hatton made his pro debut only the two boxer's families and the sports centre cleaners were there to witness it. Hardly the best way to start growing a fan base. But from that day onwards the crowds would grow. Eventually thousands would regularly follow him to fill stadiums both in the UK and 'across the pond'.

In only his second fight in December 1997 Hatton got a taste of what was to come. He fought in Madison Square Garden, New York on the undercard of the famous slugfest between Naseem Hamed and Kevin Kelly. From Widnes leisure centre to MSG in his first two bouts. Some leap.

Under the wing of boxing promoter Frank Warren, Hatton was fighting on the undercards of some big events in the UK. Warren's stable included world champions 'Prince' Naseem Hammed, Carl Thompson and Richie Woodhall. In only his eighth fight, in September 1998, Hatton again fought outside of the UK, in Germany on an undercard that included future heavyweight champion Wladimir Klitschko.

After 21 fights Hatton had won all 21, knocking out 17 of them. He then faced Jon Thaxton for the vacant British supe-lightweight title. It was a classic domestic slugfest, neither man giving quarter. The fight went the twelve-round distance with Hatton winning by four rounds in a referee's decision.

In his next fight Hatton stopped Tony Pep in four rounds for the vacant World Boxing Union (WBU) super-lightweight "world" title. It was a title Hatton went on to defend 15 times leading up to (arguably) his biggest success in the Kostya Tszyu fight.

The WBU was a very lightly regarded "world" title. Indeed, Floyd Mayweather scoffed at the WBU reference during the promotional tour for their fight, saying that he had never even heard of it. He probably hadn't. Whatever the merits of the WBU title fights, Hatton continued his undefeated streak, and the events were getting him noticed. His following continued to grow.

In the sixth defence of that WBU title Hatton fought another classic domestic dust-up against Northern Ireland's Eamon Magee. It was a tough 12 round decision victory for Hatton, but he learnt a lot from that fight. Although he had been knocking out most of his opponents, he realised that, against the ever-increasing level of opposition, he also had to use his boxing abilities. And despite his 'Hitman' moniker, Hatton did have considerable boxing skills.

Three fights later Hatton faced the tough and experienced American Vince 'Cool' Phillips. The American was probably past his best when he fought Hatton in April 2003, but he was tough. Phillips proved to be an immovable object for Hatton. Although the Manchester fighter could not stop Phillips, he did however win comfortably on all three scorecards.

Vince Phillips shot to fame winning the IBF world super-lightweight title by stopping the then unbeaten (18-0) Kostya Tszyu in May 1997 at the Trump Taj Mahal in Atlantic City, New Jersey. The fight was named Ring magazine's 'Upset of the Year'. Phillips won with a brutal technical knockout in the 10th round. Ironically it was only one of two losses (both by stoppage) suffered by Kostya Tszyu. The other was at the hands of Ricky Hatton – but that was still a long way off.

Phillips lost his IBF title in his fourth defence against fellow American Terron Millet in February 1999. He had mixed fortunes for the following three years but always lost when facing top opposition that included Vernon Forrest and Sharmba Mitchell.

Eight months after beating Vince Phillips, Hatton faced another solid fighter in Ben Tackie of Ghana. The two boxers faced off in a packed MEN Arena in Manchester, UK in December 2003. No matter how hard Hatton hit Tackie he could not shake him. Once again, Hatton showcased his boxing skills to win by unanimous decision, winning almost all of the 12 rounds on every scorecard. This was Hatton's 34th victory (25 by KO) and he was still undefeated.

The following year, 2004, Hatton fought four times. In April, June, October and December. All four were good Hatton victories. Three finished via KO plus another impressive boxing performance in a unanimous decision. The last of these 2004 fights was a KO win over the veteran Ray Oliveira. Hatton's record now stood at 38-0 and there was a clamour for a huge career defining fight. There was only one man that Hatton and his trainer Billy Graham wanted. And despite Hatton's impressive record it would be a real step up in class for the increasingly popular Mancunian.

The main man in the super lightweight division at that time was the fearsome Russian born, Australian based boxer, Kostya Tszyu. "The Thunder from Down Under" had been a bona fide world champion for over ten years winning the IBF world super lightweight title in only his 14th fight back in 1995. Since then, he had unified the division winning three of the major belts (WBC, WBA and IBF). Along the way he had beaten Floyd Mayweather's uncle (and trainer) Roger, the great Julio Cesar Chavez, Sharmba Mitchell and Zab Judah. Tszyu had beaten the very best and stopped most of them.

Since his spectacular KO of Zab Judah in November 2001 however, Kostya Tszyu had been less than active. He had only fought three times - once a year – in the three years leading up to the Hatton fight. Since that highlight reel knockout of Judah (the so called "chicken dance" performed by Judah is one of the most replayed knockouts of that era) Tszyu won two fights by KO and one points win over the ever durable Ben Tackie. Despite Kostya Tszyu's fearsome record even he could not stop Tackie. It is worth noting that Tackie was only ever stopped once and that was in his last fight in 2015 at the ripe age of 42. Knowing that Tszyu had an equally tricky time with Tackie, would certainly have given some encouragement to the Manchester fighter.

Hatton vs Tszyu was scheduled for May 4th, 2005, at the MEN Arena in Manchester, UK. By the time the fighters engaged in the ring it was the early hours of May 5th.

While Tszyu may have been the bookmakers' favourite it was Hatton who set the pace fighting at his own furious tempo to constantly pressure the Aussie boxing icon. Tszyu was a great fighter and tried his best to contain the force of nature that was being roared on by 22,000 fans in the Manchester Arena. Hatton's close work took away Tszyu's most potent weapon as the Russian born fighter was unable to unload his biggest punches from a safe distance.

Hatton was unyielding round after round. He took some good shots from Tszyu but managed to maintain his own rhythm. After eleven relentless rounds of action Hatton finally wore his opponent down. Tszyu failed to come out for the twelfth and final round. Exhausted in his corner, Tszyu retired on his stool. The great Kostya Tszyu never fought again.

Outside of Hatton's camp, while most were certainly hopeful, very few expected the result. Hatton joined the likes of Henry Cooper and Frank Bruno; boxers who transcended their sport to become national treasures. This victory was the stuff of sporting legend. In all of UK sport, not just boxing. This was the fight that truly made Ricky Hatton.

Four months after the Kostya Tszyu fight Hatton split with long time manager and promoter Frank Warren and moved over to Sheffield based promoter Dennis Hobson. Warren had done a great job with Hatton steering him to the Tszyu fight. Now it was Hobson's turn to take Hatton on the next stage of his career. A journey involving multi-million-dollar fights in Las Vegas.

Having defeated Tzsyu, Hatton's opponents would all be top level. There would be no easy fights now. Not that there were many (if any) before, but from now on Hatton would not necessarily be the favourite.

Hatton defended his newly won IBF title in a unification bout against the recently crowned WBA titlist Carlos Maussa. The wild swinging Columbian fighter had surprised many boxing fans in winning the vacant WBA belt by stopping American Vivian Harris inside of seven rounds. (That fight was a co-feature on Floyd Mayweather's first Pay-Per-View TV appearance against Arturo Gatti.)

Hatton was cut above both eyes in the first few rounds – both caused by accidental clashing of heads — but managed to survive and drop Maussa in the ninth round with a vicious left hook to the chin. It was a successful first defence of his super lightweight title, but Hatton was about to make the step up to welterweight.

Dipping his toes into the welterweight division, Hatton could hardly have picked a more difficult opponent. The tough as nails American, Luis Collazo was already a fully-fledged welterweight while Hatton was seeking to become a two-weight champion. The pair met in Boston, USA on May 13th, 2006, for the WBA world welterweight title that Collazo had won a year earlier.

The fight began well for Hatton. He caught Collazo slightly off balance in the first round scoring a knockdown. It was that extra point margin in that first session that probably made all the difference. The fight ebbed and flowed in favour of both fighters over the course of the twelve rounds. It was one of those fights where many rounds were difficult to score and could have gone either way. Collazo was comfortable sitting back for periods, with a high guard and soaking up Hatton's onslaughts. Hatton by contrast almost always looking to go forward. His higher intensity and more consistent work rate proving just enough to win the day. After the Tszyu fight this was a standout win making Hatton a two-weight champion. But in reality, he was never at his best in the welterweight division. Not even close. The signs were there for all to see. Ricky Hatton did not truly belong at welterweight. After the fight Hatton himself said that he was a natural junior welterweight (super-lightweight).

Hatton moved back down to super lightweight for his next fight against the Florida based Columbian, Juan Urango. This was for the IBF world super lightweight title Hatton had won from Tszyu. It was also Hatton's first taste of topping the bill in the boxing capital of Las Vegas on January 20th, 2007. Due to the date of the fight Hatton trained right through the Christmas and New Year period.

At the weigh-in for the fight Las Vegas got its first taste of Hatton-mania. Hundreds, if not thousands, laid siege to the weigh-in area chanting their now familiar Ricky Hatton songs.

Urango had not lost in 18 fights (one of those being a draw) and appeared very well built with plenty of upper body muscle. Hatton boxed smart and used his boxing skill when it became apparent that Urango was going nowhere. Urango was indeed a tough opponent for Hatton, but it gave boxing fans a chance to see a different side to Hatton's fighting abilities. It was a unanimous decision verdict with Hatton winning comfortably on all three scorecards. While Hatton's fan base had grown largely thanks to his go forward brawling style and his high knockout ratio, it is fair to say that his pure boxing ability had probably gone underrated.

Once again in the post-fight interview Hatton made it clear that he felt better stepping back down in weight class to super lightweight. Meanwhile, the growing army of Hatton fans was being noticed in America.

Five months later Hatton – with an even bigger following – would be back in Las Vegas to fight José Luis Castillo. This was the man who had twice fought Floyd Mayweather Jr. More importantly than that, many observers had Castillo winning their first encounter.

Castillo had fought on the same card at the Paris casino, Las Vegas, as Hatton vs Urango. The Mexican warrior won a split decision against the Cameroon born, Canadian based, Hermann Ngoudjo. Those fights were seen as two semi-finals for the vacant WBC world super lightweight title. The winner of that contest could stake claim to being the true king at super lightweight.

Hatton and Castillo met on June 23rd, 2007, at the Thomas & Mack Centre in Las Vegas. The result was clinical. A devastating body shot from Hatton ending the fight in only the fourth round. Castillo, the man who had gone two, full 12-round fights with Floyd Mayweather was chopped down mercilessly by a rampant Hatton. The comments from Hatton in the post-fight interview (as described above) led to the Mayweather-Hatton showdown less than six months later. The fight between the two boxers from opposite sides of the Atlantic Ocean was on. One of the two boxers was destined to lose their cherished unbeaten record.

The fans...

At the time Hatton began fighting in America, Manchester City football club were not the force they would become only a few years later. Despite lack of success on the field the football club still had an army of loyal fans and they identified with Hatton - himself a big Manchester City fan. As they had little to cheer at the football stadiums many of those football fans looked for sporting success to cheer elsewhere and became keen boxing fans. At least where Hatton was involved.

Initially at least, many were football fan converts. There has always been a certain cross-over with boxing and football fans. Football (soccer) is by far the most popular sport in the UK. It was always considered the working-class game and it's fair to say that many football fans also have an interest in boxing. Especially when it comes to the big fights.

Several years earlier boxers Lennox Lewis and Prince Naseem had brought thousands of fans over to the USA. A decade earlier Frank Bruno generated a large following when he twice fought Mike Tyson in the USA. While all of those were popular for their sporting achievements Hatton offered something else. Hatton was just like those sports fans, and they could identify directly with him. He enjoyed a few beers – maybe a few too many – and frequented pubs. Especially between training camps. He went to the same places as the paying public and did the same things. Such behaviour was not uncommon in bygone eras but is unheard of for the top sports stars of today. Being that 'ordinary man in the street' and accessible to the public made Hatton a working-class hero with what became something of a cult following.

Hatton's trainer Billy 'Preacher' Graham said in one of the HBO '24/7' documentaries in the lead up to the fight, that if Floyd Mayweather went to the part of town that he (Graham) came from, with all his fur coats and flash jewellery, that Mayweather would be stripped naked and left with no money in no time at all. That is probably true. The streets of Salford (and several other parts of the Manchester area) may indeed pose problems for someone flashing their Rolex watches as Mayweather is wont to do.

It is worth mentioning that Mayweather could also never go back to the place of his own upbringing for fear of being stripped bare – and much worse, if he wasn't very lucky. There are many tales of top boxers in the USA going back to their old neighbourhoods and getting into trouble.

It is a sad fact of life that once you have made it big it is very hard to be accepted in such areas. Not so for Ricky Hatton. He could go wherever he liked in the UK and the people would accept him without question.

Ironically Hatton's beloved fans could have had an impact on the judges' scorecards had the fight gone the distance. Before the fight many of the British fans had booed the American national anthem. Years later (in one of his books and several interviews) Hatton himself expressed how the American judges and the referee might have been affected listening to the travelling fans disrespecting their nation's anthem.

Over enthusiastic fans can sometimes be problematic for a 'celebrity' sportsman. In some cases, they can prove destructive. Take the case of the legendary footballer George Best as an example. Best played for the other Manchester team, United, not Hatton's beloved City. But Best was admired by everyone who loved football. Best was undoubtedly football's first real superstar. He transcended the sport. Not only was he blessed with exceptional footballing talent. He was a fashion icon, playboy and attracted attention wherever he went. He even had pop-star status, often being referred to as 'the 5th Beatle' in many countries.

In his various books Best often spoke openly about his drinking problem. He revealed that being George Best meant he never had to worry about money if he wanted to go out and get drunk. He knew that he could go down to a pub and there would always be people there who recognised him and would immediately offer to buy him a drink. Then have their photo taken doing so. How many of those "fans" have photographs of themselves having a beer with George Best? A beer that they would have bought for him. Such 'fans' were ultimately doing George Best no favours. If anything, they were a big part of the problem.

Hatton liked a drink – he is the first to admit it. But he was never an alcoholic like George Best. That said, it would have done Hatton no favours going out and drinking to excess in between fights with his adoring fanbase. Eventually such ballooning up in weight between competition catches up with every sportsperson. The question everyone involved in boxing was asking (if not openly) was; when would it catch up with Ricky Hatton?

While Hatton was still winning there was no issue with having a huge following. And kept winning he did. The crowds that followed him home and away just kept on growing. By the time of the Mayweather fight fans were filling charter flights all over the UK to fly over to Las Vegas. Most of them knowing full well there was no chance of a fight ticket; just wanting to be a part of the special sporting event. Male. Female. Boxing enthusiasts. Casual boxing fans. Some who barely had an interest in boxing - but still knew who Ricky Hatton was. They all wanted to be a part of the event. They were going to Vegas to support Hatton, the boxing star who was just like them. And they were going to have a good time doing it.

José Luis Castillo

Most great fighters eventually meet their nemesis. An opponent who they find hard to dominate. A rival that (by necessity) brings out the best in them. Or even, as the saying goes, a rival that "has their number". For Mohammed Ali that could be Joe Frazier or Ken Norton. Sugar Ray Leonard's nemesis could be Roberto Duran and/or Thomas Hearns. For Floyd Mayweather that nemesis came in the form of José Luis Castillo. They fought twice in 2002 and many people thought Mayweather was lucky to get the decision against Castillo in their first fight.

Castillo was the only common opponent shared by Hatton and Mayweather. Castillo fought Mayweather twice in April and December of 2002 (with another fight sandwiched in between in August 2002). Many boxing pundits and fans alike thought that Castillo should have been given the nod in the first Mayweather encounter. Floyd made sure there was no margin for error in their rematch, however. Regardless of the results Castillo had proven he could go the full twelve round distance -twice - with the all-conquering Mayweather.

In 2005 Castillo was involved in two awesome slugfests with Diego Corrales; both of which could have taken place in a telephone booth. The first fight (which Castillo lost by TKO in round 10) is widely considered one of the best fights of the decade. Castillo avenged that loss by stopping Corrales in the fourth round five months later. Although he won the rematch Castillo came in 3½ pounds over the lightweight limit of 135 lbs. That weight cost Castillo financially. It also meant that he was drifting into Ricky Hatton's weight class.

A third (decider) fight with Corrales was arranged but Castillo again failed to make the weight and the fight had to be cancelled. In turn this caused the Corrales team to sue Castillo for punitive damages.

By the time Castillo fought Hatton he had taken part in 63 bouts as a professional compared to Hatton's 42. Not only had Castillo been in far more fights, but many of them had been tough slugfests.

It is widely thought that by the time of the Ricky Hatton fight, Castillo was in debt. Financial troubles had followed him from his fights against Diego Corrales (who died less than 7 weeks before this fight) and Corrales' family were basically asking for Castillo's purse from his fight with Hatton.

The consensus among the TV commentators was that Castillo was a shot fighter when he fought Hatton. That is not to take away from Hatton's performance. He did what he trained to do and executed his own plan to the letter. But if the expert opinion was even close to being accurate then there was a chance that Hatton would be going into the Mayweather fight with a false impression, perhaps even over-confident. Such talk would not have affected Hatton. He simply wanted the opportunity to prove himself against the man universally recognised as the best boxer on the planet.

Serafim Todorov is one man who can make a serious claim to being the only boxer to beat Floyd Mayweather. Todorov was the Bulgarian boxer who beat Mayweather in the 1996 Olympic semi-final in Atlanta. That decision remains contentious, due to the scoring system used at the time. The rules required five judges to watch the fight and press a button if they saw what they deemed to be a scoring punch. If three of the five judges (a majority) pressed their buttons within a second of one another, a point was awarded to the fighter landing the punch. This system was not ideal in a number of ways – one being that it relied on the reaction time of judges of varying ages who were sat around the ring with differing vantage points from which to see (or not) punches land. The Olympic scoring system has since been changed, although it is probably never going to be perfect as further Olympic boxing controversy has demonstrated. Naturally both fighters thought they had scored more points (landed more punches) – and they probably had. Whatever opinion says, the records show that Mayweather was beaten.

After the Olympics Todorov was offered a professional contract to box in the USA. He claims it was similar to the offer Floyd received but how he would know that is anybody's guess. He returned to Bulgaria believing his country's boxing federation would look after him. When that failed to materialise drink and depression followed. He tried to change nationality to fight for

Turkey after he had been promised more financial help from the Turkish boxing federation. Politics got in the way of that plan and he remained in Bulgaria where he eventually turned pro just to make ends meet financially. His record was a mere 7 fights 6 wins and one loss against poor opposition. There was almost 12 years between his final two fights. He was never managed properly and ultimately failed in a sport in which he had clearly excelled as an amateur. With the correct financial backing and management who knows what he could have achieved in the professional ranks.

While he may not have been the only man to ever beat Mayweather (amateur or professionally) he was certainly the last man to do so. Floyd became the richest athlete in the world while Todorov had a very different future struggling to make ends meet. That is the hand that life can deal. Todorov's is a tale of what might have been; but more than that it is a tale of 'how the hell did that happen?' How did the sport of boxing allow a gifted and decorated amateur like Todorov – Olympic silver medal winner and three-time world champion – to fall by the wayside?

At that time Bulgaria was struggling economically with the transition from the fall of communism to the more capitalist "western" system. Todorov took any odd job he could find before trying to win some money in the ring. Years later, it is unlikely that an amateur boxer with Serafim Todorov's record would not be correctly guided into the paid form of the sport. There have been plenty of successful and talented fighters from Eastern Europe since those 1996 Olympics.

Meanwhile that Olympic semi-final loss only served to galvanise Mayweather's resolve. "I'm happy with how the result went. I'm really happy because that made me strive and work hard to get to where I'm at today," Mayweather said, when interviewed about it before his mega fight with Pacquiao.

The Fight

The main event was billed as "Undefeated", between two fighters who had amassed 81 wins with no defeats. It could have been billed as anything by the time it started. The MGM Grand was packed out. The bars in Las Vegas were full of Ricky Hatton fans. All over the city the atmosphere was electric

Hatton started fast and was straight in on Mayweather's chest. Looking to press the action but being unable to do much solid work. Despite all the talk about the referee, Joe Cortez, not allowing Hatton to do his work inside, the British fighter won the round on most people's scorecards. Half-way through the round Hatton caught Mayweather moving backwards and it looked to many as if he had almost knocked the pound for pound king over. But it was as much a stumble as a clean punch. Mayweather was not running as many expected he might. He was watching his opponent and engaging him at close range. By the end of the round Mayweather was cleanly connecting with left hooks and solid straight rights.

The second round was much like the first. Lots of clinching most of it justifiably being broken up by the referee. After five breaks the referee called a timeout and told both fighters to stop holding. A pattern was already emerging, however. Mayweather was quick enough to score with straight right-hand punches and follow up into a clinch. The single shots were accurate and powerful and would take their toll as the fight wore on.

These early rounds saw some success for Ricky Hatton. Mayweather seemed content to engage at close quarters despite having a huge 6-inch (15cm) reach advantage. It was as if he wanted to fight and win Hatton's style of fight. Ominously, by the third round it was clear that Mayweather was beginning to adapt to Hatton's style.

The third round was similar to the first two. The referee allowed Hatton to fight on the inside for long periods, even warning Mayweather about using his elbows. Again, Hatton failed to capitalise and Mayweather picked him off whenever he could. So much so that Hatton was cut over the right eye as the round came to a close. If Hatton wanted this to be a rough fight, then that is exactly what he was getting.

In the fourth round the referee basically allowed both fighters to go nose to nose. For the first two minutes Hatton had Mayweather exactly where he wanted him but failed to do any real work. In the final minute of the round Mayweather broke free from his opponent to launch attack after attack. Every time Hatton tried to get back in Mayweather's face he was met with solid leather. Mayweather was beating Hatton at his own game. They were mostly single shots, but they were hard and accurate. There were also some combinations coming from Mayweather. The master boxer turned brawler was beginning to break the British fighter down.

Round five was fought almost entirely as Hatton would have wanted. The odd breaks by the referee in that round were, if anything, saving Hatton from Mayweather's fouls. The round went to Hatton on all the scorecards, but it did not seem to bother Mayweather. He was biding his time and was never in trouble. In between rounds five and six Cortez went over to Floyd Mayweather's corner to warn him about holding. Apart from the first round this was probably the only other session won by Hatton.

By the sixth round Hatton's frustration was showing. After a minute of action Mayweather spun and slid through the ropes. Hatton charged in and appeared to hit the American on the back of the head while he was doubled over. Replays showed that Hatton never really connected but the intent was clearly there. To the referee – who was seeing this from behind Hatton – it must have looked like a foul. He deducted a point from the Englishman. Hatton frantically sought to even the round, but the remainder of the session was scrappy and difficult to score.

Round seven was notable for one thing. The referee let the fighters clinch, roll and maul for almost the entire round. It was very messy. Referee Cortez only separated the two near the end of the round when Hatton's armpit became a holding point for Mayweather's neck – and quite rightly. Note that quite a few of the separations in the early rounds were for the same infringement. Mayweather won round seven because he was the only boxer landing anything. Hatton was now getting peppered in the clinches by the much faster American. Mayweather was systematically breaking Hatton down as he fought part of the seventh with a smile on his face.

In round eight Hatton took a real beating. All credit to Hatton for trying. He managed to land a few cleaner shots in the eighth period but despite being in close for most of the round it still seemed like he wasn't trying to land any of his trademark body shots. Easier said than done of course when your opponent is a defensive genius. It was such a big round for Mayweather that after the bell the referee went over to Hatton's corner to check if he was ok to continue. Hatton did continue but the writing was now clearly on the wall. One U.S. commentator wondered if round eight was the beginning of the end for Hatton.

On any scorecard the early success of Hatton had been turned at this point. But none of that was to matter. In the corner at the end of the eighth round Roger Mayweather told his nephew in no uncertain terms, "You don't have to run from this motherf*#ker. You can beat him on the inside". It was both an accurate and prophetic statement. Mayweather Jr was now landing almost at will and from almost any distance.

The ninth was a clear Mayweather round. Every time Hatton got in close and into a position to take a shot, Mayweather hit him with a straight jab and Hatton was forced back to square one. Yet Hatton was still in the fight. He was not particularly tiring and showed great courage to come forward in the ninth, always trying to make a brawl of the event. If there were points for sheer persistence, then the fight would have been stopped and the referee would have raised Hatton's arm. But when guts and determination are met with clean, solid punches, the ending can be brutal. And so it proved… The end was in sight with three rounds remaining.

Hatton's corner clearly thought their man was behind as they urged him to win the final rounds. Hatton emerged from his corner just like every other round with a spring in his step. He was not tired despite the steady punishment that had been meted out to him. For the first minute of the round, it was the same as the previous rounds. The same perhaps, but never boring. Then just after one minute, with Mayweather retreating towards his own corner Hatton attempted to launch a right hook. Mayweather skipped out of the corner to his left and threw a perfect left hook that caught Hatton coming in. A combination of the check left hook and Hatton's own momentum sent the British fighter crashing into the corner post. Down went Hatton.

Hatton quickly rose first to his knees then stood at the count of eight. With more than half of the round remaining survival would have been a difficult task against any fighter. But Mayweather was not just any fighter. He was the best in the world. A superb exponent of the art of boxing. He could taste the finish and went for it immediately. It was time to close the show.

The end was brutal but thankfully swift. After twenty seconds Mayweather connected with four clean accurate punches that had Hatton rolling against the ropes. As Hatton stumbled and eventually fell for the second time the referee was already pulling Mayweather away and waving off the fight.

Should the referee have allowed it to continue? Or did this (final) intervention by Cortez ultimately save Hatton from serious damage? Maybe that question should be aimed at anyone who believes that Joe Cortez interfered too much in the early rounds.

The official end was 1 minute 35 seconds of round ten.

In an article for Boxing News magazine in April 2020, award winning boxing journalist Thomas Hauser recounted the Mayweather vs Hatton fight. His article focussed, in part, around the theory that referee Joe Cortez did not allow Hatton to fight in close. It was a theory that had seemingly become accepted fact for Hatton fans and for Hatton himself. Hauser noted that Cortez broke the fighters 11 times in round one, 13 times in round two and 14 times in round three. At the same time claiming that on many of these breaks one or both fighters had an arm free and was punching.

This account of the fight challenges any suggestion that the referee was unreasonably breaking the fighters – giving an apparent advantage to Mayweather. Furthermore, it is contested that Mayweather was never even trying to get away from Hatton. Rather, the exact opposite.

Hauser's article mentioned a total of 38 occasions when referee Joe Cortez broke the fighters during the first three rounds. However, it was purely a count and there was no attempt to analyse them in detail. When examined individually it is difficult to make a case against more than 11 of those (38) refereeing interventions. Out of those 11 possibly contentious breaks, almost half could be considered subjective; 50-50 calls.

In rounds two and three the referee allowed the fight to continue for several spells while the two fighters were in close. But only when there was no solid clinch. All fight fans are encouraged to watch those early rounds closely, with an open mind and probably with the commentary turned off. Only on a few occasions did Cortez break up the clinches unnecessarily and even some of those are subjective. The majority of the referee's interventions were perfectly justified. Many of the breaks were because either one fighter had an armpit around the other's neck or one (mostly Mayweather) had the other fighter completely tied up. Some breaks were made *after* allowing the two fighters to clinch and maul, for between 10 and 20 seconds, when they finally tied each other up and clearly needed separating.

It could well have turned into a farcical wrestling match had the referee not called for the majority of those breaks.

As a further challenge to that supposed refereeing issue it is only fair to offer this alternative viewpoint. The whole thing was greatly exaggerated during the post-fight analysis on the British TV coverage. Their man had lost and naturally during the 'post-mortem' the British TV panel were, to a certain degree, searching for excuses. This view of the fight soon took on a life of its own once Hatton's fans had listened to it. Very soon afterwards that topic of conversation became something of a myth surrounding this fight.

Moreover, Hauser's article only mentioned the number of breaks for the first three rounds. Only one quarter of the scheduled fight. From round four onwards there were very few breaks by the referee, and Joe Cortez clearly allowed the boxers to fight up close for long periods. It is also worth noting that on the occasions when the referee allowed them to fight in close Hatton was mostly ineffective. This fact was never widely discussed after the fight, nor in Hauser's article.

In addition, Hatton's trainer Billy Graham was heard between rounds instructing his own fighter not to get too close in order to avoid smothering his own work.

In fact, some breaks by the referee were actually protecting Hatton from Mayweather's less than legal use of the elbows. But this was a brutal prize-fight and there were fouls from both fighters. As Hatton himself was heard to say on more than one occasion during post-fight interviews; "It's not a tickling contest."

The harsh truth is that even if Ricky Hatton's own mother had been referee that night in Las Vegas, the result would not have been any different.

Mayweather did exactly what he needed; when he needed – as he so often did. Quick punches then grabbing his opponent. Then boxing sharp on the breaks. Hatton's early success was soon overrun by the much cleaner, crisper work from the American. By the third round the boxer having most success fighting on the inside was Floyd Mayweather. Not only had Mayweather nullified Hatton's supposed strengths – the 'Hitman's' best and probably only chance of winning – but the American went one better. He had taken that weapon and turned it against the British fighter.

Mayweather was winning the inside fighting and wearing down the determined Hatton. By the end of the fourth round Hatton was taking a beating and looked like he had been in a fight. Mayweather looked completely untouched.

In the end there was no shame in defeat for Hatton. Like so many of Floyd Mayweather's opponents he was completely outclassed by a much better boxer. Mayweather fought Hatton's own fight, not a style he was used to it has to be said. Mayweather adapted very quickly to that style of fight and simply took control early in the proceedings.

Mayweather had fought Hatton on the inside as well as on the outside and won both contests. In the interview immediately after the fight, he said that he was aware that he had recently given the fans a couple of dud fights. Mayweather wanted to show how sharp and effective he really was. He wanted to put on a show and that is exactly what he did.

Floyd Mayweather controlled the fight. Totally. He wanted this Hatton style, toe-to-toe duel. He could have easily done an exhibition job, boxing and dancing his way to a comfortable points decision. (He did just that in several other bouts years after this fight.) There was a determination in Floyd Mayweather for this fight. As if he felt the need to prove he could adapt to any style, and not only fight that style, but *win* doing it. Take Hatton's own style and use it against him.

Great fighters tend to make good fighters (even **very** good ones) look ordinary. That is exactly what happened in this fight.

Mayweather was never known as a knockout artist. In the final third of his career, he won most of his fights on points. Between April 2006 and the end of his last (real) fight against Andre Berto in September 2015, Floyd Mayweather had fourteen fights. Only two of those fights never went to the scorecards. One of those was a fourth-round knockout of Victor Ortiz in September 2011 (see later). The only other stoppage that Mayweather managed in that fourteen fight, nine-year period was the KO victory over Ricky Hatton.

Back in 1998 Floyd Mayweather was named The Ring magazine's Fighter of the Year when he won seven fights including his historic first world title against Genaro Hernandez and the defence against Angel Manfredy. After beating Oscar De La Hoya and Ricky Hatton in 2007, Mayweather was again named Ring magazine Fighter of the Year. An incredible nine years after his first award. In 2010 he was named Ring magazine Fighter of the Decade.

In one interview after the dust had settled on the Mayweather–Hatton fight, Mayweather sang his own version of the 'Winter Wonderland' tune. The tune that had become the anthem for the travelling hordes of Hatton fans.

There's only one May - Weather,
One May - Weather,
Walking along,
Singing a song,
Walking in a Money wonderland

The days of 'Pretty Boy' Floyd were gone. The new era of 'Money' Mayweather had truly arrived.

Aftermath...

Following the Hatton fight Floyd Mayweather announced his retirement saying that he wanted to concentrate on his promotional company. It was almost two years later when he made his return to the sport, and it was around that time that his past began to catch up with him.

Mayweather had a history of brushes with the law long before fighting Ricky Hatton. Several involved acts of violence against women.

In 2002, Mayweather was charged with two counts of domestic violence and one count of misdemeanour battery. He escaped jail receiving a six-month suspended sentence. Ironically 2002 was the year that Mayweather twice fought Jose Luis Castillo, famously struggling in the first bout.

In 2004, Mayweather was given a one-year suspended jail sentence, ordered to undergo counselling for "impulse control" after being convicted of two counts of misdemeanour battery against two women that occurred in a Las Vegas hotel nightclub.

In 2005, Mayweather pleaded no contest to a charge after hitting and kicking a bouncer, for which he received a 90-day suspended jail sentence.

Four years after the Hatton fight jail time finally caught up with Mayweather. On December 21st, 2011, just three months after the infamous victory over Victor Ortiz (see below), a judge sentenced Mayweather to serve 90 days in the county jail.

The original charge involved battery of his former partner Josie Harris. Just like one of those US legal agreements that you see in the movies Mayweather struck a deal with the prosecutors, pleading guilty to one charge and no contest to another. In return the prosecution dropped a more serious charge. In addition to the 90-day sentence Mayweather was ordered to do 100 hours of community service, complete a 12-month domestic-violence program and to pay a fine of $2,500.

Somehow the deal also delayed the jail term for some six months. This allowed Mayweather to remain free to train for and fight the biggest boxing match-up of the year when he took on Puerto Rican warrior Miguel Cotto. The fight took place in Las Vegas on the

Cinco de Mayo weekend. Mayweather won comfortably on all three scorecards.

On June 1st, less than one month after the Cotto fight, Mayweather began serving his county jail sentence. He was released on August 3rd, 2012.

Mayweather's past again caught up with him in 2015 when a planned tour of Australia had to be cancelled. Mayweather was denied a visa on the grounds of having a criminal record and having served jail time.

Mayweather went on to fight 11 times more over the next 10 years. Fighting many future Hall of Famers; including Shane Mosely, Miguel Cotto, Marcos Maidana (twice), Manny Pacquiao, Saúl 'Canelo' Álvarez and Juan Manuel Marquez.

Ten of those fights were held at the MGM Grand in Las Vegas. The place had become home to Mayweather and he made lots of money for himself and his opponents whenever he boxed there.

During Mayweather's various retirements other boxers scrambled for a version of the welterweight world title. Mayweather fought once In September 2011 Mayweather challenged the recently crowned WBC welterweight champion Victor Ortiz.

The then WBC title holder Ortiz, famously dropped his guard after the referee had called a timeout and deducted a point from Ortiz for charging in with his head. Ortiz was still too busy apologising when the referee allowed the fight to resume. Ortiz forgot the golden rule of boxing: "Protect yourself at all times." When Ortiz dropped his hands to apologize (again), Mayweather struck, dropping him with a left hook followed by a big right hand. Ortiz was unable to rise and was counted out.

The bizarre ending to the Mayweather-Ortiz fight was somewhat eclipsed by the post-fight ring interviews. With many of the crowd clearly unhappy with the way Mayweather had behaved and booing the new champion, HBO commentator and interviewer Larry Merchant quite rightly wanted to delve into the fight's conclusion. What Mayweather had done was not illegal, but most people agreed that it was unsporting. Mayweather was upset at Merchant's line of questioning and lost his temper telling Merchant that HBO needed to fire him and that he (Merchant) didn't know shit about boxing. Finishing up with the insult "You 'aint shit. You 'aint shit." Merchant, who was 80 years old, retorted by saying "I wish I was 50 years younger, and I'd kick your ass!". Over the years the fighter and commentator had become something of an unofficial double act with several spats of verbal jousting, mostly during post-fight ring interviews. That particularly heated exchange received as much attention as the fight ending itself and proof of that old adage; There is no such thing as bad publicity. As Larry Merchant later reflected; he (Merchant) was just another guy in Floyd Mayweather's movie.

As for Victor Ortiz, like so many Floyd Mayweather victims, his career was never the same after that defeat. In his last seven fights he never reached the heights of world title bouts again, winning three and losing three and finally going out with a majority draw.

Floyd Mayweather has been accused of playing it safe in his final run of fights. A little unfair perhaps, at least when you consider his first fight against Marcos Maidana. Floyd took a fair bit of punishment in that fight and still gave Maidana a rematch. But Mayweather was a safety-first type of fighter at this stage in his career and avoided (where possible) getting involved in toe-to-toe battles. He had seen what boxing can do. His long-time trainer, uncle and friend Roger passed away in March 2020 but his health had been in decline for some years. Roger's last appearance as Floyd's trainer was the Miguel Cotto bout in 2012. Floyd Senior returned to the fold as Junior's trainer for the next fight against Robert Guerrero in 2013.

Over the years Roger had suffered from memory loss among other things and Floyd opened up about the problems in 2015. Floyd said that boxing had played its part in Roger's decline. Floyd was fully aware of the dangers of the sport that he dominated. He always said that he wanted to retire from boxing, not for boxing to retire him.

Mayweather's last real fight was on 12th September 2015 against Andre Berto. Another comfortable points win for Floyd. After that he retired (again) but came back into the ring for a fight against the UFC (cage fighting) champion Connor McGregor in August 2017.

This was more of an exhibition bout than a genuine boxing match as McGregor was making his boxing debut. For what it's worth Mayweather won the "fight" via a tenth round TKO.

Regardless of the opponent it was definitely all about making money as far as Floyd was concerned. Something he was now highly proficient at. Initially, Mayweather was guaranteed $100 million while McGregor was guaranteed $30 million. However, the eventual purse for the two fighters was widely reported to be much higher, with Mayweather said to have earned $280 million from the fight and McGregor earning $130 million.

Floyd 'Money' Mayweather then retired with a perfect professional record of 50 fights, 50 wins and no losses.

In the immediate aftermath of the fight, Hatton's trainer Billy Graham was interviewed by Sky Sports (UK) inside the ring.

Graham explained how he had told Hatton that closing down Mayweather wasn't going to be a problem. As fast as he (Floyd) was, he wasn't that fast. The problem for Hatton was going to be what to do when he got close to Mayweather. "Ricky smothered his own work" and "Ricky was too close to work" were the immediate reactions from Hatton's long-time trainer. That analysis is all too apparent on watching the fight. Regardless of any refereeing criticism (which only emerged later) two things are clear to see: Mayweather was smarter and more relaxed when the fight was fought at close range, while Hatton not only 'smothered his own work' but also never attempted to capitalise with his famous body shots.

Perhaps more tellingly Graham finished that interview by saying "I told you, he's a junior welterweight. I told everyone, he's a junior welterweight." It later became common knowledge that Graham was not happy with Hatton fighting at welterweight because he thought that he (Hatton) was too small. This is something most boxing insiders agreed with. Was this the first sign that the famous partnership was about to fall apart? The only other time Hatton had stepped up a division was against Luis Collazo and while Hatton won a famous victory, it was a tough and close fight where he needed to box on the outside to keep the naturally bigger man at a distance.

After that first career loss to Mayweather, Graham would be in Hatton's corner for his comeback bout against Juan Lazcano. But it would be his last fight with Hatton. The fight was six months after the loss to Mayweather and Hatton won by unanimous decision although it was a tough contest.

Less than a year after the Mayweather fight Hatton was again fighting inside the MGM Grand in Las Vegas. This time he was facing former titlist, New Yorker, Paul Malignaggi. Soon after the fight was made Hatton revealed that Graham would not be able to make it through the 12 weeks of training. Hatton announced that his new trainer would be Floyd Mayweather Sr. The father of the man who had given Hatton his first defeat.

It seems an odd thing to say about the man who had been his only trainer. Graham's hands may have been fragile, but he would not have necessarily be the one holding the pads to give Hatton the required workouts. The physical tasks could easily have been given to another person with Graham instructing and demonstrating when needed.

It is easy to speculate but Hatton maintained that he (Hatton) was the boss, and it was his decision alone. However, rumours abounded, and it wasn't long before Graham sued Hatton. (This dispute was settled out of court several years later.)

Graham initially said he was retiring but then came out in the newspapers saying that he had been sacked. Hatton quickly countered with a newspaper interview in which he said that he had to let Graham go because his body was "shot" and he was struggling getting through training sessions. It was long known that Graham had been having pain killing injections to get through training camps. It was an openly discussed topic in the HBO 24/7 series building up to the Mayweather fight. What was not clear was how much other people – notably Hatton's father – had in the decision.

Under new trainer Floyd Mayweather Sr., Hatton won on his return to the MGM Grand. The fight was stopped in the eleventh round by Malignaggi's corner – much to the annoyance of the Brooklyn fighter. Hatton was way ahead on the scorecard and Malignaggi was never going to knock his British opponent out. But he still wanted to go the distance and not have the TKO loss on his record.

Six months later and Hatton's fans returned to Las Vegas in bigger numbers for arguably a much bigger fight. Hatton took on the Filipino sensation Manny Pacquiao. Since the Hatton-Mayweather fight the "Money" man had been in retirement. Mayweather didn't fight again until September 19th, 2009, when he took on Juan Manuel Marquez. During this time Manny "Pacman" Pacquiao had taken over the mantle of best pound-for-pound fighter on the planet. It was another huge task for Ricky Hatton. Floyd Mayweather Senior would again be Hatton's trainer.

This time there was no talk of poor refereeing. The result was both decisive and devastating. Pacquiao flattened Hatton at the end of the second round with a perfect left hook to the chin. It took several worrying minutes before Hatton was back on his feet. The proud British fighter had already been floored twice in the first round. This, after claiming that he was unbeatable at super-lightweight – his best and usual fighting weight. The loss seemed to embarrass and humiliate Hatton.

Having Floyd Mayweather Sr as trainer did not work out too well for Hatton. The two parted company and Hatton went into retirement in all but name.

Following the loss to Pacquiao Hatton's personal life was far more publicised than his sporting success. There were reports of much drinking and even drug use. While Hatton found his first ever defeat (to Mayweather) very hard to come to terms with, the manner of the loss to Pacquiao was even more difficult to handle. The dispute with Billy Graham was still ongoing and soon after Hatton fell out with his parents.

'The Hitman' Hatton and 'The Preacher' Graham even sounds like a hardworking double act. It was. In some ways they overachieved. Ricky Hatton never had exceptional boxing skills. He was a good fighter, sometimes very good but he was never great. Yet with Graham's help and plenty of hard graft the two managed to accumulate a record of 44 wins and 1 defeat*. That one loss was to the best fighter in the world (at that time) and arguably the finest boxer of his generation. A true great, in Floyd Mayweather. More than that, it was in a weight class that Hatton was never really big enough for.

(* - Hatton lost twice more after Graham's departure)

Hatton did not box for over three years and many thought he had retired for good. But he hadn't officially announced any such thing. He had to know if there was anything left and needed one final hurrah in front of his adoring fans.

It was an emotional night in Manchester on November 24th, 2012. Three and a half years after the devastating knockout loss to Manny Pacquiao, Hatton made his return to the ring against the tough Ukrainian, Vyacheslav Senchenko. The fight took place in the MEN Arena in Manchester, UK. The scene of Hatton's greatest triumph, his stoppage of Kostya Tszyu, a long seven years earlier. This time Bob Shannon was Hatton's trainer.

After such a long lay-off there was no way Hatton was going to make his best fighting weight of super lightweight. He had ballooned more than ever in the three year lay-off. The fight was held at the welterweight limit of 147 lbs and was scheduled for ten rounds. In the end the fight only lasted nine rounds. Ironically, a hook shot to the body – Hatton's own trademark punch - sent Hatton down and he could not recover. Although the fight was closely contested up to that point it was clear that the Hatton of old was no longer there.

Hatton announced his retirement in an emotional post fight interview. It was the end of a great career in which he had achieved more than he could have ever dreamed of when he first started boxing.

Hatton was honest with himself as his words after his final fight revealed. "I got what I wanted from my comeback even though it ended in a defeat. I needed to find out if I still had it, and I didn't. It allowed me to move on with my life," he said.

At that juncture Hatton should have been content. He should have been happy with his career inside the ring and looking forward to a new career outside the ring as a trainer and promoter.

But something was clearly wrong. For some time after retiring Hatton suffered from bouts of depression that got so bad at times, he even contemplated taking his own life. There was something gnawing away inside him.

Although Hatton states in his book that the depression began following the loss to Mayweather in this legendary fight, things obviously got worse following the rift between Hatton and his long-time trainer (and friend) Billy Graham.

Following the loss to Pacquiao he had also fallen out with his own parents. Such family disputes are very personal, and this text is no place to analyse what went on between Ricky Hatton and his parents. Suffice to say that Hatton probably felt very lonely at that point.

What exactly Hatton was looking for at that time perhaps only he himself can say. But the fall from adored sports star to potential suicide victim was a steep and dark descent.

Did Hatton feel that he had let his fans down? After those one-sided defeats to Mayweather and Pacquiao he seemed to be very confused. It seems that Hatton was looking for answers. But was he asking himself the wrong questions?

In reality he was never at the level of Floyd Mayweather and Manny Pacquiao. He had not been disgraced by either of those defeats. He achieved more than most just by being able to get those fights. Very few reach those dizzy heights, but he had done it. And he had done it with Billy Graham at his side for 45 professional fights.

Eventually Ricky Hatton made up with Billy Graham. It happened in 2015 at a celebration to mark the tenth anniversary of Hatton's most famous victory over Kostya Tszyu. A few years later Hatton also made amends with his parents.

Following the reconciliation with his parents and his former trainer Graham, Hatton finally found peace with himself and was able to concentrate on the training and promotional sides of the sport. The sport that he blessed inside the ring for so many years.

Undercard:

The undercard was not too inspiring. It didn't need to be as the main event was so huge.

Ricky Hatton's brother Matthew had a workman-like unanimous points win over eight rounds against Puerto Rican, Frankie Santos.

The chief support was a WBO super bantamweight world title fight between two tough Mexicans, Daniel Ponce De Leon and Eduardo Escobar. It was the aggressive Ponce De Leon who overcame a defensive sound Escobar for a unanimous points win over 12 rounds. He would lose the title only six months later in his next fight but remained a serious contender fighting many of the top boxers in his weight division.

New Yorker Daniel Jacobs made his debut beating Mexican Jose Jesus Hurtado. Jacobs won with a first round KO in a scheduled 4 rounder. Jacobs went on to become a top fighter involved in some big bouts. He has been a multiple world title challenger, winning a couple of versions of the middleweight world title along the way. Jacobs also lost a few title bouts against the very best.

Danny Garcia had his 2nd fight beating fellow American Jesus Villareal by second round TKO. Garcia enjoyed an outstanding career winning versions of the super lightweight and welterweight world titles. His record includes wins over Erik Morales (twice), Zab Judah, Amir Khan, Lucas Matthysse and Paul Malignaggi. Garcia's only losses have been in recent years at the tail end of his career and against the very best in the welterweight division.

Another bout worth noting was a super-middleweight clash between two recent Joe Calzaghe victims. Jeff Lacy and Peter Manfredo had both been well beaten by the Welshman within the previous eighteen months. Lacy dropped Manfredo in round four on the way to a unanimous points victory over 10 rounds.

Chapter Three

'I Would Never Lose to a White Boy Either'

The Story of Joe Calzaghe vs Bernard Hopkins
19th April 2008. Thomas & Mack Centre,
Las Vegas, Nevada, USA.

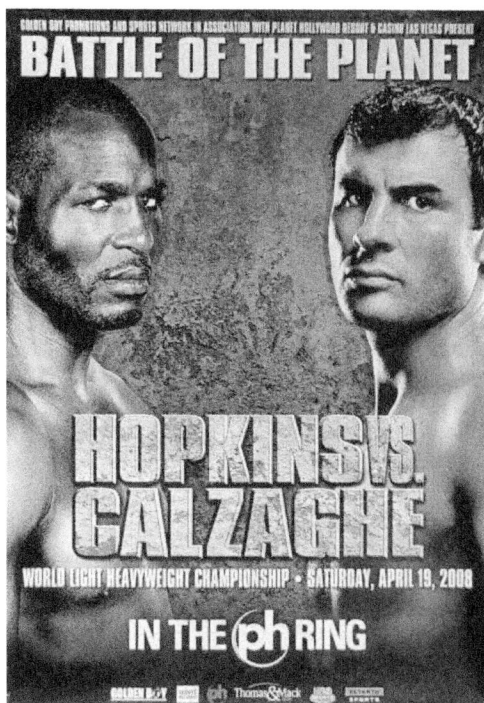

Race, and more specifically skin colour, has played a major role in some of the biggest fights in the history of boxing. There are examples across every era of the sport. Larry Holmes vs Gerry Cooney in the 1980s; Joe Louis vs Max Schmeling during the build up to the second world war; Jack Johnson vs Jim Jeffries back in 1910.

Those were all heavyweight world title fights. The blue-ribbon event of boxing and arguably of all sport. It had been over a quarter of a century since any mention of skin colour had been a major factor in the build up to a big boxing match. It was present for some time following the Holmes-Cooney fight albeit lurking in the background rather than in the spotlight. ('The Great White Hope' narrative was spun out for a couple of decades after that fight.) But things had largely moved on and if anything, the media were far more likely to play down such tensions rather than hype them up.

But when a boxer says something deliberately to attract the media's attention things can get out of control very quickly. Once it is spoken and broadcast you can't *un*say something. You can only try to explain away a remark or make excuses. This was the case when Bernard Hopkins confronted Joe Calzaghe during the build up to the Floyd Mayweather Jr. vs Ricky Hatton fight in Las Vegas in December 2007. Hopkins uttered that controversial and now infamous phrase, "I would never lose to a white boy".

From that moment the fight was on. This time it was not for the heavyweight crown but for the right to be called the best light-heavyweight on the planet. Despite the best efforts of the media to play it down, Hopkins' mischievous, racially motivated rant continued to hang over the bout and remained a talking point among boxing fans. As the saying goes; "you can't *un*hear something."

Joe Calzaghe's response to that comment was calm and collected and utterly (skin) colour blind. He simply said, "I would never lose to a white boy either. Or a green boy or a brown boy, or a red boy. Or whatever other colour they want to bring to me."

History shows that Bernard Hopkins' comments were nothing new to boxing. Even in the relatively modern era, racial tensions, or more specifically skin colour, had threatened to overshadow a world championship boxing event.

Some 26 years earlier on June 11th, 1982, the Larry Holmes v Gerry Cooney fight was overshadowed by several racial overtones. Largely spurred on by the media hype of Cooney being 'The Great White Hope'. Holmes said that if Cooney wasn't white, he would not be getting the same purse as the champion. It was even said that the then President, Ronald Reagan, had a phone installed in Cooney's dressing room so he could call him if he won the fight while Holmes had no such arrangement. Right up to the first bell the champion Holmes was being made to look like the 'B' side of the fight. Boxing tradition dictates that the champion be introduced to the crowd last, but the challenger, Cooney, was introduced *after* the champion Holmes. That level of disrespect for a champion is very rare in boxing.

Going further back, 70 years earlier, to June 22nd, 1938, Joe Louis vs Max Schmeling was more than a racial boxing issue. It turned into a political conflict. The fight came to symbolize the struggle between democracy and Nazism. A fight between the USA and Hitler's Germany. Louis was already a hero to African Americans. Even though there was racial segregation in the USA at that time, the 'Brown Bomber' went on to fight in the second world war for his country and became a true national hero to all Americans.

The whole Louis-Schmeling rivalry was unfair to Schmeling who had no affiliation to the Nazi party in Germany at that time and was used by the regime for political gain. Schmeling bore no animosity to Louis. In fact, the two boxers became friends later in life outside the ring. Their friendship endured until Louis died in April 1981. Schmeling was a pallbearer at Louis' funeral.

Almost 100 years before Joe Calzaghe fought Bernard Hopkins, Jack Johnson retained the world heavyweight title on July 4th, 1910, beating James Jeffries amidst the immense racial tension being whipped up by the media. There were even death threats for the champion from the white and unnervingly hostile crowd. The result even sparked race riots that evening.

Only two years later Johnson was twice arrested and accused of transporting women across state boundaries. The charges and trial were shaky at best. The verdict clearly racially motivated. Johnson was sentenced to more than a year in prison but skipped bail and left the USA. He lived several years in exile before returning to serve his sentence. Since 2008 there have been several attempts to gain a presidential pardon for Johnson. Despite these efforts not even Barak Obama, the first black president of the United States, saw fit to pardon the first black world heavyweight champion.

It was not until May 24th, 2018, that the then President, Donald Trump, pardoned Jack Johnson posthumously. One hundred and eight years after that famous fight. President Trump had taken part in many top boxing promotions before his jaunt into politics. It is fair to say that Trump had closer links to the sport of boxing than previous presidents, having helped stage many big fights in his role as businessman before entering the political arena. That particular campaign to pardon Johnson was spearheaded by Sylvester Stallone (of the "Rocky" movies) and former heavyweight world champion Lennox Lewis.

Similar to Bernard Hopkins comments to Calzaghe, was another example of a racially motivated comment made by British fighter, the late Alan Minter, in 1980. It happened during the lead up to his defence of the world middleweight crown in London against the challenger, the late, great Marvellous Marvin Hagler.

Minter was quoted as saying "I do not intend losing my title to a black man". When the press made a story out of the incident Minter quickly tried to make amends. He claimed that he had been misquoted and what he had really said was "I do not intend losing my title to *that* black man" – referring specifically to Hagler.

The problem in such circumstances, is that once something is said, the flames have been fanned. Just as in Minter's case, Hopkins' comments did not go unnoticed.

Bernard Hopkins

Few boxers rise to the top of their profession when they start off late in the sport. Bernard Hopkins started boxing at 18 years of age but made up for the relatively late start by boxing up to the age of 51. His last fight was just one month before his 52nd birthday.

Hopkins was 18 years old when he was sent to jail for a period of between 5 and 12 years for multiple crimes. He had been in court many times during the previous two years, so the prison sentence seemed inevitable. It was during his incarceration that Hopkins learned to box.

During his 56 months in detention Hopkins connected with another convict and former boxer Michael 'Smokey' Wilson. A former street gang member Wilson had been jailed for having shot and killed a 15-year-old back in 1970.

'Smokey' Wilson had also crossed paths with an uncle of Hopkins. His uncle Art 'Moose' McCloud – now deceased – had a professional record of 11 wins and 8 losses before the street life took a hold of him. McCloud and 'Smokey' Wilson had apparently faced off against each other in the ring. So, when Wilson learned that McCloud's nephew was in the same prison, he took Hopkins under his wing and began to train him as a boxer. The two convicts went on to form a bond that has lasted until the present day.

It was training with 'Smokey' Wilson that led to Hopkins building a solid amateur record fighting in tournaments against other prisons. Hopkins became a formidable boxer and middleweight champion of prisons for the state of Pennsylvania.

Hopkins spent just over four and a half years in Graterford state penitentiary, before being released on parole. There was no room for error and no time to wait for the seemingly inevitable descent back into crime. Hopkins decided to become a professional boxer.

He took his first professional fight on October 11th, 1988, losing a four round points decision to Clinton Mitchell and then all but disappeared for 16 months.

This was a testing time for Hopkins. He could have easily retreated into his former life of street crime. It was then that he decided to live, think and eat boxing. It became his life and he dedicated himself to the sport with great self-discipline and single bloody-mindedness. He had decided that he did not want to go back to prison and definitely did not want to end up dead. He knew what he wanted, and boxing was a large part of it.

That pro debut was strangely as a light heavyweight. When he decided to return to the ring it was as a middleweight and he won that fight by unanimous decision against Greg Paige on February 22nd, 1990. Between that second fight and December 1992, Hopkins scored 21 wins with no losses. He won 16 of those fights by knockout, 12 coming inside one round.

It was not until his 23rd fight against Gilbert Baptiste that Hopkins fought a full 12 rounds for the first time.

Then came a career defining fight against Roy Jones Junior for the vacant IBF world middleweight title on May 22nd, 1993. Although a relatively late starter in the sport, Hopkins had this huge fight over four months before Joe Calzaghe had even made his professional debut.

Roy Jones was the biggest star in boxing at that time, having been a phenomenal amateur, and he was now a fast and exciting pro. Hopkins was generally outclassed throughout most of the fight, losing by a unanimous decision. All three judges scored the fight 116–112 for Jones. Hopkins, ever the willing student, learned from his loss and was now even more determined in his quest to become the middleweight champion of the world. This was Hopkins' second loss. Having started his pro career with a defeat was not such a bad thing. It meant that Hopkins was not worried about protecting a precious "0" in the loss column of his record. Something that too many fighters are accused of when they appear to be avoiding the toughest fights. Hopkins proved time and again that he would fight all-comers.

Curiously, many casual fight fans believe that Roy Jones Jr. was a dominant middleweight when in fact his most successful and entertaining fighting years were at super-middleweight and light heavyweight.

Over the next twelve months Hopkins fought four decent fighters winning the first three by TKO. Then in May 1994 Hopkins faced the tough and experienced Mexican Lupe Aquino who had a record of 46 wins, 6 defeats and 2 draws. Most of those defeats were at the hands of top-level world titlists such as Marlon Starling and Donald Curry. Hopkins dominated the fight winning a total shut-out. Hopkins won all twelve rounds on all three judges' scorecards.

Opportunity came knocking at Hopkins' door again following the Aquino victory. The IBF world title was once again up for grabs after being vacated by Roy Jones Jr. in November 1994. A month later Hopkins fought Segundo Mercado in Mercado's hometown of Quito, Ecuador. Mercado knocked Hopkins down in the 5th and 7th rounds but the Philly fighter rallied in the late rounds and the fight was scored a draw. Many believed Hopkins would struggle in this fight because he had not fully acclimatised to the local conditions – Quito being at an altitude of 9,350 feet (2,850 metres). At the end of an exciting fight however, it was the local fighter who tired and Hopkins who was unlucky not to get the decision.

The IBF ordered an immediate rematch for April 29th, 1995, and this time the fight took place in the USA. Hopkins won by a 7th round technical knockout and became a world champion. It was another exciting fight in which Hopkins hit the Ecuadorian with everything but was unable to put him on the canvas. It was the referee who stopped the brave Mercado taking any more punishment.

The first defence of his newly won title was not until January 1996, almost 9 months after winning the belt. While the fight was a relatively long time in coming the result was not. Hopkins starched the challenger, Steve Frank (who had taken the fight with only seven days' notice) in less than 20 seconds. Hopkins dropped the challenger 10 seconds into the fight. Frank just beat the 10-count but the referee could see that he was in no fit state to continue.

In his second defence Hopkins fought the unbeaten Joe Lipsey in March 1996. With a record of 25 wins, 20 of those by knockout, Lipsey was seen as an exciting finisher although he had not fought at the same level as the champion. Hopkins stopped Lipsey with a brutal uppercut in the fourth round. Lipsey was already out on his feet when Hopkins followed up with lefts and rights sending the challenger to the floor. The referee was waving the fight off before Lipsey hit the canvas. That was Lipsey's last ever fight.

Meanwhile Hopkins made it known that he wanted to unify the middleweight division but that was a long time in coming. By the end of 2000 Hopkins defended his IBF title a further 10 times – beating some standout fighters in the likes of John David Jackson, Glen Johnson, Simon Brown and Antwun Echols (twice) - before a unification bout materialised. This run of defences included two bizarre meetings with Robert Allen.

In August 1998 Hopkins fought Allen in Las Vegas, Nevada. The fight was ruled a 'No Contest' (NC) when Hopkins was injured after being accidentally pushed out of the ring by referee Mills Lane right at the end of the fourth round. The referee was only trying to break up one of the many clinches in the fight. Trying to remain active Allen took another fight only three weeks later – an easy one round win but it did not help him. Six months later the two boxers met again in another messy fight. This time Hopkins was victorious with a seventh-round stoppage. The fight was just as controversial as the first meeting however. In a foul filled fourth round there were low blows, punches on the break and what can only be described as acting by Robert Allen. As the bell sounded to end the round, he went down, faking being hit by a punch after the bell. It seemed to most observers that Allen was trying to get Hopkins disqualified rather than win the fight. After being dropped at the end of the sixth and taking a lot of punishment in the first minute of the seventh, Allen was in real danger and the referee correctly called the bout off.

Incredibly, over four years later Robert Allen would get a third fight with Hopkins at the MGM Grand in Las Vegas where he managed to go the full twelve rounds losing a unanimous decision.

Antwun Echols is definitely one of those boxers who should not have fought on for as long as he did. But Echols had good reason to fight. As long as he was making some money. Any money! He was famously reported as having at least 23 kids. In an interview with his home-town newspaper he was asked how many kids he had to which he replied, "Twenty-three, I think". When pushed on the subject he admitted it could be more and that he really wasn't sure how many children he had fathered. That interview caused some to joke that Echols should sue boxing, because he obviously had some kind of head trauma that rendered him unable to walk into a store and buy condoms.

Away from the ring Echols had a chequered past including several brushes with the law. Early in his pro career he was arrested twice on assault charges. He has had numerous other encounters with the police including the inevitable drugs related incidents. He has allegedly been shot at least twice. In July 2015 Echols was shot in the leg while trying to break up a fight. He sustained a minor injury after being shot with a handgun and was taken to hospital. Echols was later charged with possession of crack cocaine. He was also reportedly issued with outstanding warrants for child support issues. With the number of kids involved there must have been many such issues.

Before the first Hopkins fight at the end of the millennium, Echols record was a very respectable 22-2-1. After the second fight (twelve months later) Echols went on to win five bouts before challenging for a world title again in 2003. He lost that fight (to Australia's Anthony Mundine) and his form went downhill rapidly. Between 2003 and his last fight in 2016 Echols record was 3 wins, 18 losses and two draws. He lost his final ten bouts, ending with eight straight third round knockouts and the final fight lasting less than a round.

After the second Echols fight Hopkins fought the WBC world middleweight champion Keith Holmes in a unification bout.

Holmes had first won the WBC world middleweight title back in March 1996 beating fellow American Quincy Taylor. It was Taylor's first defence after winning the title by stopping hard hitting US Virgin Islander Julian Jackson.

Holmes first defence was against British contender and future Joe Calzaghe opponent Richie Woodhall. Holmes won by 12th round TKO in October 1996. Two fights later in May 1998 Holmes travelled to France to fight the tough Hacine Cherifi in his own backyard. Holmes lost a unanimous points decision and had to wait almost exactly one year to get his revenge in the rematch. On April 24th, 1999, Holmes stopped Cherifi in the seventh round to become a two-time middleweight world champion.

Two successful defences later – including a TKO victory against future Anthony 'AJ' Joshua trainer Robert McCracken at Wembley Arena, London – Keith Holmes was ready for a unification bout.

Holmes was as tough as they come and had never been stopped. His only two defeats being on points. Nevertheless, Hopkins dominated Holmes for the full twelve rounds and won widely on the scorecards. Hopkins was now the unified IBF and WBC world middleweight champion.

The fight with Keith Holmes was part of a middleweight tournament organised by the flamboyant, opinion-splitting promoter Don King.

The arrival of former welterweight and light-middleweight champion Félix Trinidad into the middleweight division enabled King to set up a series of unification fights between the three major middleweight title-holders plus Trinidad. While Hopkins fought Holmes with the IBF and WBC belts on the line, the undefeated Trinidad would fight the WBA champion, American William Joppy. The winners of those two bouts would meet to decide who would be the undisputed middleweight champion of the world.

William Joppy had first won the WBA world middleweight title in June 1996, travelling to Japan to defeat the previous holder Shinji Takehara in Yokohama. Takehara had a solid 24-0 record and was fighting at home, but Joppy refused to leave it to the judges and stopped him in round nine. Joppy defended the WBA title twice then lost it to Julio Cesar Green via unanimous decision in a close fight in August 1997. He won back the title in January 1998 by reversing the unanimous decision over the same fighter (Green, from the Dominican Republic) to become a two-time champion. In the first defence of his second reign Joppy fought the legend Roberto Duran in August 1998. At that time Duran was 47 years of age with a record of 101 wins, an incredible 70 by knockout and 13 losses. Duran was no match for the man twenty years his junior. Joppy stunned Duran midway through the third round and proceeded to use him as a punchbag with Duran unable to respond and barely able to hold on at times. Joppy won by TKO when referee Joe Cortez stopped the fight with only eight seconds of the round remaining. It was good refereeing by Cortez.

Joppy made six more defences of his title between July 1999 and December 2000, winning four by knockout and the other two by wide points margin. The stage was set for a fight with the undefeated Trinidad.

Felix Trinidad had not fought at middleweight before facing Joppy. He made his name at welterweight. After 19 wins, 16 by knockout and no defeats Trinidad fought Maurice Blocker for the IBF world welterweight title on June 19, 1993. Trinidad – widely called 'Tito' – was ten years younger than Blocker and dominated him for the short duration of the fight. The bout lasted less than five minutes when the referee stopped the action in the second round. Tito had arrived at boxing's top table. After winning the IBF title Tito went on a huge winning streak making thirteen defences up to February 1999 winning all bar one of those by knockout. The one fight that went the distance in that period was against former champion and Puerto Rican legend Hector 'Macho' Camacho at the MGM Grand in Las Vegas, Nevada in January 1994. Trinidad won a clear points victory and Puerto Rico had found a new hero. That fight was not even top billing. The main event that night featured the great Julio Cesar Chavez against Frankie Randall. Chavez in his 91st fight not only lost for the first time in his career - by split decision - but was also floored for the first time by Randall in the eleventh round.

In February 1999 Tito fought the excellent Pernell Whitaker in Madison Square Garden, New York. Whitaker had been lightweight and junior welterweight world champion before stepping up to welterweight to become a three-weight world champion in October 1994. He lost the WBC world welterweight title to Oscar de la Hoya in April 1997. Trinidad convincingly beat Whitaker, winning by unanimous decision. Two fights later Trinidad faced Oscar De La Hoya in an eagerly anticipated welterweight unification bout between the two undefeated boxers whose combined record was 66 wins and 0 defeats. The fight took place in Las Vegas, Nevada on September 18th, 1999. Trinidad won a very close majority decision with two judges having him just ahead of De La Hoya and the third scoring it a draw. De La Hoya seemed to be winning the early rounds but gassed out towards the end with Trinidad winning the all-important 'championship rounds'.

Instead of defending the unified IBF and WBC world welterweight titles (as well as the lineal welterweight title) Trinidad moved up in weight and beat the then undefeated David Reid for the WBA super-welterweight (a.k.a. light-middleweight) world title in March 2000. Tito won by a comfortable unanimous decision. He then defended the super-welterweight title, twice beating two good opponents in the French based Senegalese Mamadou Thiam (then with a record of 33-1) and the American Fernando Vargas who was unbeaten at 20-0. 'Tito' won both fights by knockout. It was then that Don King invited Trinidad to join his middleweight unification tournament.

In an exciting fight Trinidad floored Joppy with a solid left hook, straight right combination (twice) at the end of the first round. Joppy somehow held on and recovered to make a fight of it in the second and third rounds. In the fourth with the fighters going toe-to-toe, Trinidad dropped Joppy again with a huge left hook and with two minutes of the round remaining the end seemed inevitable. Yet Joppy showed amazing resilience to make it out of the round. In the fifth round however 'Tito' hurt Joppy with a huge right hand to the side of the face. Joppy went down but bravely got right back up. The referee had no option but to save Joppy from himself and waved the fight off with about forty seconds remaining. Felix Trinidad had become a three-weight world champion and boasted a record of 40 wins no losses with thirty-three wins by knockout. More importantly, he had successfully taken his punching power up into the middleweight division and was now on a collision course with Bernard Hopkins for the undisputed middleweight title.

The fight took place at Madison Square Garden, New York city on September 29th, 2001. It was supposed to have been held on September 15th but was postponed following the 9/11 terrorist attacks on the World Trade Centre in New York City. Don King managed to convince enough people that the show should go ahead, and the controversial promoter deserves a lot of credit for that.

Trinidad was eight years younger than Hopkins but had had almost as many fights and possessed a better knockout ratio than the Philly fighter. Despite their age difference, Trinidad had been boxing as long as Hopkins. He began boxing at 12 years of age, making his professional debut at 17; the age at which Hopkins was facing a long prison sentence.

Following Trinidad's exciting and decisive victory over William Joppy he became the pre-fight betting favourite. For the first time in many years, Hopkins was the underdog. This led Hopkins to place a large bet of $100,000 on himself to win the bout (allegedly). The $100K came from a sponsorship deal Hopkins had with online casino site Golden Palace; 'GoldenPalace.com' can clearly be seen displayed on Hopkins' back for the fight.

Hopkins caused huge controversy while promoting the bout. He threw the Puerto Rico flag on the floor in press conferences in both New York City and Puerto Rico. This led to a riot in Puerto Rico where Hopkins had to be ushered to safety from the angry mob. It is unlikely that this stunt would have sold more fight tickets. Hopkins and a Puerto Rican hero fighting in New York City for the undisputed world middleweight crown was always enough to guarantee a full house. Therefore, one has to question Hopkins' intentions. Did he just like flirting with controversy?

The fight was vintage Hopkins. On his way to a unanimous decision the Philly fighter floored Trinidad in the twelfth and final round. Referee Steve Smoger stopped the bout when Trinidad's father (and trainer) jumped into the ring to save his son. It was the first loss of Trinidad's career.

When the fight was over Hopkins put on a little display of American patriotism. Perhaps unhappy with a largely American born crowd favouring Trinidad over himself he led a chant of 'USA! USA!' from inside the ring. Hopkins had cause to be a little annoyed. Most of the pro Felix Trinidad crowd were not Puerto Rican. They were probably born and bred in New York, USA albeit with Puerto Rican heritage. Yet they were very much for the Puerto Rican fighter. It was also only weeks after the 9/11 terrorist attacks. Maybe the crowd just did not like Hopkins. Especially after his disrespectful display in Puerto Rico. His persona and antics outside of the ring were definitely becoming as infamous as his winning style inside the ring was famous.

He may not have been the most universally popular fighter, but he was now the unified IBF, WBC and WBA word middleweight champion. Hopkins had just become the first undisputed world middleweight champion since Marvellous Marvin Hagler in 1987. To end the year, 'The Ring' magazine and the 'World Boxing Hall of Fame' named Hopkins as the 2001 Fighter of the Year.

Hopkins then defended the undisputed title six times. He beat Carl Daniels in February 2002 (by technical knockout in the tenth round) and surpassed Carlos Monzón's division record of 14 defences. He then beat Morrade Hakkar in March 2003, by eighth-round TKO, William Joppy in December 2003, by unanimous decision; and Robert Allen (for a third time) in June 2004, also by unanimous decision. Then for his fifth defence Hopkins fought 'The Golden Boy' (*El Chico d'Oro*) Oscar De La Hoya. Hopkins reportedly earned $10 million for the fight but De La Hoya was boxing's biggest draw at the time and reportedly earned an incredible $30 million. De La Hoya had just won the (still slightly less regarded) WBO middleweight title from Germany's Felix Sturm, a fight that many believed Sturm won. All four sanctioning bodies world titles were on the line as well as the Ring magazine and lineal middleweight titles.

The fight took place at the MGM Grand in Las Vegas, Nevada and was held at a catch-weight of 158 pounds (two less than the middleweight limit) so should have slightly favoured the naturally smaller De La Hoya. It didn't. Hopkins won by ninth round knockout with a viscous left hook to the liver. Bernard Hopkins became the first boxer ever to hold all four versions of the world title simultaneously.

Hopkins followed his historic victory over De La Hoya with another historic victory over British fighter Howard Eastman in February 2005. This win tied Hopkins with Larry Holmes' record of 20 consecutive successful title defences. Hopkins was now 40 years old. It was to be Hopkins last successful defence and his final win as a middleweight. In his next fight Hopkins lost all of the titles to Jermain Taylor by split decision on July 16th, 2005. It was a close fight that could have gone either way and a rematch was set for December 2005. Hopkins lost that one by a unanimous decision. There's an old saying in boxing that no matter how good you are 'there's always that guy out there who has your number'. For Bernard Hopkins, at middleweight, that guy was Jermain Taylor.

Hopkins then decided to move up in weight but did not stop at super-middleweight as many top middleweights (including the likes of Roy Jones Junior) had done. He moved up to light heavyweight and so avoided a potential clash with one Joe Calzaghe.

Antonio Tarver had become the dominant force at light heavyweight having beaten tough Jamaican Glen Johnson and twice beaten Roy Jones Junior. The first victory over Jones Jr. was a devastating second round knockout in revenge for losing the light heavyweight world title to Jones via a majority decision. A fight which most observers thought Tarver had won. Despite these victories Tarver was stripped of the world WBC and WBA world light heavyweight titles and was left holding only the lightly regarded IBO world light heavyweight belt when he faced off against Hopkins. Boxing politics aside this match up was for the (now increasingly rated) Ring Magazine title and the winner would be universally recognised as the best light heavyweight in the world. Going into the fight Tarver was a 3-1 favourite having been the first man to knockout Roy Jones Jr. and an established light heavyweight. On June 10th, 2006 Hopkins beat Tarver by a lopsided unanimous points decision – all three judges scoring the bout 118-109 in favour of Hopkins.

Hopkins had said that he would retire after the Tarver fight, but he came back the following year. On July 21st, 2007, at the Mandalay Bay Resort & Casino in Las Vegas, Nevada, Hopkins defended The Ring light heavyweight championship against former undisputed junior (light) middleweight champion Ronald 'Winky' Wright.

Controversy was never far away however as Hopkins again played the part of villain. During the weigh-in, Hopkins shoved Wright with an open-hand to the face. This initiated a brawl between both fighters' teams. A Month later Hopkins was fined $200,000 for instigating the brawl – the fine amounted to 6 percent of the $3 million purse Hopkins received for the fight. Hopkins comfortably won the contest with a unanimous decision over the twelve rounds.

Emboldened by his latest victory Hopkins was in no mood for retirement. He immediately stated his intent to fight Calzaghe when he told reporters, "I want Joe Calzaghe next. Tell him to come on over here and we'll fight. I'll beat him, too, and then he won't be undefeated."

Joe Calzaghe

A proud Welshman, Calzaghe was actually born in Hammersmith hospital, London. His Welsh mother and his father, a Sardinian (Italian), made the move to Sardinia less than a year later but Calzaghe's mother was homesick and the family soon moved to Wales where they eventually settled in the small town of Newbridge.

In complete contrast to Bernard Hopkins, Joe Calzaghe followed the traditional route to the top of boxing. He started early. At the age of ten he joined his first boxing club, Newbridge Amateur Boxing Club, and immediately took to the sport. He even gave up playing football two years later. It wasn't long before he was making a name for himself in the amateur ranks.

Calzaghe won four schoolboy Amateur Boxing Association (ABA) titles, followed by three consecutive senior British ABA titles (British Championships) between 1990 and 1993. Those titles were won in three different weight categories, welterweight, light middleweight and middleweight. His amateur record is reportedly 110 wins to 10 defeats.

While he finished with a perfect record as a professional Calzaghe did lose a few amateur fights; mostly as a boy. It says a lot about Calzaghe's character and determination in the professional ranks that he remembers every detail about his last defeat. It was against a Romanian called Adrian Opreda in the European Junior Championships in Prague (then still part of Czechoslovakia) in 1990. That was back when headguards were introduced in the amateurs and Calzaghe was never comfortable wearing them. In a close fight the Romanian got the decision in a country that was then, still (just), part of the old Soviet Bloc. It may or may not have been a factor, but by his own admission a devastated Calzaghe cried following that defeat. However, that disappointment only strengthened Calzaghe's determination and he made up his mind that he would never lose another fight. Calzaghe was 17 years old. Nearly twenty years later having not lost another fight as an amateur or pro, Calzaghe was set to face a ring legend in Bernard Hopkins.

At the time of Calzaghes last defeat Hopkins had already lost his first professional fight and had started adding some wins to his record. Losing his first fight meant that Hopkins was never preoccupied with protecting his "0" ('Oh') Trying to remain undefeated can put undue pressure on a fighter. Often boxers pay too much attention to the zero losses on their record. Losing it late in a boxer's career can have a disproportionately negative effect on their confidence. A career can unravel once a fighter finally gets that first loss on their record.

What hurt more than any of those amateur defeats was not being picked to go to the Olympic games in Barcelona in 1992. After the loss to Opreda the Newbridge based fighter won three consecutive senior ABA titles in Great Britain between 1990 and 1993. Calzaghe was also ranked number one in his weight category by the ABA in 1992. Yet despite all this they decided to take Robin Reid to the Olympic s instead of Calzaghe. Their decision was said to be because Calzaghe had not fought in a senior international tournament. Calzaghe had been prevented from doing so by a wrist injury. Hand injuries would continue to dog his career right to the last.

Robin Reid did well at the Olympics winning a bronze medal at light middleweight and the two boxers would cross paths some years later in a world title bout. Would Calzaghe, with the superior domestic amateur record, have done better and maybe won gold? It was a question that bothered Calzaghe for some time. Yet on reflection it was probably a blessing in disguise. If Joe had won an Olympic gold, he would have been offered a million-dollar contract to sign professionally. He may not have fought with the same determination while attempting to climb the professional ranking.

As things turned out he turned professional in September 1993 for a pittance and within weeks made his debut in Cardiff on the undercard of the Lennox Lewis vs Frank Bruno WBC world heavyweight title fight. Calzaghe beat Paul Hanlon inside the first round.

A victory on his professional debut, Calzaghe sat ringside to witness the huge Lewis-Bruno showdown close up. Calzaghe now had his eyes firmly set on the prize. He, Joe Calzaghe, wanted to be topping the bill at big events like this. *"This is what I want. One day"* he said to himself.

There then followed eight more quick victories, six inside the first round with two in the second, before a boxer named Bobby Joe Edwards took Calzaghe the distance in an eight rounder in February 1995 at Telford, England. That night local hero Richie Woodhall won the vacant European middleweight title. Woodhall had boxed for Great Britain in the 1988 Seoul Olympics winning a bronze medal at light-middleweight – losing to none other than Roy Jones Junior in the semi-finals – and later became WBC Super Middleweight world title holder. He would also be one of 9 world or former world champions to lose to Joe Calzaghe.

After three more quick victories and in his 14th professional fight, Calzaghe fought Stephen Wilson at the Royal Albert Hall, London for the vacant British Super-Middleweight title. Wilson had by far the best record (11-1) of any opponent to date. Oddly, Wilson had come down in weight as a professional, having represented Great Britain at light-heavyweight in the 1992 Olympics in Barcelona. Calzaghe dominated after an early slow start and stopped Wilson in round eight to become the British Super-Middleweight champion. Calzaghe had started 36 rounds and completed only 23. His record was 14-0 with 13 KOs.

After two more quick and easy wins Calzaghe fought someone with a better record than his own. Mark Delaney had a record of 21-0 (17 wins by KO) and was highly tipped to go all the way to the top by the tough world champion, Ireland's Steve Collins. Calzaghe fought Delaney of West Ham, London, in his own backyard and convincingly beat him inside five rounds. It was an excellent performance against a very good fighter. Calzaghe moved to 17-0 (16 KOs) and still the doubters questioned his ability.

After Delaney came Warren Stowe. A game, durable fighter who had never been stopped in 19 fights losing only 2 of those on points.

Then came a fight against Pat Lawlor from San Francisco. If the doubters were still critical of the quality of Joe Calzaghe's opposition the same could not be said of Lawlor's. The American had gone the distance with Hector 'Macho' Camacho and also lost to 'Terrible' Terry Norris. He had beaten Wilfred Benitez on points and stopped the 'Hands of Stone' himself, Roberto Duran, in six rounds. Calzaghe stopped Lawlor inside of two rounds.

Three more quick wins followed. First a second-round stoppage of journeyman Carlos (Peter) Christie. Next came a one round victory against unbeaten American Tyler Hughes in June 1997. Then four months later a third round TKO against Brazilian Luciano Torres who had only been stopped once in 47 fights. The calls for a world title fight were growing louder with each fight.

Shortly after successfully defending the world WBO Super middleweight title against Craig Cummings in July 1997, Steve Collins retired rather than fight Joe Calzaghe. Collins was 33 years old as was Nigel Benn who had also recently retired following back-to-back defeats at the hands of Collins. One other fighter remained active from that British dominated era of 1990s super-middleweights; the flamboyant 31 year old Chris Eubank. Calzaghe and Eubank met in Sheffield England on October 11th, 1997, for the vacant WBO world super-middleweight crown.

Calzaghe (then aged 25) entered the Eubank fight with a record of 22-0, 21 KOs after taking part in only 54 rounds of boxing as a professional. Compare that to Chris Eubank whose record stood at 45-2-2 with 23 KOs. Eubank had fought an incredible 360 rounds including twenty-one world title bouts. If the Calzaghe critics were wanting him to step up in class, then this was surely it. Eubank was durable, had never been stopped and had only lost twice in 49 fights in close decisions against the rugged Steve Collins. Chris Eubank promised to take Calzaghe "into the trenches" and that is exactly what he did.

As career defining fights go the Eubank bout proved to be the making of Calzaghe.

The fight began fast with Calzaghe flooring Eubank in the first minute. That knockdown proved to be a false dawn. Calzaghe thought that this might be a quick night's work. It was not to be. Eubank acknowledged the knockdown as a good punch, but he was a shrewd campaigner and he dug in to make it a tough fight.

By the end of the sixth round, with half the fight still to go, Calzaghe later admitted that he "was knackered". But the Welshman stuck to his task and fought through his fatigue to earn a well-deserved unanimous points victory. The fight turned out to be a huge wake up call for Calzaghe. Eubank was as tough as they came as bloody battles against Benn and Collins had already proven. He was also a very slick and skilled boxer.

Calzaghe was now WBO world Super-Middleweight champion and still undefeated in 23 fights.

The opposition in Calzaghe's first 9 defences had a combined record of 248 wins 19 losses and 4 draws. One fighter was responsible for eight of those (combined) losses; the Paraguayan perennial contender Juan Carlos Gímenez. The doubters were already on Calzaghe's case and made a lot of the standard of opposition for that title fight. But none of this was Calzaghe's fault. Gímenez was the WBO mandatory challenger. He may have lost eight fights, but he had never been stopped. He had been the distance with Nigel Benn, Chris Eubank in the 1990s and even Juan Roldan and Roberto Duran in the late 1980s. He was a tough and seasoned pro with 51 wins under his belt but in a one-sided affair Calzaghe forced him to retire on his stool at the end of the ninth round. Calzaghe won every round on all three scorecards and became the first man to stop Gímenez in 60 fights.

January 2000 and the start of a new millennium. Joe Calzaghe was set to fight fellow British boxer David Starie in Manchester in front of a huge sell-out crowd. This fifth defence of his WBO world super middleweight title was officially the main event of the evening, but it was not the main attraction. The majority of the crowd was there for another reason. While even most casual boxing fans were aware of how good Joe Calzaghe was, there were many in the crowd who were only interested in another fighter that night.

The final fight of the evening featured the one and only 'Iron' Mike Tyson making the first of two appearances in a British ring as part of a short UK tour (the other being in Glasgow five months later). Tyson demolished British heavyweight champion Julius Francis in the second round of what was never really a contest. Not that it mattered. The vast majority of the crowd had only ever seen Tyson on TV (many times) and this was their chance to see him in the flesh. Meanwhile Julius Francis had his 4 minutes of fame – for that is exactly how long the fight lasted. Francis' camp also came up with an ingenious way of making extra money even if he lost, as most people expected him to. He had sold the space on the soles of his boxing boots as advertising space. The idea is said to have come from Frank Maloney – most famous for being Lennox Lewis' manager. Nobody expected Francis to stay on his feet for long, so the comical but cunning idea was taken up by the Daily Mirror (a prominent British tabloid). He was sure to be knocked out and when flat on his back the name of the newspaper would be there for all the world to see. They certainly got their money's worth. The British heavyweight was down twice in the first round and three times in the second before the referee stopped the contest. For that short fight Francis earned the biggest payday of his career - around £350,000 – plus an additional £20,000 for the advert on the soles of his shoes.

Also on the undercard that night was another British boxer who would go on to fill stadiums on both sides of the pond. The 21-year-old Ricky Hatton, winning his 17th fight in his home-town via a third round TKO, incredibly went almost unnoticed.

David Starie was an interesting character. He had built up a solid enough record and had now fought his way to a world title shot at a huge arena. Yet Starie was not a full-time boxer like Calzaghe. He was also a part time fire-fighter.

Starie was an accomplished amateur. In 1993 he was the ABA light middleweight champion and the following year won the ABA middleweight title. As a professional he had a solid record of 22 wins (15 by KO) and only one defeat. Starie won the British super middleweight title by stopping Sam Storey in 1997. He lost the title to Dean Francis three months later via KO. That was his only ever stoppage loss.

In March 1998, Starie won the Commonwealth super middleweight title, beating future world titlist Clinton Woods on points. He retained that title until his penultimate fight in March 2003. In November 1998 Starie regained the British super middleweight title in November 1998 when he beat Ali Forbes by KO to win the vacant title. In his last fight in June 2003, he again challenged for a world title facing Sven Ottke for the WBA world super middleweight title, losing on points and announcing his retirement from the sport.

Following retirement from boxing Starie became a full-time fire fighter. The combination of brave fire fighter and former top boxer proved to be an excellent role model for youngsters. Starie retained an involvement in boxing by working with a local amateur boxing club.

It was a disappointing fight for the Calzaghe camp, but Starie never really came to fight. He was in survival mode from the first bell, trying to keep Calzaghe at long range and grabbing when in close.

In the end Calzaghe won a convincing enough points victory but it was a missed opportunity. Mike Tyson still generated huge interest both sides of the pond so it was a pity that Calzaghe couldn't have put on one of his better performances with such a huge captive TV audience for the evening. Calzaghe's record was now 28-0 with 23 KO victories but his talent was still not recognised in American boxing circles.

For his 6th defence in August 2000, Calzaghe took on a young upcoming American Omar Sheika at Wembley, London. Calzaghe had come in for a lot of criticism from the media for under par performances in his last few fights. The truth was that Calzaghe had been dogged by hand injuries for the previous two years which had seen him go the full twelve rounds against Robin Reid, Rick Thornberry and David Starie. Now fully healed he needed a big performance and that is exactly what he gave against Sheika. In a classic blend of styles both men put on an exciting fight that must surely now prove to the American audience that Calzaghe was indeed the real deal. Former world champion Nigel Benn said after this fight that Calzaghe was the best super middleweight in the world.

Calzaghe's next fight was in Sheffield, Yorkshire, England where he faced former WBC world super-middleweight champion and close friend Richie Woodhall. In a close and bruising encounter the game Woodhall was knocked down in the ninth. It didn't last much longer. as Calzaghe won by TKO in the tenth round in what was an exciting fight. This would be Woodhall's last fight. Meanwhile, Calzaghe was just getting better and better.

The previous fight that evening featured (local) Yorkshire fighter Paul Ingle who was defending his IBF world featherweight title he had won eight months earlier in New York's Madison Square Garden on the Lennox Lewis vs Michael Grant undercard. The events of the evening were overshadowed however by the outcome of the Ingle fight. The Sheffield fighter was carried from the ring on a stretcher and underwent brain surgery. This tragic fight and Paul Ingle's brave road to recovery are described briefly in Chapter one.

For his eighth defence Calzaghe fought the big fearsome looking German Mario Veit in April 2001. At the time both boxers had identical records of 30-0. Thirty fights, thirty wins, no defeats, no draws. That equal record lasted all of 2 minutes. Veit, who was massive for a super middleweight at just under six foot four inches tall, was blasted out in superb fashion by a determined Calzaghe. Immediately there were those who questioned Veit's thirty opponents but at that time he was the number one contender. Calzaghe was only beating the opposition that was put in front of him. And when fully fit with no hand injuries he was doing it very efficiently.

The two met again four years later in May 2005, this time in Germany. In between the first and second clash Clazaghe had defended his title a further seven times. Veit had won another fifteen fights, his record now standing at 45-1. Veit had clearly improved since their first encounter. But so too had Calzaghe. This time Veit almost made it to the half-way point in the fight before being stopped in the sixth round.

Something *had* changed however between the two Veit contests. Rather than criticise the level of Calzaghe's opposition, the media were now acknowledging that many opponents had been avoiding the Welshman. The lack of those elusive unification fights was definitely not down to Calzaghe or his manager Frank Warren.

Six months after the first Veit fight in October 2001, Calzaghe again found himself almost on the undercard of another Mike Tyson fight. While Tyson was fighting the Dane, Brian Nielson, Calzaghe made his ninth world title defence in what was billed as the "co-main event". The fight took place in Copenhagen and was Calzaghe's first fight outside of the UK. His opponent across the ring was the WBO's number nine ranked fighter, Will McIntyre from the USA. Once again, the challenger had a decent enough record (on paper) of 29 wins with only 2 defeats. Not only had he never been stopped, but he had also never been knocked down. Calzaghe dented both of those credentials and hopelessly outclassed the American. Following a third-round knockdown of his opponent, Calzaghe also showed a compassionate side. When he hit McIntyre with a huge uppercut it was clear that the challenger was in no fit state to defend himself as he fell against the ropes. Calzaghe appealed to the referee to jump in right there and then. Instead, the referee gave the American a standing count (technically marked as a knockdown) and the bell sounded the end of the round. If Calzaghe had pounced on his stunned opponent instead of giving the referee a chance to intervene the American could have been very seriously injured. There was clearly no way McIntyre was going to last much longer and sure enough he was stopped early in the fourth.

The undercard in Denmark featured the perennial heavyweight contender Ray Mercer winning by second round KO to set up a crack at Wladimir Klitschko's WBO world heavyweight title. Meanwhile 'Iron' Mike beat Nielson, stopping the Dane in the sixth round, setting up his date with destiny against Lennox Lewis.

Also on the Copenhagen undercard, and no doubt later watching Calzaghe's performance from ringside, was an upcoming Danish super middleweight by the name of Mikkel Kessler. The Dane moved to 23 fights unbeaten after a six round unanimous points win. Kessler would cross paths with Calzaghe six years later in a career defining fight for both boxers.

"I am the best super middleweight in the world. I want Roy Jones. I want Bernard Hopkins."

Calzaghe after beating Will McIntyre in Denmark (Oct 2001).

The immediate aftermath of this fight showed how much Calzaghe wanted fights with both Bernard Hopkins and Roy Jones. A few weeks earlier Bernard Hopkins had just won the middleweight tournament unifying all four belts in beating Felix Trinidad. It looked like Hopkins would step up in weight and Calzaghe made a big thing out of calling out Hopkins after the McIntyre fight. In the post-fight (ringside) interview Calzaghe insisted that he was the best super middleweight in the world.

Charles Brewer had won the IBF world super middleweight title in June 1997 – just months before Calzaghe won the WBO version – beating Gary Ballard by TKO. He defended the title 3 times including a knockout win over British boxer Herol Graham after being way behind on the scorecards.

Brewer later fought Sven Ottke in October 1998 but lost a controversial split decision in Germany against the home fighter. After chalking up three quick victories Brewer returned to Germany in September 2000 as the challenger, only to be denied again in another controversial split decision against Ottke.

Before fighting Calzaghe, Brewer was involved in a fantastic three round thriller against two-time Bernard Hopkins foe, the always interesting Antwun Echols (see above). In one of those fights that has to be seen to be believed, the action was stopped in the third round with Brewer taking punishment but still on his feet. Brewer claimed it was a premature stoppage and he had good reason. Echols had been dropped three times in the second round but there was no three-knockdown rule in effect for this fight, so he was allowed to continue. Echols was coming off his second defeat to Hopkins at middleweight to move up to the super middleweight division.

Calzaghe made the 10th defence of his WBO title against Brewer in Cardiff on April 20th, 2002. It proved a comfortable, unanimous points win against the former recent IBF champion.

Calzaghe fought twice more in 2002. First, he thrashed the American Miguel Angel Jiminez in August. Jiminez had only lost one fight in 22 and had never been stopped. Calzaghe won every round on all three judges' scorecards. Then in December, Calzaghe stopped another American, Tocker Pudwill, inside two rounds. (Pudwill was another fighter to have lost on points in Germany to Sven Ottke, although in his case by a wide margin.)

This led up to Calzaghe's first fight in 2003 and his fifth consecutive American opponent, the useful ex-WBA titlist Byron Mitchell. The two squared off on June 28th in Cardiff, Wales.

Mitchell was coming off a split decision loss to Sven Ottke in Germany. This was yet another contentious victory by Ottke in his home country. Not that it slowed Mitchell down. He dropped Calzaghe at the start of the second round. This was the first time Calzaghe had ever been floored. He recovered immediately and rallied to return the favour dropping Mitchell with a flurry of punches. Mitchell did not recover as quickly. Calzaghe poured on the punches and the referee correctly stopped the fight. This was the first time Mitchell had ever been stopped and was certain to get Calzaghe noticed across the pond.

Calzaghe had a pair of fights in each of the following two years. In February 2004 he stopped Russian based Armenian fighter Mger Mkrtchyan in the seventh round. In October the opponent was American based Egyptian Kabary Salem. Calzaghe won comfortably on points but suffered the second knockdown of his career (within three fights) when he was floored in the fourth round. It was a flash knockdown and the champion was not hurt.

In May 2005 the big German Mario Veit got his second chance to take Calzaghe's title. Veit, who was unbeaten on their first encounter, had gone on to win a further 15 fights without loss before this rematch. It did not help him in the slightest. He lasted five more rounds than the first fight but was dispatched in the sixth. Calzaghe travelled to the German's backyard for this fight and never intended leaving it to the German judges.

In September 2005 Calzaghe beat the Kenyan boxer Evans Ashira via another total points shutout. Ashira had only lost one of his previous 25 fights but was hopelessly outclassed by the Welshman. Even more impressive was that Calzaghe had injured one of his notoriously fragile hands and won the fight one handed. Calzaghe's record now stood at an impressive 40 wins from 40 fights.

That broken bone in his left hand meant that a scheduled November 2005 face off against the feared American Jeff 'Left Hook' Lacy had to be postponed. This was the fight Calzaghe had craved for a long time. A unification bout against the IBF word super middleweight champion Lacy.

German Sven Ottke crossed paths with several of Calzaghe's opponents. He defended the IBF title twenty-one times after taking the belt from Charles Brewer in 1998. But he retired in 2003 rather than defend the IBF title against American Jeff Lacy or face Calzaghe in a unification bout. Ottke retired an undefeated champion with a 34-0 record with only 6 wins coming inside the distance. Also, several of his close points victories in Germany were considered controversial "home fighter decisions". It became something of a standing joke in boxing circles that if you fought in Germany you had to knock out the home-based fighter just to get a draw. That said, Ottke remains one of only 15 boxers to retire as an undefeated champion. An exclusive club indeed.

When Ottke retired Jeff 'Left Hook' Lacy fought Canadian Syd Vanderpool for the vacant IBF title in Las Vegas in October 2004.

Lacy beat Vanderpool (who had gone the distance with Hopkins at middleweight) via an eighth round TKO taking his record to 17 wins without loss.

Lacy made four successful defences of his IBF title - two of them against former Calzaghe victims, Omar Sheika and Robin Reid – before the unification fight was made.

While winning the title against the experienced Chris Eubank was a major landmark for Calzaghe, the unification fight against Jeff Lacy was probably his first internationally recognised career defining fight. Certainly in America.

Lacy was considered a formidable opponent and many boxing pundits on both sides of the pond had Lacy as favourite going into this fight. He was also unbeaten. He had a record of 21 wins with 17 of those coming by KO/stoppage.

The fight was dubbed 'Judgement Day' and pitted the WBO champion Calzaghe in his 18th defence of his title against the man people were calling the 'mini-Mike Tyson' because of the way he was knocking people out.

Calzaghe had wanted to pull out of the fight after the hand he broke in the Evans Ashira fight was still bothering him. His father and trainer Enzo convinced him to take the fight promising his son that this would be a life changing fight. The unification bout he had craved for so long.

The story of the fight is simple. Calzaghe dominated Lacy from start to finish and put on a display that made him instantly popular with many in America. The final scores could have been a total shutout only Calzaghe, perhaps getting carried away with the crowd's excitement, had a point deducted for punching Lacy in the back during the 11th round. Long before the final round the crowd were chanting "Easy! Easy!" Calzaghe really did make it look easy. He was WBO and IBF champion but also won The Ring Magazine and lineal titles, becoming the first super-middleweight to be recognized as world champion by The Ring magazine. He was now universally recognised as the top super-middleweight on the planet.

After the fight Calzaghe had this to say: "I've never been so focused and dedicated. Eight years I've been champion and I've been written off by a lot of people. This fight has been on my mind morning, noon and night. I demolished him and outclassed him. His punches didn't trouble me in the slightest. I was expecting more. I saw them coming from miles away. I knew I was going to win the fight. How's that for a slapper? Those slaps had his legs going all over the place".

He added, "If I get a chance to fight Jones or Tarver in America, I'll go for it."

That chance to fight Roy Jones did not come until right at the end of Calzaghe's career and he never fought Tarver whose career would falter following a loss to Bernard Hopkins just three months later.

The next two fights were almost an anti-climax after the Lacy beatdown. First there was a tough 12 round win over Sakio Bika in October 2006. The tough Australia based Cameroon fighter continues to box at the time of writing and has still never been stopped in 45 bouts.

Then, in April 2007, Calzaghe scored a quick win inside three rounds against the American Peter Manfredo, the winner of a boxing-based reality TV series called 'The Contender'. It was a mismatch but guaranteed a big audience in the USA. Calzaghe chose to fight Manfredo for the WBO title rather than the IBF mandatory challenger (German Robert Stieglitz). Consequently, the IBF stripped Calzaghe of their belt.

While most of the boxing world regarded Calzaghe as the best in his division there was one man who disputed that claim. The man that held the other two belts – WBC and WBA titles – 'The Viking Warrior' from Denmark, Mikkel Kessler. A huge unification battle was set for November 4th, 2007, with three belts on the line.

The fight was unfinished super-middleweight business for Calzaghe against his closest rival in the division. The two fighters boasted a combined record of 82 wins and no defeats.

The bout took place at Cardiff's Millennium Stadium in front of 50,000 people. It was a unification bout for the WBO, WBA (Super) and WBC super-middleweight titles. Also, The Ring Magazine belt The 35-year-old Welshman was giving away seven years to the 28-year-old Dane.

For the first few rounds Kessler had the upper hand with some solid shots, jarring Calzaghe at times. Then Calzaghe took control and won most of the remaining rounds leading to a clear win by unanimous decision. It was his 21st successful title defence, surpassing the 20 title defences made by Bernard Hopkins at middleweight.

According to the punch statistics, Calzaghe had thrown an incredible 1,010 punches against 585 for Kessler, although Kessler had a higher degree of accuracy with the number of punches landed. Afterwards, when speaking about the number of punches thrown, Kessler said; "his punches weren't particularly hard, but it was confusing when he hit you 20 times." Meanwhile in Calzaghe's post-fight talk the Welshman made his intentions clear.

He wanted to move up to the light-heavyweight division and fight Hopkins.

Just over a month later, still basking in his glory, Calzaghe went over to Las Vegas to watch the Floyd Mayweather Jr vs Ricky Hatton fight. That's when Calzaghe finally met Bernard Hopkins face to face. After an infamous exchange of words and that controversial "white boy" rant from Hopkins there was no going back. The fight was on.

"Oh yes! I loved it. I knew right then that this fight's going to get made right now."

Calzaghe, after Hopkins made his infamous "white boy" comment.

The Fight

*"You're not even in my league!
I would never let a white boy beat me. I would never
lose to a white boy. I couldn't go back to the projects
if I let a white boy beat me."*

Bernard Hopkins infamous racially tainted taunt
aimed at Joe Calzaghe (December, 2007)

When Calzaghe was being bullied as a child Hopkins was forging a name for himself as a street thug. The two fighters were almost polar opposites in both their upbringing and public personas. Hopkins always tried to come across as the brash, aggressive guy with something to prove, perhaps still trying to identify with the street gangs he was once part of himself. Calzaghe was more the shy, retiring type who never felt comfortable under the media spotlight outside the ring.

This fight was a clash of two proud boxing nations on opposite sides of the Atlantic. It was a clash of personalities. But mostly it was a clash of boxing styles.

The time for talk – trash or otherwise – was over. It wasn't a full house but there was a large crowd including thousands of British fight fans who had made the long journey to the U.S. Many of those inside the stadium were, like Calzaghe, Welsh, including Sir Tom Jones who was no stranger to Vegas having sung there many times. This time he sang the Welsh national anthem. Ray J. sang the American anthem. Then the gladiators entered the arena. Finally, after what seemed an eternity, everyone apart from the referee and the two fighters left the ring. It was on.

Round 1:

Calzaghe didn't exactly race out of the blocks to get at Hopkins. It was a slow first minute and the American tied up Calzaghe when he finally rushed in with an attack. Then after only 60 seconds of the fight and a seemingly harmless looking exchange Hopkins caught Calzaghe flush on the face. The Welshman looked more embarrassed that hurt. It wasn't so much a well-timed punch by

Hopkins as an attempt to hit while moving into a clinch. But it caught Calzaghe wide open and down he went. The rest of the round was uncharacteristic for Calzaghe who only threw single punches instead of his usual high volume punch output. And every time he tried to follow up with a combination the wily Hopkins tied him up. First round to Hopkins

Round 2:

Calzaghe struggled to get into any kind of rhythm while Hopkins began turning it into his kind of fight. Single punches followed immediately by a forward head lunge into a clinch. It wasn't pretty to watch and the referee called a time-out after Calzaghe threw a low blow. It was nothing but Hopkins made it count in his favour. This was turning into exactly the kind of fight Hopkins would have wanted; slow and dirty. Despite a lack of success in landing combinations, Calzaghe was at least forcing Hopkins into fighting at a much higher tempo than the home fighter would have liked. This was definitely a difficult round to score but Calzaghe's higher work-rate and forward motion probably edged it.

Round 3:

More of the same. With nine rounds still remaining the question most commentators were asking was, when will Calzaghe adapt to Hopkins' awkward style. The Philadelphia fighter was smothering anything that remotely looked like boxing coming from the British fighter. Meanwhile Calzaghe appeared to be still in shock from that first-round knockdown. He needed to snap out of it, and fast.

Round 4:

The fight still suited Hopkins' style and the fighters were engaging in a little dirty tactics causing the referee to bring them both together in the middle of the ring for a talking to.

Hopkins was doing what he does best. He was spoiling Calzaghe's work (or at least his attempts at work) whenever he could. Such tactics had served him well, but it wasn't crowd pleasing. Hopkins was spoiling the fight but at last, in the fourth round, it looked like Calzaghe had finally woken up.

Round 5:

It was now clear that Calzaghe was the one with all the energy, but he was still unable to take full control of the fight. Hopkins, wily as ever, hardly even fought in bursts. His main tactic was single shots then, using the momentum, rush straight into a clinch. Head first.

Round 6:

More of the same with Hopkins now repeatedly fouling whenever Calzaghe tried to fight. At the end of the sixth round the referee Joe Cortez visited both corners telling both fighters to clean up their act. It was rough and messy but at the half-way mark Calzaghe had just about managed to negate the first round knockdown and edge ahead.

Round 7:

Calzaghe dominated the round, but it was still an untidy affair.

Right at the close Calzaghe almost lost his balance while rushing in to land his flurries of punches. At the time Hopkins was throwing punches to keep Calzaghe off him. The round looked like Calzaghe's but if he had fallen at that point it would have been a repeat of round one and Hopkins could have taken the two-point margin. As it was the round went to Calzaghe.

Hopkins' trainer Freddie Roach tried to rally his fighter before the eighth round by claiming that Calzaghe was ready for the taking. "It's time to start walking him down, you are the stronger man" he told Hopkins. Was it a classic case of trying to motivate his fighter or was Roach watching another fight? In reality, it was Hopkins who was running out of gas.

Round 8:

Hopkins was a cagey fighter and a very elusive target. Yet Calzaghe managed to land some flush solid shots in round eight. The tide was definitely turning Calzaghe's way. Avoiding Calzaghe and the need to be quick enough to tie him up was taking its toll on the older Hopkins.

Calzaghe ended the round with a bit of showboating as Hopkins swung wildly and missed with a couple of shots.

Round 9:

A huge round for Calzaghe catching Hopkins with several powerful punches flush in the face. Hopkins was showing definite signs of fatigue and was certainly less able to avoid some of his opponent's punches.

Round 10:

The pattern continued. Calzaghe coming on stronger while Hopkins showed more signs of tiring. Then after just thirty seconds of the round Calzaghe, while being pulled down by the head, caught Hopkins with a low blow. It looked fairly innocuous, but it was definitely below the belt. The referee called it and gave the hurt fighter time to recover. Hopkins played it for all it was worth and then some.

It was an Oscar winning performance by Hopkins. The referee was willing to allow Hopkins five minutes to recover but the Philadelphia fighter took just under two and the action resumed. However, those two minutes rejuvenated Hopkins, who was then able to fight more like he had in the early rounds. It was a difficult round to score unlike the previous few which had been all Calzaghe. The tenth could have gone either way with the judges.

Would Hopkins have run out of steam without those precious minutes to rest and recover? We will never know...

Round Eleven:

With Calzaghe again in the ascendency Hopkins seemed to be exhausted. With 35 seconds of the round remaining Calzaghe had Hopkins pinned in the corner and hit him with a body punch right in the stomach. The referee was stepping in to separate the fighters and was blindsided. Hopkins went down feigning another low blow. The referee appeared to call a timeout but then decided it was not a low blow. But critically, he also did not say the word "Box" in order to restart the action. Hopkins had almost twenty seconds of respite before they resumed the fight. If it was not a low blow – which the in-house replay on the large screens clearly showed that it was not - then why was it not ruled a knockdown? Why was Hopkins not given a standing count? That would have sealed the result right there before the final round. For the remaining 15 seconds of the round the slightly refreshed Hopkins, for the first time in the fight, tried to impress the judges and made a stand of it in the centre of the ring.

Round Twelve:

Before the start of the final round Calzaghe's trainer and father, Enzo, insisted that his charge needed to stop Hopkins. "You've got to stop him" he said repeatedly. Clearly trying to keep his son on his toes, it was mostly a way of urging for a big last round. However, considering what happened in the first round, that level of motivation should have been tempered with a little caution. Winning the last round was important but not by being reckless.

Meanwhile in the opposite corner Freddie Roach simply asked for a big last round. It seemed that Hopkins' corner thought their man was winning the fight. They were basically telling him to keep doing what he had been doing and the result would be a win. Hopkins could barely do any more than he had been doing. One punch lunging in, then hold. Holding at every single opportunity. Hopkins was exhausted. It was apparent several rounds ago that Hopkins did not have the stamina to keep Calzaghe off. There was no way the final round would be any different.

Everyone in the arena had their own version of the result but the judges' scores were the only ones that mattered. In the end it was a split decision victory for Calzaghe with one judge giving it to Hopkins by 114-112. Ironically that judge was Adelaide Byrd who a few years earlier had scored a massive win for Calzaghe against Jeff Lacy. The other two judges were closer to the reality of the fight with scores of 115-112 from Ted Gimza and 116-111 from Chuck Giampa.

HBO's unofficial ringside judge Harold Lederman scored the bout 116-111 for Calzaghe.

Hopkins definitely made it difficult for Calzaghe, but the Welshman found a way to win after a very bad start.

According to the fight statistics and punch count system CompuBox, in the 21 Hopkins fights that they had tracked, Calzaghe landed more punches on the Philly fighter than any of his previous opponents. Calzaghe landed 232 punches, almost double the number of punches landed by Hopkins (127). The previous best against Hopkins was by Roy Jones Jr. (206) in their first encounter back in 1993.

Ultimately, after all the hype that led to this fight, Hopkins did "lose to a white boy". But none of that ever came up after the fight. All the talk was about whether Hopkins would continue and who would be Joe Calzaghe's next and final opponent.

"I must win and I must win big and I must punish him, to be able to look anybody in the face and say 'I told you so'"

Bernard Hopkins before the fight

"I would never lose to a white boy either. Or a green boy or a brown boy, or a red boy. Or whatever other colour they want to bring to me."

Joe Calzaghe's full response
to Hopkins' 'white boy' comment.

Hopkins tried to explain away those controversial comments he made in an interview with one of his hometown's newspapers the Philadelphia Daily News.

Hopkins said the comments were not meant to be taken as a racial slur or a reflection of his feelings on white fighters. It was simply said to create some hype for the big fight with Calzaghe. "It's just another way of talking trash. It doesn't mean I think white guys can't fight. I know better than that" he was reported as saying.

Hopkins felt that the plan worked and made the fight with Calzaghe even bigger, based on how the public reacted. It probably did work in that respect, but does that justify what he said and how he delivered it?

In his justification Hopkins pointed to Larry Holmes and Gerry Cooney. Hopkins explained how that fight was split along racial lines, with black people rooting for Holmes and white people for Cooney. "Those guys became very good friends afterwards, but their fights sold better because of the black-white thing. This is not anything new." Hopkins explained.

It is true that Holmes and Cooney did become friends after their fight but that was in a very different era. An era where the media played heavily on such things rather than trying to down-play them. However, what if it had been the other way around? In that case there is no doubt that the press would have slaughtered Calzaghe. Even if he had merely retorted with his own version such as "I would never lose to a black man", the press would have had a field day. The event could have easily spiralled into another Holmes vs Cooney fiasco.

*"The first four rounds, and after that Calzaghe got in his groove,
much like he did when he fought Mikkel Kessler,
and from that point on it was Calzaghe.
And Calzaghe didn't fight as good a fight as he could've fought,
and he still won decisively,"*

Emanuel Steward, reporting on the fight for HBO.

Aftermath

"I don't know who I want to fight next. Maybe I'm the legend killer. I just beat Bernard Hopkins. Next maybe Roy Jones."

Calzaghe was never going to gain much from fighting Hopkins. If he lost, he would have been beaten for the first time and by an ageing champion. If, as it turned out, he won, then some people were always going to say that he just beat an old fighter who was way past his best.

Calzaghe's motivation was three-fold. He wanted to box on the big stage in the USA. He wanted to win a title in another weight category. Most of all he wanted to beat Hopkins because he knew that later people would realise what a great victory that really was.

There was of course a fourth reason. Money. Calzaghe stood to make a lot of money fighting his final two bouts in the USA against big names in the sport. This was all part of his retirement plan.

For Joe Calzaghe the aftermath of this fight was simple. One more fight in the mecca of boxing, Madison Square Garden against a top-rated opponent in Roy Jones Junior, then retire. Simple. One more win, make some money and retire at the very top. He had nothing else to prove. Simply the best of his era and on his best day probably unbeatable.

Calzaghe met Jones Jr. on November 8th, 2008, in a fight that was billed as "Battle of the Superpowers". The fight was for The Ring light heavyweight title that Calzaghe had won by beating Hopkins.

Roy Jones Jr.

After ruling at middleweight and then for a time at super middleweight in the mid-1990s Roy Jones Jr. stepped up to light heavyweight and beat the tough Jamaican Mike McCallum by unanimous decision on November 22nd, 1996. In his first defence at his new weight in March 1997, Jones lost to Montell Griffin via a disqualification. Griffin was hit by Jones while taking a knee but made far more of it than he should have. Jones subsequently felt that he had been cheated in that, his first loss. In an immediate rematch five months later Jones exacted one of the most savage revenge victories in boxing history. Only a few seconds into the fight Jones had his man taking a standing count. A couple of minutes later Griffin was dropped by a left hook from Jones. He could not recover. Famously stumbling around the ring attempting to get up while his legs betrayed him.

Jones went on to win twelve straight fights culminating with a win over British boxer Clinton Woods on September 9th, 2002. Jones then went on to do what no other boxer had done in the modern era of the sport. He won the WBA heavyweight title by convincingly beating Joh Ruiz on March 1st, 2003. Jones almost immediately relinquished the heavyweight crown in order to drop back down to light heavyweight and take on Antonio Tarver on November 8th, 2003. In what seemed a below par performance Jones beat Tarver via a majority decision. One which many observers thought should have gone to Tarver. During Jones' journey up to heavyweight Antonio Tarver had beaten the same Montell Griffin to win the IBF and WBC light heavyweight titles that had been vacated by Jones. When Tarver and Jones met for the first time the vacant WBA light heavyweight title was also on the line. Jones blamed his subpar performance in the fight on difficulty making weight despite having eight months to shed 18 pounds (8kg).

At the time of the Tarver rematch Jones had had 50 fights winning 49 with the only blemish on his record being that dodgy disqualification against Griffin. He was widely recognised as the best boxer of his generation (pound for pound) and was even talked about as being one of the best and most gifted boxers of all time. But boxing is not like other sports. Eventually even the best can come face-to-face with their nemesis. It can be another great fighter, or it can just be someone who simply 'has their number'. For Roy Jones Jr. that adversary came in the form of Antonio Tarver.

Tarver lost to Jones on points (a majority decision) in the November 2003 fight, but most observers thought that the judges had incorrectly scored the bout. Jones clearly struggled after coming back down from his excursion up at heavyweight. Tarver lost his WBC world light heavyweight title in that fight and wanted the immediate rematch. The rematch came six months later in May 2004 when Tarver famously destroyed Jones with a second round KO. The fight was equally as famous for the verbal taunt when the two fighters met to receive the traditional referee's final instructions in the centre of the ring. When referee Jay Nady asked if anyone had any questions. Tarver said, "I got a question. You got any excuses tonight, Roy?" Nady interrupted by saying "Let's not ask questions like that." But Tarver insisted on repeating the question, "You got any excuses tonight, Roy?"

Jones clearly won the first round, but Tarver forced the fight in the second being the aggressor and forcing Jones onto the backfoot. A hard left counterpunch half-way through the second session sent Jones to the canvas and he seemed to be hurt for the first time in his career. He got up just before being counted out but stumbled across the ring. The referee had no option but to wave the fight off.

Tarver had only landed six clean shots before the big left hook that ended the fight. Call it confidence, anger, or a mix of both; but on the night Tarver certainly delivered.

The two would meet in a trilogy fight 17 months later. In between that fight they fought a total of three bouts, all against the same opponent, Glen Johnson. In September 2004 Johnson knocked Jones out in the ninth round capturing the vacant IBF light heavyweight title. Johnson then beat Tarver by split decision in December 2004. Exactly six months later on June 18th, 2005, Tarver avenged that defeat with a unanimous decision victory over Johnson. The Jones-Tarver trilogy fight took place on October 1st, 2005. Tarver won by unanimous decision. The previously 'untouchable' Roy Jones Jr. had lost three successive fights. Two by KO.

After proving that Roy Jones was a mere mortal, Tarver landed the role of fictional boxer Mason Dixon in Sylvester Stallone's latest Rocky movie "*Rocky Balboa*" (also referred to as Rocky VI). Tarver beat Rocky in that movie but lost his next real fight to Bernard Hopkins, making Hopkins the lineal light-heavyweight champion. Tarver had to lose more than 40 pounds to make the light heavyweight limit after filming the Rocky movie.

After his losses to Tarver, Roy Jones regrouped and between July 2006 and January 2008 won his next three fights against opponents with a combined record of 88-4-2. The last of those three was the Puerto Rican legend Felix Trinidad who had won 42 of his 44 fights. Trinidad had not fought for over two and a half years and was floored twice by Jones who won by a clear unanimous decision. Jones demonstrated that he was still a very capable fighter and still possessed the brilliance that made him a multi weight world champion.

He had not been beaten in 50 fights before encountering his arch-rival in the shape of Antonio Tarver (not counting the disqualification vs Griffin). The Johnson loss was sandwiched in between the difficult Tarver trilogy. Going into his fight with Joe Calzaghe, Roy Jones was still widely considered a force in the sport and he was only three years older than the British boxer.

The fight with Roy Jones was expected to be Calzaghe's last and was well attended with plenty of British fight fans making their way to New York. But the opening round was not what they had expected to see. It was a classic case of *déjà vu*.

For the second fight in succession, and only the fourth time in his career, Calzaghe was caught coming in and was floored by Roy Jones in the very first round. The punch turned out to be caused by an accidental forearm by Jones. Calzaghe immediately found himself two points down on the scorecards. Exactly as he had against Hopkins.

Calzaghe managed to compose himself and soon took complete control of the fight. He won all eleven remaining rounds and even had moments to perform a spot of showboating (something Jones himself had become famous for doing while teasing opponents).

Calzaghe completely dominated Roy Jones to the point of humiliation. It was almost embarrassingly easy at times. Even though he was knocked down in the first round Calzaghe arguably had the better of that first session. Eighteen months later Jones went on to lose his rematch with Bernard Hopkins only less embarrassingly. Considering what Hopkins immediately went on to achieve, Calzaghe's emphatic victory over Jones deserves far more credit than it received at the time.

"I fought with a smile on my face"
Calzaghe recounting his final fight vs Roy Jones Jr.

How good to know that you are winning a fight while putting on a great show and that you would not have to do it again. Totally content with the situation. Going out at the very top and on your own terms.

Sadly, very few fighters get to do that. Hopkins probably boxed on far too long and Jones Jr certainly did. Many do.

Lennox Lewis and Floyd Mayweather Jr. can probably say the same as Calzaghe. That they retired at the top of their game, financially secure and with their faculties intact. Boxing is a brutal sport. Everyone knows that. But that's also one of the reasons the fans love it.

There was talk of a comeback for a short time. Two new stars had emerged at super-middleweight. One from the UK in the shape of Carl Froch and the new king of the division in the American, Andre Ward. While the 35-year-old Joe Calzaghe was leaving the super-middleweight division to move up to light heavyweight Froch was building a solid resumé having won all 21 fights since his debut in 2002. At age 30 Froch was about to fight (and win) his first world title shot against Jean Pascal. Meanwhile Andre Ward was only 23 years old with 13 straight wins and about to fight someone with a similar record, the 21-year-old Roger Cantrell (12-0). Ward was still eight fights away from winning a world title which he did in November 2009 defeating the 'Viking Warrior' Kessler. Ward dominated the fight which was stopped in the eleventh round due to Kessler's face being badly cut. By that time Calzaghe was 37 and had been retired for a year.

It is always the way in boxing. Younger boxers on their way up often pass older boxers on the decline. Sometimes meeting them in the ring and taking their titles. Other times (probably more often) destined never to fight each other.

Ever since Calzaghe's retirement comparisons have been made between 'The Pride of Wales/Italian Dragon' and Carl Froch. There have been many discussion/arguments about who would have won if they had fought. But choosing the winner between the best Calzaghe and the best Froch has never been in dispute among boxing scholars. The real "dream fight" debate from that crossover period is who would have won between Joe Calzaghe and Andre Ward.

Bernard Hopkins fought on for another eight years. The guy that some claimed was an old man of 40 when losing to Calzaghe managed to hold back father time to fight twelve more bouts. His comeback after the Calzaghe defeat came against Kelly Pavlik. The man who had beaten the man (Jermain Taylor) who had dethroned Hopkins at middleweight. Hopkins schooled the much younger Pavlik winning a wide points victory. The fight was voted Ring Magazine's 2008 Upset of the Year and immediately everyone was (once again) saying what a great fighter Hopkins was.

Two fights later Hopkins had the chance to avenge his 1993 loss to Roy Jones Jr. The two Calzaghe scalps faced off in Las Vegas in April 2010. Roy Jones had three fights after losing to Calzaghe. Two stoppage wins over former Calzaghe victims Omar Sheika and Jeff Lacy, followed by a devastating first round KO loss in Sydney to Australian Danny Green. Jones was 41 and Hopkins 45. The result was a convincing points win for Hopkins.

At the end of 2010 Hopkins fought Jean Pascal in Quebec, Canada. Pascal was the WBC world light heavyweight title as well as The Ring and lineal champion. The fight ended in a majority draw (in Hopkins' favour) but it meant that Pascal retained the titles. Many thought Hopkins won the fight despite being knocked down (twice) for the first time in 16 years. The WBC ordered an immediate rematch. Hopkins' exploits that year earned him The Ring Magazine 2010 Comeback of the Year award. Hopkins was still far from finished as a fighter.

The two met again six months later in May 2011 this time in Montreal, Canada. Hopkins, now 46 years old, defeated Pascal by unanimous decision to become the lineal/WBC/The Ring light-heavyweight champion. Hopkins famously did press ups in the centre of the ring in between rounds as if to show that he, the much older man, was fitter than Pascal. But maybe also, Hopkins did it to get into Pascal's head. Either way it worked.

With that win, Hopkins became the oldest man in the history of the sport to win a major world title. [That accolade was previously held by George Foreman, after his knockout victory over Michael Moorer in 1994 to reclaim the world heavyweight title at the age of 45.]

This was ten years after Hopkins had beaten Felix Trinidad to become undisputed middleweight champion. At that time Hopkins was 36 and already considered old.

There followed two fights with American and former champion Chad Dawson. The first was ruled a 'no contest' when Hopkins' shoulder was injured after being thrown by Dawson. Hopkins subsequently retained his WBC world title. In the rematch Dawson regained the title winning a majority decision. The second Dawson fight was Hopkins' only fight in 2012. Incredibly 2012 was the first calendar year since way back in 1989 that Hopkins did not register a win.

Hopkins fought twice in 2013. In the first of these Hopkins broke his own record of being the oldest boxer to win a world title. At 48 years of age Hopkins beat the then undefeated 31-year-old Tavoris Cloud by unanimous decision to become IBF world light-heavyweight champion. Later that year Hopkins successfully defended his title beating German-based Armenian Karo Murat by unanimous decision.

The next defence came in a unification bout in April 2014 against Kazakhstani Beibut Shumanov who was the WBA champion. Hopkins won by unanimous decision (again) and broke yet another age barrier record to become the oldest boxer in history to unify titles in a weight division. This set up another unification fight against the WBO titlist, the fearsome Russian Sergey Kovalev.

The fight took place in Atlantic City on November 8th, 2014. It was a very one-sided fight with the three judges' scoring it 120-107, 120-107, 120-106 for a unanimous decision for the Russian. A total shut-out, Hopkins lost every single round, losing his titles and even getting knocked down in the first round by Kovalev. Just two months shy of his 50th birthday it looked like father time had finally caught up with Hopkins although he had just become the first fighter to take Kovalev past eight rounds.

Hopkins never fought in 2015 but he did call out Britain's Carl Froch - again. Hopkins had previously called out Froch after losing to Joe Calzaghe. This time Hopkins wanted to fight Froch in a farewell match. Froch declined the offer calling it a "lose-lose situation" and elected to retire instead.

In December 2016, just over two years since his lop-sided loss to Kovalev, Hopkins headed into what was to be his farewell fight against fellow American Joe Smith Jr. It had been over twelve years since Hopkins had won by KO when he stopped Oscar De La Hoya back in September 2004. Hopkins had lost seven fights up to this point in his career but none by KO. That all changed against Smith Jr. The 51-year-old Hopkins lost to Smith, a man 24 years his junior, in round number eight. Not only was knocked Hopkins down, but Smith knocked him out of the ring.

Ironically, perhaps, Joe Smith Jr. is white. In his final fight not only did Hopkins 'lose to a white guy' but he was also knocked out by him.

Bernard Hopkins is still heavily involved in boxing working with Oscar De La Hoya at Golden Boy Promotions. Hopkins was inducted into the International Boxing Hall of Fame in the class of 2020, but that induction week was postponed until 2021 due to the "coronavirus pandemic". The 2021 induction week was also postponed till the following year.

Years later Joe Calzaghe is still getting long overdue credit for what was a very good victory over Bernard Hopkins.

Calzaghe could have used the same "lose-lose situation" excuse that Carl Froch made to avoid Hopkins. When they met Hopkins was 43 years old while Calzaghe had just turned 36. Over seven years difference. Yet Calzaghe gave away several years to some top-rated opponents, all of whom he beat convincingly.

Calzaghe fought the man most Americans thought would destroy him in Jeff Lacy. The American was 5 years younger than Calzaghe, but it was he (Lacy) who got destroyed. The tough as nails Sakio Bika was seven years younger but Calzaghe beat him by unanimous decision. Peter Manfredo was nine years younger than Calzaghe and was destroyed by a youthful performance of sheer speed.

Kessler was the unified WBC and WBA super-middleweight champion of the world and unbeaten. Did that not count for anything? He was also 7 years younger than Calzaghe.

Yet when Calzaghe went up against the older Hopkins these statistics were never brought up. There was only talk of similar age difference (of seven years) only this time in Calzaghe's favour.

After several years and having seen what Hopkins went on to achieve it is clear that the age difference was never a factor back in April 2008. It is also clear that Joe Calzaghe's victory over Bernard Hopkins was just another great victory for 'The Pride of Wales'.

On 5 February 2009, Joe Calzaghe announced his retirement from professional boxing, finishing with a record of 46 wins and no losses, becoming one of only fifteen world champions to retire as an undefeated world champion. The others are:

Floyd Mayweather Jr., Rocky Marciano, Andre Ward, Ji-won Kim, Terry Marsh, Pichit Sitbangprachan, Harry Simon,

Jimmy Barry, Jack McAuliffe, Ricardo Lopez, Michael Loewe, Edwin Valero, Sven Ottke, and Dmitry Pirog.

Calzaghe made 21 successful defences of his super-middleweight title(s) surpassing the 20 defences made by Bernard Hopkins at middlewcight and by Larry Holmes at heavyweight. Only former heavyweight champion Joe Louis (with 25 defences), former light heavyweight champion Dariusz Michalczewski (23 defences), former minimumweight champion Ricardo López (23 defences), and former heavyweight champion Wladimir Klitschko (23 defences) have made more title defences.

Following Calzaghe's retirement, fellow boxer and friend, Ricky Hatton, described him as "the best British fighter we've ever had." Top boxing information/database website BoxRec.com, rates Calzaghe as the greatest super-middleweight of all time, as well as the greatest European boxer, pound for pound, of all time. As is so often the case once great boxers retire, respect for Calzaghe's achievements continues to grow with the passing of time.

Joe Calzaghe was inducted into the International Boxing Hall of Fame in 2014.

Undercard

The undercard for this huge fight was not exactly filled with well-known names. At least back in 2008. However, there were several up-and-coming boxers fighting at the event that would go on to become world champions. Three of them (at this time) remain active and fighting at the very highest level.

Future star Daniel Jacobs made an appearance in only his fifth professional fight when he beat Leshon Sims by a 4th round knockout in a super middleweight contest. Jacobs went on to fight at the very highest level. At the time of writing, he has amassed a record of 37 wins with 4 defeats. His only losses being to Dmitry Pirog (by KO) and two unanimous decision losses to elite fighters Saúl 'Canelo' Alvarez, Gennady "GGG" Golovkin and John Ryder. The fight with Pirog, the tough as steel Russian, was for the vacant WBO world middleweight title. Pirog defended the title only three times and retired undefeated in twenty fights after a serious back injury (ruptured disc) cut short his promising career. Pirog remains the only man to have stopped Daniel Jacobs.

Danny Garcia in his fifth professional outing stopped fellow American Guadalupe Diaz in the first round of a scheduled four rounder. Garcia went on to great things. He fought and beat just about every top fighter at light welterweight and welterweight including Amir Khan, Caleb Truax, Sergio Mora, Lamont Peterson, Erik Morales (twice), Nate Campbell, Luca Matthysse and Zab Judah. He won WBA and WBC world light welterweight titles and moved up to claim the vacant WBC world welterweight title in January 2016 beating Roberto Guerrero by unanimous decision. Garcia lost is title in his second defence against Keith Thurman in March 2017. He continues to fight at the highest level and remains one of the world's most exciting fighters.

Jermell Charlo in just his second fight beat fellow American Jesus Villareal by a third-round knockout. The highly touted Charlo went on to become WBC world light middleweight (super welterweight) champion. Charlo rose up the ranks and won the WBC title by beating John Jackson via an eighth-round stoppage in May 2016. Jackson is the son of the legendary Julian Jackson (recognised as one of the hardest punchers in recent decades) but his genes were not enough to win the fight. Charlo was losing the fight on all three scorecards when he delivered the knockout. After three successful defences Charlo lost the title to Tony Harrison in December 2018 but won it back again (from Harrison) a year later in December 2019.

Charlo has a twin brother who also fights at the top level. The two brothers made history by becoming the first twins to hold two versions of a world title simultaneously. Jermell's twin, Jermall (note only the one letter difference) already held the IBF world light middleweight title when Jermell won the WBC version.

He continues to fight at the highest level and unified the WBA, WBC and IBF light middleweight titles on September 26, 2020, with an eighth round KO of Dominican Republic fighter Jeison Rosario. Charlo attempted to completely unify the division in a July 2021 bout with WBO title holder Brain Castano. The fight ended a draw and (at the time of writing) the rematch is pending.

One of the chief supporting bouts featured Mexican David "Destroyer" Lopez against American Ryan Davies in a ten-round middleweight contest. Lopez won with a fifth-round knockout. Both fighters had reasonable records, but Lopez was known more as a spoiler than a future champion. What happened seven years later however made for bigger news than any of Lopez's fights.

On July 6, 2017, David López was shot dead during an incident in his hometown of Nogales, Mexico. It was reported that he was travelling with a passenger just before midnight, when his truck was hit by a large volume of bullets fired by heavily armed gunmen.

Lopez died immediately before the police arrived. The Red Cross paramedics attended to the second victim. It turned out the other passenger was Lopez's 14-year-old son. Fortunately, the boy survived.

When police arrived at the scene, they soon realised that Lopez was already dead, so paramedics provided care only to his seriously injured son. Boxing can be a cruel sport with deaths and long-term brain damage never far from the headlines. Yet it is easy to forget that life itself, outside of boxing, can often be much crueller.

"Destroyer" Lopez once fought American Austin Trout for the WBA light middleweight world title in June 2011. Trout retained his belt with a twelve round unanimous decision. However, Lopez left his mark on boxing with a record of 42 wins, 16 losses, 1 draw. 24 of his victories came by knockout.

Former 2000 Olympic games super-heavyweight gold medal winner Audley Harrison also fought on the undercard. Harrison had failed to live up to the expectations that come with winning the top prize in the amateur ranks. He had fought twenty-four times but lost three of those to journeymen fighters.

He fought Jason Barnett who went by the entertaining alias of 'Half Man Half Amazing' - although disappointingly the ring announcer never used it for this fight. His record at the time of 10 wins and 6 defeats could almost be described as 'half and half.' Harrison cruised to a comfortable knockout victory stopping Barnett in the fifth session of a scheduled eight rounder. Harrison hit his opponent with two body shots half-way into the round. Barnett just beat the count, but the referee called it off.

Despite the win Harrison still received criticism from the crowd, some of whom called him 'Audrey' and 'Fraudley'. That type of criticism is unjustified, but Harrison failed to get any closer to a world title shot and finished with a record of 31-7.

In his final fight Harrison was knocked out in the first round by a genuine rising star in the division (and 2008 Olympic heavyweight bronze medal winner) in Deontay Wilder. Less than half-way through the round Wilder knocked Harrison over with the very first right-hand punch he threw. Watching at ringside was another Olympic gold medal winner who had just turned pro; one Anthony Joshua. Harrison is just one of many boxers who could not make a successful transition from Olympic success in the amateurs to the professional ranks.

Another boxer in the Enzo Calzaghe stable was Nathan Cleverly. He was one of only a few people in Joe Calzaghe's entourage for the Hopkins fight. Cleverly had won all eleven fights as a professional and in Las Vegas he fought American Antonio Baker. It was clear that Baker was a hand-picked easy victory for the rising star Cleverly. Baker finished his career with an uninspiring 7-13-1 record but at the time his record stood at 6 wins, 9 losses with one draw. Of his six defeats Baker had only been stopped twice; once by former Joe Calzaghe victim Peter Manfredo and later to future world champion Chad Dawson who would eventually go on to beat Bernard Hopkins by a majority decision in 2012. Cleverly had only won three of his eleven fights by knockout and was unable to become the third man to stop Baker. But he did cruise to a convincing unanimous points decision over eight rounds. Cleverly won every round on every scorecard. Just over two years after this fight Cleverly gained a Bachelor of Science (BSc) degree in mathematics at Cardiff University.

Cleverly went on to win a further two fights before winning the Commonwealth light heavyweight title. Three fights later he beat the unbeaten Danny McIntosh for the British light heavyweight title. In February 2010 Cleverly claimed the European light heavyweight title beating Italian Antonio Brancalion inside five rounds. Two fights later Cleverly claimed a world title winning the WBO world light heavyweight belt against Polish boxer Aleksy Kuzienski in London on May 21st, 2011. Cleverly won by a 4th round stoppage and went on to defend his world title four times. He then faced the fearsome Russian Sergey Kovalev in August 2013 and was easily beaten inside four rounds. He continued to box, moving up unsuccessfully to cruiserweight and then having some success back down at light heavyweight, winning two and losing two. Cleverly finished his career in 2017 after losing by fifth round knockout to Sweden's Badou Jack. Nathan Cleverly left the sport with a respectable 30-4 record.

Chapter 4:

Don't Judge a Book by Its Cover

The Story of Anthony Joshua vs Andy Ruiz Junior.
1st June, 2019, Madison Square Garden,
New York, New York, USA.

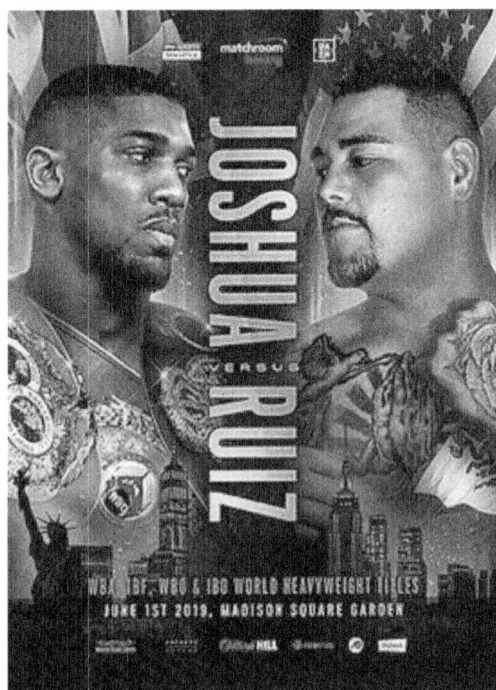

The fight between Anthony Joshua and Andy Ruiz Jr. never had a catchy billing or promotional slogan. It was a hastily arranged match-up after Joshua's original challenger, Jarrell Miller, failed three (3) drug tests in the build up to the fight for the unified WBA/WBO/IBF world heavyweight titles.

The event had already sold 17,000 tickets (as Anthony Joshua vs Jarrell Miller) with over half of those tickets being sold to British fight fans who were once again making their way across the pond in huge numbers. This time to watch Anthony Joshua's eagerly anticipated American debut.

This fight was supposed to be a stateside showcase for the unbeaten 'AJ'. The boxer. The champion. The brand.

When Miller was (quite rightly) denied a license to box the whole event was thrown into disarray as the promoters and organisers searched for a last-minute replacement. Who would fight Joshua for the heavyweight crown? Who would get their dream opportunity? Their shot at the title?

Enter Andy Ruiz Jr. A softly spoken American of Mexican descent who had lost only once in 33 fights. He was slightly shorter than Joshua but just like Miller he was heavily set and stocky. Similar in stature to the opponent that Joshua had been training for.

Joshua, the 2012 Olympic gold medallist, was the reigning WBA, IBF and WBO titlist. He boasted seemingly overwhelming physical advantages over the late substitute challenger Ruiz. Joshua also had the whole sports world backing him. Andy Ruiz was a massive 15-1 underdog. This was supposed to be an easy tune-up fight leading to the biggest possible showdown with the (then) current WBC champion, the undefeated, hard-hitting Deontay Wilder.

It was likened to Rocky Balboa being given a shot at the title against Apollo Creed in the movie *Rocky*. But this was no movie.

What happened would shock the whole sporting world and become arguably the biggest ever upset in the world of boxing. Even eclipsing the defeat of Mike Tyson by James Douglas.

Proving yet again that in any sport, particularly boxing, and especially heavyweight boxing, the most valuable advice is free. That advice, true also in life in general, comes in the form of that old adage:

"Don't judge a book by its cover".

The Rise of Anthony Joshua

Joshua's rise to become the unified heavyweight champion of the world was not just fast-tracked it was turbo-charged.

Olympic gold medal winning amateur to IBF world heavyweight champion in 16 fights. This was a whirlwind four years by any boxing standards.

Before challenging Charles Martin for the IBF world title in April 2016 Joshua fought fellow Briton Dillian Whyte in what many considered would be a tough test. Up to the Dillian Whyte fight Joshua had only boxed a total of 25 rounds in his 14 bouts. None of his fights had gone past the 3rd round. When Whyte was still standing at the start of the fourth round, he was taking Joshua into uncharted territory. One round later Whyte too was in deep. He had only ever been as far as four rounds in his previous sixteen fights and had only fought 44 rounds before the Joshua fight. Remarkably the winner of this fight was set to challenge for a world title.

Compare these statistics with some of boxing's recent legends; Mike Tyson, Lennox Lewis and Wladimir Klitschko. "Iron" Mike Tyson had 27 fights boxing some 70 rounds before he fought for a world title and everyone thought his rise to the top was fast tracked.[*] Lennox Lewis had 21 fights boxing about 80 rounds before he was awarded the title which he was actually in line to fight for, before Riddick Bowe gave up the WBC belt. Wladimir Klitschko had an incredible 34 fights and 112 rounds of boxing before he challenged for a world title.

All boxers want to get out of the ring as quick as possible. No fighter wants to box more rounds than are necessary. They can only beat what is in front of them. What did this say about Anthony Joshua? Were the durable fighters, usually so important in testing young rising stars, no longer available? Or was Joshua just something extra special?

[*] It is worth noting that although Mike Tyson had 27 fights before challenging Trevor Berbeck for the WBC world title in November 1986, there is more to Tyson's rise to the top. Incredibly, Tyson had 12 fights in 1986, beginning in January. This run included 10 wins by KO with two back-to-back wins on points. Both of those

were over ten rounds and less than three weeks apart (on 3rd and 20th of May) against good opposition in James Tillis and Mitch Green. Tyson's debut pro fight was on 6th March, 1985. He won his first world title just over 20 months later.

Historically, nobody comes close to Leon Spinks in fighting for and winning a world title after so few professional fights. Spinks won the light heavyweight gold at the Montreal Olympic games in July 1976. He made his professional debut in January 1977 and only eleven months later fought Muhammad Ali in February 1978 for the WBC and WBA heavyweight titles. (There were only two versions of the title in those days, so this was for the undisputed title). Incredibly that was only Spinks' eighth fight and he hadn't even won all of his previous seven – one being a draw. He had only boxed 31 rounds. That is half the number of fights Joshua had before fighting for one version of the title. Incredibly however, Spinks had fought only one round less than Joshua before his title shot. Perhaps even more incredible, the combined record of Spinks' seven opponents was an unimpressive 108 wins against 68 losses with 4 draws. Yet somehow Leon Spinks managed to get a shot at the title held by a legend in Ali, whose own record was 55 wins and two defeats. Maybe it was by virtue of the fact that Spinks was, like Ali, a light heavyweight Olympic gold medalist. Probably also due to some cunning matchmaking by Top Rank duo Bob Arum and 'Butch' Lewis.

Spinks was the only man to take the title from Ali in the ring. All of Ali's other losses came when he was the challenger or in non-title fights.

Seven months later however Spinks lost his title in a rematch with Ali. Spinks' was known as "Neon" Leon in the pugilistic vernacular. Possibly (initially) for his flash fighting style but probably more for his love of the bright lights and late-night parties. Ali (unlike the first fight) trained hard for their rematch, whereas Spinks spent most of the seven months partying. He even famously went missing the day of the rematch only to be found by one of his team a few hours before the first bell was due to sound. Spinks was in bed with a woman in a seedy motel room, allegedly with all the paraphernalia of a heavy night out laid out on the bedroom tables. Meanwhile many of the sixty-three thousand plus fans that had tickets for the fight at the New Orleans Superdome that day were already filling the arena. Spinks made it in time for the first bell and even managed to hear the final bell but was well beaten in a unanimous decision by the rejuvenated 36-year-old Ali. Leon's career famously imploded after that and he never reached those dizzying heights again. But none of it seemed to bother him. His easy come easy go attitude seemed to infect everyone who met him. Everybody liked him. "Neon" Leon Spinks sadly passed away in February 2021 following a long battle with cancer. He was 67 years old.

In his first 12 fights Joshua boxed in 8 different cities in the UK. A promotional dream, this was the Anthony Joshua roadshow, albeit against poor opposition. It was as much a public relations (PR) exercise as a record building one; taking Joshua around the country and building a fan base.

This was a PR masterclass by Joshua's promoter Eddie Hearn. One which would guarantee huge crowds in the next phase of Joshua's career – wherever in the UK he fought.

Carefully matched opponents are nothing new for new professional boxers being groomed for stardom. Joshua's early opponents were certainly no different. This would later be referred to as "phase one" of Joshua's career by promoter Hearn.

There is little worth mentioning about Joshua's first seven fights apart perhaps for his third bout against Croatian Hrvoje Kisicek. This was interesting for two reasons. Firstly, it was on the undercard of a Prizefighter tournament in York Hall, London, featuring some known heavyweights including one James "Lights Out" Toney. Some of the fighters in that tournament would provide three out of Joshua's next eight opponents. The other interesting thing about this match was the comedy value. It could barely be described as a training session for Joshua. It was more like a travelling circus tent fight. The records simply show however that Joshua moved to 3 (wins) and 0 (losses).

In his eighth fight in Manchester, England, Joshua was taken into the third round for the first time by the Kazak born, German based Konstantin Airich. The Kazak boxer had been in with a few decent fighters, even going the distance with the Cuban Olandier Solis and Russian Denis Bakhtov. More importantly however was the simple fact that whenever he met decent opposition, he had lost. His fight with Joshua ended in the third round after a second knockdown.

Joshua returned to London and another two-round demolition in his next fight against the aforementioned Bakhtov. In his next two fights Joshua fought two more boxers from the Prizefighter tournament on the bill of his third fight. The first was Michael Sprott who Joshua dispatched half-way through round one in Liverpool, England. This was Joshua's 7th fight in 2014. In April 2015 another boxer from that 'Prizefighter' tournament, Jason Gavern became the second boxer to take Joshua into the third round. Only half of it, however. Joshua again won with a clinical knockout.

Joshua's 14th fight was against Scotland's Gary Cornish. Cornish had had half as many fights again as Joshua and had won all 21 of them. 12 by way of knockout. Cornish had been granted six months holiday from his regular job as a carpenter in order to train for the Joshua fight. It made no difference. Joshua swatted him aside in only half a round and claimed the vacant Commonwealth title in the process.

Three months later in December 2015, Joshua had by far his toughest test in a domestic grudge match against fellow Londoner Dillian Whyte. In 2009 Whyte had beaten Joshua in an amateur fight, dropping him to the canvas on the way to a points victory. The two had history and the fight lived up to the hype with both boxers intent on landing big shots. Joshua hurt Whyte in round one and then Whyte returned the favour in round two, staggering Joshua. Whyte piled in but was unable to knock him down. There were even punches after the bell at the end of the round. The fight continued at pace until the seventh round when Joshua caught Whyte with a huge right hand that sent him back onto the ropes. Joshua followed up and floored him with a big uppercut. Joshua had defended his Commonwealth title and won the vacant British title in this bout. More importantly he had boxed for twice as long as he had ever done previously.

There was no announcement of Joshua's next contest after the Dillian Whyte fight. Up to this point Joshua's promoter Hearn, had always talked up the next fight. For a month at least Joshua was on a short break. Joshua's management team had an eye on a fight in New York for early 2016 when a new IBF champion emerged, the American Charles Martin. On paper at least Martin had a solid unbeaten record of 23 wins and one draw. He had won the IBF title on the 16th of January fighting on the undercard of a Deontay Wilder WBC title defence. Although to say he "won" the title almost flatters Martin.

After Tyson Fury defeated Wladimir Klitschko in November 2015 to become the new unified heavyweight champion, the IBF ordered him to fight their mandatory challenger Vyacheslav Glazkov – a Ukrainian fighting out of Florida, USA. However, Fury wanted to take the rematch with Klitschko and was stripped of the IBF title. The IBF then ordered Glazkov to fight Martin for the vacant world title. The fight took place at the Barclays Centre in Brooklyn, New York.

Martin fortuitously claimed the vacant title by "stopping" Glazkov in the third round, due to injury. After two mediocre rounds, in round 3, Glazkov slipped to the canvas, falling backwards after trying to dodge a right hook from Martin. The referee correctly ruled it a slip, but Glazkov appeared to hurt his right knee during the fall. When the fight resumed, Glazkov tried to throw a right body hook but instead went down again after losing his balance. It looked as though Martin was about to throw a right jab but there was never enough power to knock his opponent down. When Glazkov hit the canvas he was clearly in pain. The fight was stopped and the ringside doctor diagnosed him with a torn anterior cruciate ligament.

None of this mattered to Team Joshua however. They now had a shot at a legitimate world heavyweight title. Martin chose to make his first defence against Joshua and agreed to travel to England for the fight. The match was agreed in February and set for April. It was reported that Martin would bank £6 million ($8.5m) for the defence against Joshua. It was easy to see why Martin was willing to give the dangerous young rising star a shot. His purse for the Glazkov fight in winning the title was reportedly only $433,300. Eddie Hearn was buying his star boxer a golden opportunity. After only 14 fights and (perhaps even more incredible) having boxed in only 32 rounds as a professional, Anthony Joshua was to get his shot at a world heavyweight title.

The fight took place on the 9th of April 2016 at the O2 Arena in London. Martin was the first southpaw (leftie) that Joshua had fought, but it turned out not to be a factor. Joshua took control immediately in the first round and kept Martin at length with solid jabs before sending him to the canvas with a straight right hand in the second round. Martin got to his feet, only to be knocked down for a second time by a similar punch just seconds later. This time Martin waited until the count reached ten before jumping up. The referee saw it as failing to beat the count and waved the fight off. Martin appeared to have all his senses about him as he watched the referee making the count but just left it a little late. Martin simply never looked that interested. Joshua was declared the winner in yet another win inside of two rounds.

Martin was heavily criticized for his performance. Some observers accused him of not trying and quitting early, feeling that he could have got up quicker and fought on. Martin later placed the blame on the pre-fight distractions, claiming that he was 'mentally not there'. He also spoke to squash rumours that the fight was fixed. At just 85 days, his reign as IBF heavyweight champion was the second shortest in professional boxing history, with only Tony Tucker's 1987 reign being shorter. (Tucker lost his title to Mike Tyson.)

After just 16 fights, all but one of them lasting on average approximately only 4 minutes, Anthony Joshua was a heavyweight world champion. 'AJ' the brand, had arrived. From amateur star to world champion in just 16 fights and having started only 32 rounds of boxing. The British public embraced him as a true star of the ring.

Before the end of the year 'AJ' defended his new title twice. Just over two months after winning the title Joshua fought Dominic Breazeale in the same arena where he had won the title. It was Joshua's 17th fight while Breazeale had won all 17 of his bouts. The two boxers had almost identical records. But their abilities were not identical. 'AJ' dispatched Breazeale in the seventh round knocking him down twice.

Although Joshua dominated the fight and won every round. Breazeale proved to be a durable opponent, surviving some big shots from the champion. Breazeale's trainer for that fight was Manny Robles who would later train Andy Ruiz for the Joshua fight in New York. This was the first close-up look Robles had of Joshua.

To end the year Joshua fought Eric Molina in the second defence of his title. The Molina fight was a sideshow in reality. This event was staged as an easy win and as a build up to announcing the Wladimir Klitschko fight. Klitschko was ringside for the fight and stepped through the ropes during the post-fight interviews. It was all a perfect publicity stunt as the unification fight was officially announced to the world. It seemed completely scripted and rehearsed but nobody cared. The fans were going to get the big unification bout they wanted to see, and it was going to take place at Wembley Stadium, London.

Joshua had recently beaten four previously unbeaten fighters in four of his last five outings (with a combined record of 77 wins and one draw.) All supposedly rising stars like Joshua himself. He was a heavyweight champion but still lacked a defining fight. That fight was just around the corner in the form of a Ukrainian giant. Another former Olympic gold medal winner and the man who had become the dominant force in the sport since Lennox Lewis had retired from the ring.

The Post Lewis Heavyweight Division...and Wladimir Klitschko

It is impossible to talk about the post Lennox Lewis heavyweight boxing scene without acknowledging the overwhelming dominance of the Klitschko brothers. Particularly the excellent reign of the younger brother Wladimir.

Anthony Joshua's rise to the top was only really complete when he unified the WBA and IBF titles in beating Klitschko. In between the retirement of the great Lewis and the arrival of the new star Joshua, one name stood out in the heavyweight division. Although he may not have been appreciated all that much at the time Wladimir Klitschko is now (quite rightly) widely recognised as one of the greatest heavyweights of all time.

Wladimir Klitschko won the gold medal at the 1996 Olympic games in Atlanta, USA. He turned professional in the same year with an outstanding amateur record of 135 wins with only 6 losses. Fighting almost all of his early fights in Germany, Klitschko had a record of 24 wins unbeaten with 21 knockouts when he had his one and only fight in his homeland of Ukraine. That fight, against American Ross Puritty, would haunt Klitschko for years.

Klitschko, who at that time had never gone past eight rounds, was strangely found wanting when Puritty took him into the tenth round. Klitschko was knocked down twice but survived the round. At the start of the eleventh with Puritty again on top Klitschko's trainer jumped into the ring and stopped the fight. Meanwhile, Ross Puritty remains one of so many boxers who seem to have never fulfilled their true potential.

Klitschko regrouped and won 8 fights before appearing on the undercard of Lennox Lewis vs Michael Grant at Madison Square Garden (see chapter one).

Before the Anthony Joshua fight Klitschko had boxed once before in London. After appearing on the undercard of Lennox Lewis v Michael Grant, Wladimir also appeared on the undercard of Lewis' next defence of his titles when he fought Frans Botha in the Millwall Arena. That night Klitschko beat Monte Barret inside seven rounds.

Three months after his first fight in London, Klitschko fought and beat Chris Byrd on points in Cologne, Germany to capture the WBO Heavyweight title. From then on most of his fights were held in either Germany or the USA. The stateside fights being held in either Atlantic City, Madison Square Garden or Las Vegas. He was used to the big stage and big crowds. Wladimir had arrived at the top table of the heavyweight scene where he would remain a major player for the next fifteen years. Klitschko won his first world title exactly one day before Anthony Joshua's 11th birthday.

Lennox Lewis' last fight was on 21st June 2003 when he defeated Vitali Klitschko via a technical knockout after six rounds of boxing. In May 2003 Ring magazine published its annual ratings with Lennox Lewis still listed as their heavyweight champion. The number one ranked contender was Vitali Klitschko, the number two ranked was Chris Byrd while at number three was South African Corrie Sanders. Wladimir Klitschko the younger brother of Vitali was ranked in eighth place. The previous year Vitali Klitschko was ranked at number seven with his brother Wladimir, then the WBO heavyweight champion, being ranked as the number one contender.

The first year and a half of the post Lennox Lewis era proved to be difficult for Wladimir Klitschko. In March 2003 an early knockout loss to the South African Corrie Sanders started rumours that would persist throughout much of the remainder of Wladimir's career. The talk in boxing circles was that he was "chinny". Basically, that he could not take a punch. This was more than a little unfair to Klitschko as Sanders was an experienced fighter with a record of 38 wins and two losses and was known to have a heavy punch with 23 KO wins.

The rematch never happened as Sanders gave up the WBO belt in order to pursue the more highly regarded WBC belt. Just over a year later Sanders fought the older Klitschko, Vitali, for the vacant WBC heavyweight title at the Staples Centre Los Angles, the same venue where Vitali had lost to Lennox Lewis. Vitali avenged his brother's loss and won the WBC belt in the process with an eighth-round stoppage victory.

Sanders only fought four more times after that defeat and finished his career in 2008. Then in 2013 during a family party at a restaurant in Brits, South Africa, Sanders was shot during an armed robbery. Three armed men entered the party and immediately started shooting. Sanders was shot in the stomach as he was shielding his daughter. As he fell to the floor bleeding heavily but still protecting his daughter, he told her to pretend that she was dead. Cornelius "Corrie" Sanders died in hospital in the early hours of the following day. Three Zimbabweans were later arrested and found guilty. They were each given a 43-year prison sentence.

Just as the old saying goes, 'if you fall off a horse get right back on'. Klitschko did exactly that by fighting less than four months after the loss to Sanders and again at the end of 2003. Although these were two very one-sided wins against weak opposition it set up a fight for the vacant WBO heavyweight title against American Lamon Brewster.

Enter Emanuel Steward. The man who had steered Lennox Lewis back to the top spot after his loss to Oliver McCall became Klitschko's trainer for the Brewster fight. It was not the best of starts for this fighter-trainer partnership. Wladimir Klitschko lost in round 5 despite knocking Brewster down twice in the previous round. The first time Brewster had been knocked down. In the fifth round Klitschko suddenly appeared to be worn out, his mouth gaping wide for air during the quieter moments of the round. He looked gassed. Completely exhausted. Brewster seized his chance with aplomb.

Despite the defeat Klitschko and Steward remained a team for eight years until Steward's death in 2012. Steward transformed Klitschko from an aggressive puncher to a more defensively oriented boxer, emphasising his strengths as a way of defence as well as attack. Following Lennox Lewis' domination of the heavyweight division under Steward's tutelage between 1995 to 2003, Steward guided Klitschko to similar heights. Klitschko went on to rule the division between 2006 and 2015. That loss to Brewster would be Klitschko's last defeat for almost 12 years. A run of 22 wins, 15 by KO (68%) which included 10 previously unbeaten opponents and

19 world title fights. Wladimir Klitschko fought all the top contenders (some twice) and never dodged anyone in that period. The only top boxer he never fought was his own brother.

Then in November 2015, Klitschko lost to British boxer Tyson Fury who became unified WBO, WBA, IBF, IBO and lineal heavyweight champion. Fury famously won by unanimous decision but shortly afterwards went through a bout of depression and drug abuse and needed serious help. Unable to prepare for, let alone fight, a rematch with Klitschko, Fury was eventually stripped of all belts. This left the door open for the unlikely Charles Martin to fight for the IBF belt - and then subsequently lose it to Anthony Joshua.

Wladimir Klitschko's record was 64 wins, 4 losses and 1 draw when he fought Joshua. An impressive 53 of those wins were by KO. His alias "Dr. Steelhammer" was well earned.

By the time Klitschko met Anthony Joshua in the ring, anyone who had beaten Wladimir Klitschko was either beaten in a rematch (Lamon Brewster) or beaten by his brother Vitali (Corrie Sanders and Ross Puritty). The one exception being Tyson Fury.

To understand how the heavyweight landscape was shaped in the post Lennox Lewis era it is necessary to go back to the time when Lewis was still competing as an amateur and just starting out as a professional boxer.

By the end of the 1980s practically the whole world knew these two Russian words; *perestroika* and *glasnost*. The word *perestroika* is widely translated as "restructuring", referring to the reforming of the political system. *Glasnost* meant "openness". The world also knew the name of the leader of the old Soviet Union at that time. Michal Gorbachov set in motion events that would lead to the break-up of the Soviet Union and the old Warsaw Pact countries of Eastern Europe. Among other things this would allow the people of the newly free countries to travel to other parts of the world. It also meant that sportsmen (and women) from the old

'Soviet Block' were able to move from the unpaid amateur ranks to the professional world of sport.

By the early 90s countries such Ukraine, Uzbekistan and Russia were self-governing counties once more. In the 1996 Olympic games in Atlanta, USA, these countries competed for the first time under their own flags. The boxers from these newly re-formed countries won a total of eleven medals in the Atlanta games. After the games they were free to turn professional and some did so. One of those was the super-heavyweight gold medal winner Wladimir Klitschko.

By the turn of the new century the former Soviet Union countries had tasted over a decade of freedom and boxers from these nations were now making their mark in the professional ranks. Boxing titles were now truly "world" titles as former Soviet Union countries and even China now producing professional boxers.

At the time of his last fight in June of 2003 Lennox Lewis was universally regarded as the best heavyweight on the planet by anyone who knew anything about boxing. Despite this fact, even before Lewis had officially retired in February 2004 the heavyweight titles were already fragmented. In 2003 Lewis was still the WBC and lineal world champion. He had been stripped by the WBA for refusing to fight John Ruiz and instead fighting Michael Grant (see Chapter One). Ruiz was the WBA champion until March 2003 when Roy Jones Junior – a true legend who had come through the weights from middleweight - took the title from him. The IBF title had been held by Chris Byrd since 2002. Also, Lewis had never held the WBO version of the heavyweight championship as it was still not highly regarded at that time. Wladimir Klitschko was the WBO champion until he was knocked out by Corrie Sanders in March of that year. Sanders subsequently vacated the title in order to challenge for the more highly regarded WBC version once Lewis finally retired.

At the end of 2003 this was the state of the heavyweight titles: The WBC and WBO championships were vacant, the WBA champion was Roy Jones Junior and the IBF champion was Chris Byrd.

In April 2004, two months after Lewis' retirement, Vitali Klitschko beat Corrie Sanders for the vacant WBC title. Two weeks earlier Vitali's brother Wladimir lost in his bid to recapture the WBO belt, being stopped by Lamon Brewster.

John Ruiz was declared the interim WBA champion when Roy Jones Jr. vacated his title in order to move back down to the light heavyweight division. Meanwhile Chris Byrd had successfully defended his IBF title twice plus one draw (where the holder retains the belt). At the end of 2004 the titles were held by four different boxers. Vitali Klitschko was the new WBC champion, John Ruiz was the interim WBA champion, Chris Byrd was still IBF champion and Lamon Brewster was the new WBO champion.

In November of 2005 Vitali Klitschko vacated the WBC title when he announced his retirement after withdrawing from a fight with Hasim Rahman due to injuries. The WBC then promoted Rahman as their interim champion. Just over a month later John Ruiz lost the WBA championship belt to the oversized seven-foot-tall Nikolay Valuev, who became the first ever Russian to hold a heavyweight title. At the end of 2005 there were still four different champions. Hasim Rahman was WBC champion, Nikolay Valuev was the WBA champion while Byrd and Brewster were still IBF and WBO champions respectively.

Things started to get very interesting in 2006. On April 1st, Lamon Brewster lost the WBO title to the relatively unknown Belarussian boxer Serguei Liakhovich. On the 22nd of April Wladimir Klitschko won the IBF version of the heavyweight title, beating Chris Byrd by unanimous decision in Mannheim, Germany. Following a draw against blown up middleweight James "Lights Out" Toney in March, Hasim Rahman suffered a 12th round knockout loss to Russian based Kazakhstani, Oleg Maskaev, on August 12th. Maskaev became the new WBC champion and all four versions of the heavyweight title were held by boxers who were born in the former Soviet Union.

Serguei Liakhovich subsequently lost the WBO belt in his first defence to the veteran American and perennial contender Shannon Briggs on the 4th of November.

In the Ring magazine ratings for 2006 five of the top ten ranked heavyweights were born in the former Soviet Union; the above mentioned Klitschko, Maskaev, Valuev and Laikhovich being joined by Russian Ruslan Chagaev

By June 2nd, 2007 all four belts would once again be held by boxers born in the former Soviet Union when Russian Sultan Ibragimov beat Shannon Briggs in Atlantic City, New Jersey. At the end of 2007 the Ring magazine heavyweight division ratings had only two boxers in the top ten who were not born in the former Soviet Union. Only one of those (Tony Thompson) was American while the other 'non-Soviet' fighter was "The Nigerian Nightmare" Samuel Peter. A few years later Wladimir Klitschko would go on to beat both of these fighters by knockout. Klitschko was ranked the number one heavyweight with Samuel Peter second.

In February 2008 Wladimir Klitschko began to unify the world titles. He beat Sultan Ibragimov by a wide unanimous points decision at Madison Square Garden, New York. Two weeks later on March 8th Samuel Peter won the WBC championship title beating Oleg Maskaev by a sixth-round knockout in Cancún, Mexico. Peter lost the WBC belt in his first defence against Wladimir's big brother Vitali on October 11th in Kreuzberg, Berlin, Germany.

Meanwhile Chagaev had been stripped of the WBA title for being unable to fight the giant Nikolay Valuev. This meant that Valuev fought and beat John Ruiz on August 30th for the vacant title and became a two-time heavyweight champion.

After unifying the IBF and WBO titles the younger Klitschko defended them twice in July and December beating Tony Thompson and Hasim Rahman respectively – both by KO. Despite his achievements Wladimir Klitschko was still not widely accepted by the American boxing fraternity.

At the end of 2008 the Ukrainian Klitschko brothers held three of the four belts - WBC Vitali and WBO/IBF Wladimir. While the WBA title was held by the enormous Russian Valuev. Even more staggering was the Ring magazine heavyweight rankings for that year. Just as in 2007 only two of the top ten ranked heavyweight boxers were born outside of the old Soviet Union. The aforementioned Samuel Peter ranked 7th, and the Cuban and former cruiserweight champion Juan Carlos Gomez ranked 9th. Sitting in first and second place were Wladimir and Vitali Klitschko. Not one American fighter, or even one from western Europe, made the top ten.

This must have been the first time ever that "the boxing bible", a USA based publication, had no American fighters in its end of year top ten heavyweight rankings. Less than two decades after the collapse of the Soviet Union, boxers from that part of the world totally dominated the heavyweight landscape. They would rule the division for almost a decade.

When Anthony Joshua started boxing at the age of 18 in 2007, all the heavyweight title belts were held by boxers who would not have been able to fight professionally when he was born back in 1989.

It is worth taking a closer look at these former 'Soviet Block' heavyweight fighters who completely transformed the division in the post Lewis era.

Apart from the two Ukrainian brothers there were three Russians, an Uzbekistani and a Belarusian: Ruslan Chagaev – Russia, Sultan Ibragimov – Russia, Oleg Maskaev – Usbekistan, Serguei Lyakhovich – Belarus and Nikolay Valuev – Russia

Ruslan Chagaev had boxed at two Olympic games, in Atlanta in 1996 and also in Sydney in 2000. He failed to win a medal on both occasions. However, Chagaev won gold at the 1997 World Amateur Boxing Championships heavyweight, defeating the great Félix Savón in the finals, but later he was stripped of the championship for having 2 professional bouts in the United States before the tournament. Chagaev is the only non-Cuban boxer to defeat the legendary amateur Félix Savón twice, and the only one to do it at the world championships. Savón suffered his first international defeat in more than a decade, when he met Chagaev for a first time. Chagaev was never stopped as an amateur.

Sultan Ibragimov was a relatively late starter in boxing. He began at the age of 17 but quickly established himself on the international scene. He won the heavyweight silver medal at the 2000 Sydney Olympic games being beaten in the final by the legendary Felix Savón. A year later Ibragimov took bronze in the world championships in Belfast, Northern Ireland. He turned professional with a highly impressive amateur record of 135 wins against 6 losses and was never stopped. He made his professional debut in May 2002 and after six fights became the student of legendary trainer Angelo Dundee. The great trainer was spotted in Ibragimov's corner for his sixth fight against American Chad Butler. When reporters asked Dundee if he was returning to the sport of boxing, he reportedly said, "Yes, it was this Russian guy whom I took out to the fight today that made me return to the ring. Sultan's talent, his human charm and ability to see and understand boxing, combined with the character of a real fighter, give me confidence that that we are dealing with a future world champion." Angelo Dundee was correct. In his 22nd fight Ibrigamov did indeed become a world champion.

After winning the WBO title Ibrimaov defended his crown once, comfortably outpointing an ageing Evader Holyfield over 12 rounds in October 2007. He then lost the WBO title to Wladimir Klitschko in February 2008.

Oleg Maskaev was known for his powerful right-hand punch. He has twice knocked out former WBC heavyweight champion Hasim Rahman. However, he was also known for having a 'weak chin'. He suffered knockout losses to known contenders Oliver McCall, David Tua, Kirk Johnson, Lance Whitaker, Corey Sanders and also to journeyman Nagy Aguilera.

His most famous victories were his two wins over Hasim Rahman. In their first fight Maskaev knocked Rahman off balance, sending his rival out of the ring in the 8th round on November 6th, 1999. This fight is also notable for the famous "chair incident", in which noted referee, Steve Smoger, who was backup referee for this fight, was struck in the head by a chair thrown by a fan. Maskaev beat Rahman again in August 2006, knocking him out in the 12th and final round. That result, preceded by a run of 10 victories since a defeat by American Corey Sanders (not to be confused with South African Corrie Sanders) earned Maskaev the "Comeback Fighter of the Year" award in Ring magazine for 2006.

Born in what is now Kazakhstan during the days of the Soviet Union he later took Uzbekistan nationality before taking up Russian nationality. Maskaev never fought in the Olympics but he did win gold in the 1994 Asian games boxing for Uzbekistan.

The little known Serguei Lyakhovich was another accomplished amateur boxer from a former Soviet Union country. Born in Belarus he represented his country in the 1996 Olympics but was defeated in his first bout by the Tongan, Paea Wolfgramm, who went on to lose in the final to Wladimir Klitschko. The following year Lyakhovich won bronze in the world championships in Budapest, Hungary. He turned professional in 1998 with an impressive 145-15 amateur record. Several years after holding one of the world titles and very much in the twilight of his career, he was knocked out in one round by the fast-emerging Deontay Wilder. Just over a year later Lyakhovich lost a 10-round decision to the almost anonymously emerging Andy Ruiz Jr. It was Ruiz' 24th fight.

Last but not least, the most striking of all was 'The Beast from the East', Nikolay Valuev. At seven feet tall he was easily the biggest heavyweight title challenger in history.

Valuev twice held the WBA heavyweight title beating John Ruiz both times in 2005 and 2008. In his first stint as champion Valuev retained the title four times before losing a majority decision to Ruslan Chagaev in April 2007. In his second term as champion he made one successful defence outpointing the eternal Evander Holyfield before losing another majority decision to Great Britain's David Haye in November 2009. Valuev retired shortly after his defeat to Haye citing serious bone and joint problems as the reason. Clearly moving such a huge frame around the boxing ring had taken its toll on the giant Russian. Following retirement, thanks to his distinctive appearance as well as his boxing fame he became something of a novelty act and appeared in movies and TV shows. He also signed several promotional contracts to advertise various products.

Valuev later took up politics and in the December 2011 Russian parliamentary election he became a member of the State Duma (the Russian Federation's lower house) as a member of the United Russia Party.

Valuev, along with above mentioned, fellow Russian Sultan Ibragimov, is one of only five heavyweight champions to have retired without having suffered a stoppage loss during his career. The other three are Americans Gene Tunney, Rocky Marciano and Riddick Bowe.

Wladimir Klitschko's career is covered elsewhere in this chapter, but the post-Lewis heavyweight scene was dominated by both Wladimir *and* his older brother Vitali. Here is a closer look at Vitali's career:

Standing at two metres and one centimetre tall (6 feet 7 inches), Vitali Klitschko was an intimidating warrior. He was a champion kickboxer as well as an accomplished amateur boxer. He boxed as an amateur at the same time as his brother Wladimir who was almost five years his junior. While Vitali boxed at super-heavyweight the younger Klitschko fought at heavyweight. In 1995 Vitali won a silver medal at the world championships in Berlin, Germany. He lost in the final to a Russian, Alexei Lezin who went on to win bronze at the Olympics the following year while Wladimir won gold. Surprisingly with such a good amateur pedigree, Lezin never turned professional. Vitali looked set to represent his country in the 1996 games but was dismissed from the Ukrainian team after testing positive for a banned steroid (which he later claimed came from a drug he was using to treat a leg injury). That left the door open for his brother Wladimir to step up to super-heavyweight and go on to win the gold medal. Vitali turned professional in the same year. During his amateur career he amassed an impressive 195 wins against 15 losses.

His professional boxing record stands at 45 wins with only 2 losses. He won 41 fights by knockout and with an 87.23% knockout percentage, he holds the fourth highest knockout-to-fight ratios of any world champion in heavyweight boxing history, behind Deontay Wilder, Anthony Joshua and Rocky Marciano. His only two losses came via a shoulder injury and a deep cut above his eye, both of which were recorded as stoppages rather than outright knockouts; in both fights he was leading on the judges' scorecards. The first loss was to Chris Byrd in April 2000. It was Vitali's third defence in 10 months since winning the WBO world heavyweight title, beating Great Britain's Herbie Hide in June 1999. Klitschko could not come out for the 10th round and retired with a shoulder injury. It later turned out that he had torn his right rotor cuff muscles. Vitali received a lot of criticism for quitting the fight as he was so far ahead on all the judges' scorecards at that stage of the bout. Klitschko rebounded from his first defeat to Byrd by boxing to five victories in a row. One of those wins came against Ross Puritty in December 2001. (The same Puritty who three years earlier had handed Wladimir Klitschko his first defeat in Wladimir's only fight in his home country Ukraine.) This run of victories earned Vitali a shot at WBC Heavyweight Champion Lennox Lewis. This would be Vitali's second loss but more famously it was the last fight in Lewis' illustrious career. This time it was a deep cut over the left eye that stopped the fight. Vitali was again ahead (just) on all three scorecards but this time he wanted to continue and complained bitterly that the fight should not have been stopped. The cut was caused by Lewis' punches and therefore he won by technical knockout. The cut was so severe that with six rounds still to go it is doubtful that Klitschko would have been able to continue winning rounds as it would have seriously impeded his vision.

In April 2004, with Lennox Lewis retired, Vitali stopped Corrie Sanders (another man who had beaten Wladimir) to take the vacant WBC world title. After making just one defence Klitschko retired in November 2005 to concentrate on politics. The WBC awarded Vitali their "champion emeritus" status, which meant that he would be assured to become the mandatory challenger if he decided to return to boxing.

He returned to the ring in October 2008 when he got an immediate shot at his old title and defeated the then reigning WBC champion Samuel Peter. Vitali Klitschko then went on to defend the WBC title through 9 defences before retiring again in 2013.

Klitschko is a three-time world heavyweight champion, the second-longest-reigning WBC heavyweight champion of all time and has the fifth-longest combined world championship reign in history at 2,735 days.

He is one of nine boxers to defeat at least ten different fighters for the world heavyweight title. Vitali has defeated 15 boxers for the world heavyweight title, the fifth-most in history (tied with Lennox Lewis). He is the only heavyweight boxer to have reigned as world champion in three different decades. He is also one of only three world heavyweight champions to have never been knocked down in any fight (along with Oliver McCall and Nikolai Valuev). Vitali Klitschko and George Foreman are the only heavyweight boxers in history to defend a world title after turning 40. He was also the first professional boxing world champion to hold a PhD degree.

He was still the reigning WBC world heavyweight champion at 42 years of age when he finally announced his retirement in December 2013.

There is no doubt that Vitali would have been a formidable force in any boxing era and rightly deserved his nickname "Dr. Ironfist". From 2006 until 2015, Vitali and Wladimir dominated heavyweight boxing in a period that is now generally referred to as the "Klitschko era".

Vitali became heavily involved in politics in his native Ukraine. He served as a member of the Ukrainian parliament while still boxing. His first political post was in 2012. When he finally retired from boxing, he became mayor of Kiev and is still an active politician.

"Even though an athlete or a fighter will always say, 'I have to focus solely on my opponent on June 1,' I'm not going to lie and say I haven't always looked at that bigger picture..."

Anthony Joshua, a few days before the Ruiz fight.

The Klitschko fight...

The Joshua vs Klitschko fight was announced immediately following Joshua's second defence against Eric Molina. But both parties had been discussing the fight for a couple of months, ever since Klitschko's proposed rematch with Tyson Fury was called off. The main sticking point was that both fighters wanted the WBA title (stripped from Fury) to be up for grabs. A decision which the WBA kept postponing. When the WBA finally agreed the fight was on – for Joshua's IBF title, the vacant WBA (super) title and the lesser regarded but vacant IBO title.

Wladimir Klitschko weighed 240¼ pounds for this fight, the lightest he had weighed since 2009. The much younger Joshua was heavier at 250 pounds. After ruling the division for so many years, Klitschko had not won a boxing match for over two years – albeit he had only one fight in that time, losing it to Fury.

In front a huge Wembley Stadium crowd of 90,000 Joshua won by TKO in a roller coaster battle full of drama. Both boxers giving no quarter.

The first four rounds were close as both men were cautious. In the fifth round, Joshua came out and immediately threw a barrage of big punches. The Ukrainian seemed to take them well but eventually fell to the canvas. Klitschko rose up and dominated the remainder of the round with Joshua struggling to make it to the bell. In round six Klitschko landed a straight right hand that knocked Joshua down for the first time in his professional career. The next few rounds were understandably cautious with both men now wary of each other's power.

In round eleven Joshua attacked Klitschko with an upper-cut blow to Klitschko's face which stopped the Ukrainian in his tracks. Joshua hurt his opponent with a few combinations and down went Klitschko for the second time in the fight.

The old warrior rose at the count of six but on very shaky legs. Some fifteen seconds later Joshua knocked him down for a second time in the round by firing in seven unanswered punches culminating in a left hook that floored Klitschko. This time Klitschko got up at the count of five, but he was clearly exhausted and hurt. With just over half a minute of the round remaining Joshua pinned Klitschko on the ropes and let fly with a cluster of punches. With the former champion not returning any punches the referee decided that Klitschko had taken enough punishment and correctly stopped the fight.

There was a return match clause in the contract and there was much talk of a possible rematch, but it never came to fruition.

The importance of beating Klitschko...

Anthony Joshua who was now universally known simply by his moniker and own initials 'AJ', had risen from Olympic Gold medallist to world super star in less than five years. He was now the unified WBA, IBF and IBO heavyweight champion of the world. He had just beaten a true heavyweight great. The importance of beating Wladimir Klitschko should not be underestimated.

Wladimir was under-rated for quite a few years with many (mostly) casual boxing fans remarking that he was not as good as his brother Vitali. They based this mainly on Vitali's performance against Lennox Lewis, a fight which the older Klitschko actually lost! If Wladimir Klitschko was not being appreciated then maybe Lennox Lewis finally was.

There's an old saying that you don't appreciate what you have till it's gone. With great boxers this is so often true. Lennox Lewis was a great heavyweight champion, and even though the younger of the Ukrainian brothers had lost his belts to Tyson Fury, so too was Wladimir Klitschko.

Wladimir Klitschko has the longest reign of any heavyweight boxing champion — not Joe Louis, Jack Dempsey, Muhammad Ali or any of the other great names associated with the heavyweight title.

The Ukrainian heavyweight held the title for 4,383 days over 12 years over two different title reigns. (Note: Neither Mike Tyson nor Rocky Marciano ranks in the top 10 list of longest reigns.).

Louis, the "Brown Bomber," holds the record for title fight wins, 27-25 over Klitschko (Louis fought several boxers on more than one occasion). Ali is third with 22 championship wins. Klitschko's brother, Vitali, is tied with Lennox Lewis for fifth on the list with 15 title fight wins.

As of 2020, Wladimir Klitschko holds the record of most boxers beaten for the world heavyweight title, with 23, one more than Louis (on 22).

Joshua's deserves a lot of credit for his victory over Klitschko. The size of that achievement has been greatly undervalued by many and that is unfair to both Joshua and the Ukrainian.

It is true that Klitschko was over 41 years old and had not fought in over a year while Joshua was a young and hungry 27 year old. But Klitschko was always the consummate professional and would have prepared just as hard for this fight as for any other. It is also worth considering Klitschko's impressive record in recent fights. It would be wrong to say that Klitschko was no longer a top contender.

A month before AJ won his Olympic gold medal final in London, Klitschko had just knocked out the veteran Tony Thompson, beating him for the second time in four years.

Between Joshua winning Olympic gold and the end of 2015, Klitschko had seven fights culminating in the famous loss to Tyson Fury in November of 2015. In the lead up to the Fury fight, five of Klitcshko's opponents were unbeaten with a combined record of 120 and 0 including a total of 69 KOs. Klitschko knocked out three of these and clearly outpointed the others. Tyson Fury was himself also unbeaten with a record of 24-0 (with 18 victories by KO) when he met Klitschko. The other (7th) fight, sandwiched in between the six unbeaten opponents, was against the lesser-known Samoan born Australian Alex Leapai.

At this late stage in his career between the ages of 36 and 39, Wladimir Klitschko was remaining very active with two fights per year against top class opposition.

There will always be detractors eager to play down the performance of the new unified champion. Klitschko himself was subject to much of the same for most of his career. The fact is that Joshua came back from adversity, climbed off the canvas and knocked out the Ukrainian boxing legend in an exciting fight. The fight was named 'Ring Magazine Fight of the Year' and Anthony Joshua was now widely considered to be the top heavyweight in the world.

At the end of 2017 Ring Magazine rankings had Anthony Joshua at number one. He was the WBA and IBF champion. Deontay Wilder the WBC champion was ranked at number two and Joseph Parker the WBO champion was ranked at number three. Andy Ruiz Jr. had anonymously crept into the rankings at number seven.

The lineal world champion was still Tyson Fury – a fact that Fury was always quick to remind Joshua of.

Anthony Joshua was now on top of the world; literally. But his life could have so easily gone in a different direction.

In March of 2011 while Wladimir Klitschko was preparing for his fight with British boxer David Haye, Anthony Joshua was arrested for possession of a class B drug with intent to supply. With the Olympic games in London only a year away Joshua's amateur career looked to be in tatters. He was pulled over for speeding, and when police searched his car they found 8oz (227 grams) of cannabis hidden in his sports bag.

Everyone can wonder about this and ask the obvious question. What the hell was a promising Olympic games medal prospect doing with such drugs in the first place? But the fact was that the drugs were found in his possession, and he would have to go to court. At that time possession with intent to supply illegal drugs carried a maximum of 14 years in prison. But this wasn't the 'French Connection' nor was it some large Mexican drug cartel deal. Joshua pleaded guilty which often helps when it comes to sentencing, and due to the small amount of drugs involved, he received a much lighter sentence. He was given a 12-month community order which included having to perform 100 hours unpaid work in the community (often referred to as 'community payback').

He was temporarily suspended from the British Olympic team but allowed to continue his preparation for the coming games. It was a wake-up call for Joshua and a major turning point in his life. All his energy and focus would now be thrown into boxing. If he didn't have the Olympic boxing tournament to focus on who knows what might have happened. As it was, Joshua became another stereotypical 'bad boy' who was saved by the sport of boxing.

After the Klitschko fight there would be no easy fights for Joshua. Six months later he fought the French based Cameroon born Carlos Takam in Cardiff, Wales in front of nearly 80,000 spectators. The Frenchman proved a tough opponent for Joshua's first unified title defence. Takam recovered from a good knockdown in round four and by round ten looked like taking Joshua the distance for the first time in his career. But after Takam took some solid shots to the head in the tenth round the referee stopped the fight. Many thought the fight was stopped prematurely. Nevertheless, it was another TKO victory for Joshua.

The stage was set for another unification bout with the WBO champion Joseph Parker. The fight was arranged for March 31, 2018. Once again Joshua fought at the Principality Stadium in Cardiff. The fight was a comfortable unanimous points victory for Joshua who was taken the full twelve rounds for the first time in his career. His twenty fight KO streak had come to an end. Parker never really looked like trying to do enough and seemed more content to try and be that first man to take Joshua the distance. Joshua for his part maintained good discipline and used his jab throughout to good effect. Parker won only two rounds on the scorecards of two judges. The third judge only gave Parker one round.

The fight was relatively uneventful with both huge boxers perhaps showing too much respect for each other's size and power.

Joshua now held the WBA, IBF and WBO titles. He also held the IBO heavyweight title. Meanwhile in the USA Deontay Wilder was still the WBC champion. Weeks earlier Wilder had successfully defended his title against the big Cuban, Luis 'King Kong' Ortiz, via a tenth-round stoppage.

All the talk was then of a total unification clash with all the belts on the line. But Joshua vs Wilder was not going to happen. Just over two months after Joshua beat Parker and after more than two and a half years out of the ring, Tyson Fury made his comeback fighting the unknown Albanian, Sefer Seferi, in Manchester, UK. It was an easy win for the man who was still the lineal heavyweight champion and it was Fury, not Joshua, who was on a collision course with Wilder.

There was no shortage of options for Joshua however. Next to step up to the plate was the big Russian Alexander Povetkin who had a good record of 31 wins and one loss. His only loss was five years earlier to a division dominant Wladimir Klitschko which the Ukrainian won by a unanimous points decision. Povetkin was the WBA mandatory challenger and while Eddie Hearn was in talks with Deontay Wilder's team for a possible unification/undisputed bout the WBA threatened to strip Joshua of their title unless he faced Povetkin.

The fight was set for September 21st, 2018, at Wembley Stadium, London. Another huge crowd of around 80,000 were at the venue to watch Joshua defend all of his belts.

At the end of the first round Povetkin let go a flurry of three punches catching Joshua, breaking and bloodying his nose. Povetkin, spurred on by this early success, went for the head in round two and caught the champion again. Rounds three through to six were similar with the Russian looking to get in close to launch his hook shot while Joshua used his longer reach to jab off his opponent. Half way through the seventh round Joshua hit Povetkin with a few single but solid shots. As the Rusian went backwards Joshua fired a left hook followed by a big right hand. Povetkin hit the canvas but beat the count. Joshua immediately went in for the finish and had Povetkin pinned against the ropes taking combination punches. The referee stepped in with a minute still remaining of the round. That was the first time that the 39 year old Russian had been stopped.

On December 15th, 2018, Joshua accompanied Eddie Hearn to New York for a fight between Saúl 'Canelo' Alvarez and (Hearn fighter) Rocky Fielding. There was a crowd of over 20,000 in Madison Square Garden with Joshua sitting ringside. It was widely reported that Joshua enjoyed the electric atmosphere and was warming to the opportunity of fighting in the USA and at this iconic venue.

Promoter Hearn just needed to find a suitable opponent.

Andy Ruiz Jr.

"Yeah I think I've always been the underdog. When they see me, they're like 'yeah who is this short chubby kid? He's gonna get tired really fast. I don't think he can last"'

Andy Ruiz Jr. on how people see him.

Andrés (Andy) Ruiz Junior was born September 11th, 1989, just one month before Anthony Joshua. Unlike Joshua however, Ruiz started boxing at a very early age. He first went to a boxing gym at 6 years of age and had his first amateur fight at the age of seven. Ruiz has been a boxer all of his life. Even at the age of seven he was a big heavy kid. Always bigger than those his own age. The only fights he could get at that young age were against kids several years older.

As the years went by it was more of the same. Travelling between the USA and Mexico to amateur fights, Ruiz was fighting in two countries and was very much a part of both. Born in the USA to Mexican born immigrant parents. His name translates in various languages as 'brave' and 'manly'. His father (Andy Sr.) moved to the USA when he was eight years old and became a construction worker eventually starting a construction business. The family lived in the small southern California town of Imperial, a small place where everyone knew each other, located roughly thirty minutes from Mexicali, Mexico. Like any border town it has its fair share of problems. But fortunately for Ruiz his father made sure that he never had time to spend hanging around on the streets. When Ruiz was kicked out of high school for fighting his father would take him to work and put a hammer in his hand. Ruiz was raised in a churchgoing home with a nuclear family and was well grounded.

According to Ruiz, "My father and I used to argue. Because all I was thinking about was boxing." Eventually his father told him to choose between (construction) work or boxing, one or the other, and go for it. Do it properly. Ruiz decided on boxing and headed south.

Ruiz's grandfather owned a boxing gym in Mexicali, and it was in Mexico where Ruiz started his amateur career that, over the years, saw him build an outstanding record of 105-5.

In 2008 with the Olympic games in China on the horizon, Ruiz was still living in Mexico and tried to represent the country in the Beijing games. He would qualify for the Mexican team as his parents were born there. But Ruiz just missed out on the Olympics losing a close decision in Guatemala during the qualifying rounds.

The 2008 Olympics came and went while Ruiz remained unknown to the wider boxing world. The following year, armed with an impressive amateur career Ruiz made his pro-debut.

Ruiz not only represents Mexico and the United States. He stands for anyone who is underestimated because of the way they look. Ruiz is quick to tell anyone he speaks to of all the "chubby kid" quotes (and worse) that he had to put up with all through his career. All kids who grow up not looking like an Adonis can look up to Andy Ruiz as a role model and inspiration. As Ruiz so often says himself, "Anything is possible man".

"Andy Ruiz, at best, is a little bit above average as a heavyweight"
Bob Arum, Ruiz' former promoter.

Ruiz made his professional debut in March 2009.

When boxers turn professional, they do not suddenly switch from three rounds to boxing 10 or 12 periods (or 15 as it used to be). They are eased into the professional ranks with four and six round matches before moving on to eight rounders. Then as they gain more experience, they will fight ten rounds, then twelve.

There were no high-profile names nor were there any experienced veterans on that early fight list. Like most fighters making their way to the top the opposition is generally carefully picked. Ruiz fought ten fights in his first two years as a professional winning all ten. Four in the first round plus a second and a third-round knockout victory. What is more important however is that four of those first ten fights went the distance. Two of four rounds and two six rounders. Ruiz won these fights with almost perfect points scores. He hardly lost a round in the judges' eyes. Andy Ruiz may have been tough, he may have been a puncher, but he could also box. Right up to his first world title shot versus Joseph Parker in 2016, Ruiz never left any doubt in any fight that went to the scorecards. He was not only accumulating wins with a good knockout ratio he was winning fights convincingly on sheer boxing skill.

Ruiz fought mostly journeymen opposition up to his 20th bout. But in his 15th fight he knocked out a former amateur star from the 2006 US amateur championships in Jonte Willis (record 8-3-1). That was in July 2012. Ruiz followed up that stoppage victory with a win over Maurenzo Smith (record 11-2-2) two months later and at the end of the same year Ruiz fought again beating Elijah McCall by TKO.

In an interview following the win over McCall (son of former heavyweight champion Oliver) back in 2012 Ruiz seemed focussed and intent on moving up the rankings. He spoke of getting "a shot at the Klitschkos". Joshua was yet to make his professional debut. Ruiz finished the interview with these words for his fans: "Thanks for supporting me and I am going to go to the top baby".

At the time of the McCall fight Ruiz was 24 years old. It would be four years and 13 more fights before Ruiz finally got a shot at a title, but it would not be against either of the Klitschkos. That first shot at a world title turned out to be against Joseph Parker. Earlier that same year Anthony Joshua had won the IBF heavyweight title. Joshua made the second defence of his IBF title (against Eric Molina) on the same day as Ruiz challenged Parker in New Zealand.

After his first three fights in Mexico Ruiz boxed his next sixteen in several cities in several different states, including Las Vegas, Nevada. Then in his 20th fight, just three months before Anthony Joshua made his professional debut, Ruiz stepped out of his comfort zone. With Bob Arum's Top Rank, Ruiz travelled 7,000 miles to fight unbeaten Joe Hanks (21-0) in Macao for the vacant World Boxing Organisation Inter-Continental heavyweight title. While not a recognised "world" title this was a stepping-stone to recognition and possible future world title challenges. This was a high-profile contest and one that Ruiz came through with flying colours. He dropped Hanks twice in round four. Patiently stalking his opponent throughout Ruiz used his fast hand speed landing quick combinations to bring the fight to an early end. Ruiz won the WBO Inter-continental title in the process and was now on a lot of people's radar. This was still three months before Anthony Joshua made his professional debut.

Four months later Ruiz again fought in Macao on the Manny Pacquiao-Brandon Rios undercard, defending his WBO Inter-Continental title and fighting for the vacant NABF heavyweight title against Tor Hamer (21-2). Seemingly another rising star, Hamer was the 2008 Golden Gloves champion and a 2012 Prizefighter winner. Ruiz forced Hamer to quit on his stool after three one-sided rounds.

After 21 fights and 70 rounds of boxing Ruiz looked set to challenge for a world title or at least fight a top contender. But he would be made to wait a further three years and 8 fights. Some boxers are destined to rise quickly through the ranks and onto big fights, while others like Ruiz are made to do it the hard way.

In May 2014 Ruiz was ranked as the WBO number 2 contender when he fought Manuel Quezada in Fresno, California. Ruiz destroyed Quezada inside of two rounds.

In October of the same year Ruiz destroyed Kenny Lamos in the first round (also in Fresno). Both were good victories, but Ruiz needed to be fighting better opposition.

That step up in class came two months after the Lemos fight when Ruiz fought former WBO heavyweight champion, 38 year old Siarhei Liakhovich in Phoenix, Arizona. Ruiz was taken to the ten-round distance for the first time in his career by Liakhovich, who trained hard for this fight and tried to win. Ruiz won by unanimous decision. Ruiz revealed he fractured his right hand during the second round. He fought most of the fight one handed against a determined former champion, and still won on all three scorecards.

In June 2015, Ruiz began training with well-known trainer Abel Sanchez. Three months later in September Ruiz beat journeyman Joell Godfrey winning by unanimous decision over eight rounds. Only four weeks later Ruiz beat veteran Raphael Zumbano also on points over eight rounds. Zumbano had been destroyed by Anthony Joshua inside of two rounds, only five months earlier. It is odd that often, common opponents are no indicator of how a fight may turn out.

By the time they met in the ring Anthony Joshua and Andy Ruiz had shared three common opponents. Two of those, in Zubano and Kevin Johnson, were brushed aside with frightening ease by Joshua yet both took Ruiz the distance. Ultimately it would be the third common opponent - Joseph Parker - that should have set the alarm bells ringing in the Joshua camp.

Six months before Ruiz fought Ray Austin in May 2016, Tyson Fury had just upset the odds by beating Wladimir Klitschko. When Fury was stripped of the belts he had won from Klitschko the heavyweight scene became fractured once again as all belts were up for grabs.

One month after Anthony Joshua won the IBF belt having boxed only 34 rounds as a professional, Andy Ruiz beat Ray Austin stopping him after four rounds. Ruiz had boxed over one hundred rounds as a professional, was still unbeaten and yet still seemed to be a long way from getting a shot at the title.

But Ruiz sensed that there would soon be opportunities. "I am just focused on this guy and after the fight we will talk soon after. Fury has left the division wide open for all of the division including myself. I am willing to fight anybody and will take advantage of it" Ruiz told reporters before his fight with Austin. This fight was also the first time that Ruiz had weighed in lighter than his opponent. Ray Austin also stood at 6' 6" (198cm) - the same as height as Anthony Joshua.

Two months later in July 2016, Ruiz faced an ageing fighter in 42 year old Josh Gormley. With a record of 23 wins and 4 defeats

Gormley had won 22 of those victories by stoppage. However, the only known names he faced had beaten him. It seemed that Gormley's biggest claim to fame was being the great grandson of the legendary 'Manassa Mauler' Jack Dempsey. His mother was Dempsey's granddaughter and Gormley used the alias 'Josh Dempsey'. Facing an opponent with such famous boxing genes in his DNA never bothered Ruiz, who demolished Gormley in three savage rounds. Gormley continued to fight in extreme fighting contests such as bare-knuckle and mixed martial arts (MMA) right up to (and after) the Joshua-Ruiz bout.

Less than two months later in September 2016 Ruiz was back in the ring to fight Franklin Lawrence who had a record of 21 wins, two defeats and two draws. Although Lawrence was 40 years old he had won his last nine fights inside the distance dating back to 2009. His only losses were against veteran and ex-champion Oliver McCall and, in only his fifth professional fight, against future WBC world champion Bermane Stiverne. The Stiverne fight being stopped after Lawrence injured his arm in round one. Ruiz beat Lawrence by unanimous decision over ten rounds with the scores being almost a complete shutout. This was the fifth defence of his WBC-NABF title. The win also set up a future WBO eliminator bout with Hughie Fury (cousin of Tyson Fury) to be fought on the undercard of the planned Tyson Fury-Wladimir Klitschko rematch. That Fury-Klitschko rematch never happened and the WBO belt was vacated by Tyson Fury, who was battling depression and drug issues.

Just as Andy Ruiz had predicted before his fight with Ray Austin, opportunity came knocking on his door.

"This 'aint my first rodeo"

Andy Ruiz on his arrival in New Zealand,
when asked about fighting away from home.

Joseph Parker was the WBO number one ranked contender while Klitschko was their number two. But Klitschko decided to set his sights on the WBA version – another title that Tyson Fury had to vacate. This left the door open for the WBO's number three contender Andy Ruiz.

Joseph Parker was one person who would definitely **not** judge a book by its cover. He had sparred with Ruiz two years earlier in America and did what so many others had done in underestimating Ruiz because of his size and body shape. Ruiz proceeded to punch the New Zealander around the ring, and it is said that Parker spent the following three days sipping his meals through a straw.

The fight took place in Auckland, New Zealand on the same day that Anthony Joshua made the second defence of his IBF title against Eric Molina. Due to the location the Parker-Ruiz bout would take place about twelve hours ahead of the Joshua fight.

Finally, Ruiz was getting the recognition he deserved. He had trained hard for this fight losing some 15kg during training camp at Big Bear in California, USA. By the time he arrived in New Zealand he was ready for the full twelve rounds. Parker, following his previous encounter with Ruiz, was also expecting a tough twelve rounds. Both men were undefeated, Parker had won all 21 of his fights, 18 by KO, while the more experienced Ruiz had 29 victories with 19 KOs. The stage was set for a very evenly matched contest.

While Ruiz was trying to become the first Mexican world heavyweight champion, Parker was attempting a first for New Zealand. The closest a Kiwi boxer had come to winning a heavyweight world title was David Tua who lost to Lennox Lewis 16 years earlier.

The New Zealand media was understandably excited by this fight and seemed to be looking for an advantage for their fighter when they continually asked Ruiz if he felt any extra pressure being so far from home and fighting in another country. Ruiz was always polite and told them he had fought (twice) in China. He killed that line of questioning by calmly adding, "This 'aint my first rodeo."

The fight proved to be every bit as tough as both fighters expected. After twelve rounds of action the fate of both boxers was left in the hands of the three judges.

Ruiz started off well, pressing Parker in the early rounds but slowed down during the middle rounds. Then the fight swung back in Ruiz' favour in the championship rounds. Ruiz showed his faster hand speed when the fighters got close while Parker wisely tried to keep Ruiz at distance by using his longer reach and quick jab. Parker also tried to hold when the two fighters got in close in order to smother Ruiz' advantages on the inside.

Both men showed great respect for each other throughout the contest. There was a case for both fighters and not many would have argued if the fight had been scored a draw.

In the end two judges had Parker winning by one round while the third judge scored the fight a draw. A majority decision.

Ruiz stated he would like to have a rematch in the future but there was no rematch clause in the contract. Parker's camp did not want another fight with the dangerous Ruiz and instead looked towards bigger fights in England with Hughie Fury and later, a unification fight with Joshua.

It was certainly a close fight with many potential 'swing rounds'. Ruiz' trainer Abel Sanchez claimed that Ruiz easily won saying, "I thought we won. I thought we were a couple of rounds up. I thought he (Ruiz) won the first four or five rounds and easily won three more of the last seven. I felt Parker maybe got four rounds at the most." Sanchez added, "If he won the first four or five rounds, it's impossible for him to lose the rest of them…"

Sanchez was not alone in thinking his fighter had been robbed. Most notably New Zealand Professional Boxing Association (NZPBA) president Lance Revill, described the majority decision by the WBO-appointed independent judges as "bullshit". Revill added that he was embarrassed to be a New Zealander after watching the fight. Rather than score the fight close, Revill had it 118–111 to Ruiz. Most experts ruled it a close Parker win or draw.

Following his comments, Revill resigned as president of the NZPBA, stating; "I was getting criticised by members of my own association who were saying 'Lance is out of line' and saying I shouldn't be saying that as president. Well, if I can't say it as president, who can say it? I want to be able to say what I like and speak my mind because I don't like the way boxing has been run at the moment."

Ruiz had failed to become the first heavyweight of Mexican ancestry to win a world title but did not seem too down-hearted "I came closer than any of the others," said a magnanimous Ruiz. "I have to do better next time."

After the loss to Parker, Ruiz talked up a rematch and said, "The only thing to do is work hard and get back in the gym". Despite this seemingly stoic attitude, just when it seemed that things were about to take off for Ruiz, he almost disappeared for over fourteen months and did not box at all the following year (2017).

Of his long absence from the ring, Ruiz explained, "I just wanted to take a break. I already have 30 fights. I wanted to be with the family, I started investing my money. I started building houses. But every boxer needs that little break and now I've got to come back harder." He also added that he needed to get the hunger back.

Ruiz was certainly not being paid the huge sums of money that Joshua was now making. Ruiz's biggest career purse up to that point was the $1m he took home from his bout with Parker. Investing in construction with his father's company appeared to be a sensible option. But to be inactive for so long suggested that his heart was no longer in boxing.

Ruiz changed trainer after his self-imposed break when he began working with the well-respected Emanuel (Manny) Robles. His first fight under Robles' tutelage was against Devin Vargas. He showed no sign of 'ring rust' when he stopped Vargas half-way through the first round. Ruiz now needed to box some rounds in his next (comeback) fight.

Just over four months later Ruiz fought the experienced Kevin 'Kingpin' Johnson over 10 rounds in Fresno, California in July 2018.

Johnson had been around. He had recently taken some capable fighters the distance including Kubrat Pulev and Derek Chisora. Johnson also took Tyson Fury the full twelve rounds in a WBC title eliminator, losing a lop-sided decision. Fury famously went on to beat Wladimir Klitschko to become the unified IBF, WBA, WBO, IBO and lineal world champion. Johnson had even taken Wladimir's brother Vitali the full twelve rounds fighting for the WBC title, again losing every round. But that was nine years before facing Ruiz.

Perhaps the most notable loss for Johnson was a 2nd round TKO defeat to the upcoming Anthony Joshua. That fight was supposed to be the first real test for Joshua in his 13th bout. Far from being tested, Joshua blasted his opponent with two knock downs in the first round and one again in the second before the referee decided that Johnson had received enough punishment. It was the first time Johnson had been stopped and he barely landed a punch on Joshua.

Ruiz fought his typical style trying to close down the ring and letting his hands go whenever he got the chance. He dominated Johnson and won convincingly on all three scorecards.

After beating Kevin Johnson, during the ring interview, Ruiz called out Jarrell Miller. The man he would ultimately replace in the Joshua fight. At that point Miller was 22 fights unbeaten and already on the radar of the Joshua team. While Ruiz had slipped out of the Ring magazine top 10 that year (no doubt through inactivity) Miller had sneaked in at number 8.

"Andy has the fastest hands that I've seen in a heavyweight since Muhammed Ali"

Bob Arum (Pre Parker fight presser in Auckland)

On January 11th, 2019, it was reported that Ruiz had signed a deal with boxing advisor Al Haymon, and would now be part of the Premier Boxing Champions (PBC) stable, with his fights being aired on Showtime and FOX. It was also reported that Ruiz had bought out the remainder of his promotional contract with Bob Arum at Top Rank. Ruiz believed that he would now be guaranteed more exposure and hence bigger fight purses. More importantly it should lead to bigger fights. Ruiz's PBC debut was on the Danny García vs. Adrián Granados undercard on April 20th in Carson, California. His opponent was the 36 year old German based Russian, Alexander Dimitrenko (record 41-4, 26 KOs) in a bout scheduled for ten rounds. When Andy Ruiz Jr. stepped into the ring he displayed a new tattoo across his broad heavyweight shoulders. Its message was simple. "Victorious."

Dimitrenko possessed huge height and reach advantages but could not stop Ruiz moving forward. Using his quick hands and throwing punches in bunches, Ruiz wore his opponent down in the first four rounds almost knocking Dimitrenko down in the third and fourth. The fifth round was all Ruiz and at the end of that round Dimitrenko's corner called a halt to the bout. Ruiz had won all five rounds on the judges' scorecards.

> *"Every fight I always eat a Snickers before I get in the ring.*
> *It just gives me that extra boost and energy.*
> *So, I'm really happy man."*

Ruiz, self-parodying after beating Dimitrenko.

Post-fight, Ruiz perhaps surprised people by not calling out the top names in the division. "For my next fight there's somebody like me, a chubby exciting fighter I want," said Ruiz. "Adam Kownacki I'm ready, let's do this."

As things turned out Ruiz' next fight would be his dream come true. Fate, destiny, luck - call it what you will - events transpired to give Andy Ruiz Jr. his golden opportunity. Two and a half years after failing to become the first Mexican heavyweight champion of the world he would get a second chance. This time in the spiritual home of boxing, Madison Square Garden, New York, New York.

> *'Don't underestimate this chubby kid I am coming for you'*

Andy Ruiz Jr. when the fight deal was finalised.

Jarrell Miller…

> *"The game plan is to stop his behind in the seventh round"*

Jarrell Miller's strangely prophetic prediction
at the London press conference

Joshua vs Ruiz would not have happened if it was not for one Jarrell Miller. Not only did Miller fail a drug test; not only did he fail a second drug test. No. Miller managed to fail **three** drug tests just five weeks before a shot at the world heavyweight title.

The proposed 'AJ' vs Miller fight was born out of a heated exchange during the Joshua vs Povetkin launch press conference in New York City on July 17, 2018. Miller gate-crashed the party and began hurling insults at Joshua. The British fighter visibly lost his composure when he made a move for Miller and returned a series of insults. Only promoter Eddie Hearn's intervention prevented an altercation. This was grudge match gold, and it was not lost on Hearn. With Miller referencing Joshua's mother in the string of insults it would be an easy fight to make and even easier to promote. Add to that Miller's uncanny ability to trash talk and this was a fight promoters dream for an 'AJ' stateside debut.

Miller made his professional boxing debut in July 2009 but then took almost two years out of boxing before his second fight. He then took almost one year more out before his third fight.

Following his 16th victory in January 2016 Miller called out the then IBF champion Charles Martin who went on to lose his title to Anthony Joshua just over two months later. Miller was then ranked just outside the top ten by most governing bodies. In the Ring magazine 2017 heavyweight rankings Miller came in at number ten and by the following year he had risen to number eight.

Between 6th October and 17th November 2018 Miller won two fights in six weeks against good boxers. This put him firmly in the sights of Joshua's management team as an opponent for Joshua's American debut. In February 2019 Miller was indeed announced as Joshua's next opponent. At the time Miller had a solid record of 23 wins and no defeats, with one draw in a four round bout early in his career.

Miller had always done his fair share of trash-talking in the build up to fights. It was part of his persona; he was that type of fighter. During the build up to the fight that never was, he insulted Joshua multiple times during their New York press conferences and physically pushed him during one. Miller, as he would often say himself, enjoyed being the 'bad guy', the 'villain'. His style of trash talking was also about getting inside his opponent's head to get that psychological edge. It seemed to be working with Anthony Joshua, who resorted to hurling insults back at Miller during a long press conference in New York. How much it actually affected Joshua only the man himself would know but there were signs that it was getting to him. Miller was much calmer during the London press conference but made a bold prediction saying: "The game plan is to stop his behind in the seventh round." That prophecy was partly correct, but it would not be Miller stopping Joshua's "behind" in the seventh round.

But away from the showmanship, the bravado and trash-talking, Miller was hiding a very dark secret. Soon after all the hype of the press conferences had faded away that secret was revealed.

On 17 April 2019, both camps confirmed the Voluntary Anti-Doping Association (VADA) had informed them that Miller had tested positive for the banned substance GW1516. The test results were from a random VADA-conducted urine test Miller submitted to on March 20. Further tests taken on March 31 proved positive for the same substance, GW1516 again, plus two others, EPO and HGH.

Miller was denied a boxing license by the New York State Athletic Commission and Joshua's promoter Eddie Hearn announced that Joshua was looking for a new opponent.

The announcement that Miller had failed anti-doping drugs tests came just three days prior to the Ruiz-Dimitrenko fight (April 20). On hearing the news Ruiz put his name forward as a replacement challenger for the unified WBA, IBF, WBO, and IBO heavyweight titles on June 1st, 2019. Reportedly calling promoter Eddie Hearn directly.

On April 22, two days after beating Dimitrenko, Ruiz and his team had a meeting scheduled with Eddie Hearn. It was reported Luis Ortiz's team had rejected two offers of career-high purses to fight Joshua. (This was probably because Ortiz had plans to fight Deontay Wilder in a rematch for the WBC title. That fight went ahead in November 2019, Wilder winning by a 7th round KO.) This meant that Ruiz became the frontrunner. Terms were agreed quickly and on May 1st, with only one month to go before fight night, Joshua vs. Ruiz was confirmed and announced.

Only six weeks after beating Dimitrenko, Ruiz was to fight for the unified titles against arguably the biggest name in Boxing at that point in time.

For a short period in 2018 it looked like a fight between Miler and Andy Ruiz may materialise. That old boxing saying immediately springs to mind; "Styles make fights." Had Ruiz and Miller squared off against each other it would have been a fantastic fight. Similar physique and styles. Both are pressure fighters who like to go forward and not put a foot back.

That fight may also have been possible after Ruiz losing the rematch to Joshua and when it was announced that Miller would return to the ring in July 2020. But then, incredibly, Miller failed yet another drug test with just two weeks to go before his comeback. Even more incredibly he failed for the same three illegal substances he had tested positive for just a year earlier. This would surely be the end of Jarrell Miller's boxing career. It is doubtful he will ever be seen again anywhere near the top level.

The Fight

> *"I think being so tall he fights like a big robot.*
> *I think with my style, my speed, my movement,*
> *I don't think he's fought anybody like me.*
> *It's going to be a whole different ball game.*
> *All the guys that he's fought,*
> *they usually run around from him.*
> *I don't think he's good going back.*
> *I'm going to bring the pressure, the speed, and the combinations*
> *to him."*

Andy Ruiz Jr. on fighting Joshua.

When Ruiz was picked as the replacement for Jarrell Miller most people said things like, "who is he? I have never heard of him" or "I have never seen him fight". And worse. "He looked like he had just rolled off the couch" joked one American football player.

Joshua was introduced as 'the heavyweight fighting pride of the United Kingdom' by the incomparable ring announcer Michael Buffer.

When the crowd got their first look at the two fighters standing face to face in the ring, everyone thought this was going to be an early night. Joshua was seen as the King from across the pond and this was meant to be a coronation ceremony stateside. Or so they all thought.

Joshua seemed strangely out of sorts as he was being introduced to the crowd in 'The Garden'. Fidgeting with his mouthguard and looking almost confused. Almost as if he did not understand what was going on. Many rumours surfaced post fight but whatever the reasons for this strange behaviour they were kept quiet and remain a bit of a mystery.

> *"This is going to be one of the most one-sided*
> *ass whippings in pugilistic history"*

Sylvester Stallone's pre-fight thoughts.
(And so it was, but not how most people thought.)

Round 1:

The fight began with understandable caution by both fighters. Extreme caution in fact, almost to the point of boring the viewing public. Neither fighter was throwing many punches. Joshua kept Ruiz at long-range using his considerable 8-inch (20cm) reach advantage to fire the left jab. Meanwhile Ruiz looked composed and patient. Walking his opponent down always looking to go forward but still throwing very few punches. Both warriors were just sizing each other up, trying to gauge the range. There was good reason, because these guys were not there to score points. They were there to knock each other out. Yet after three minutes of boxing neither fighter had landed a good clean punch.

At the break the advice from Joshua's corner was already, oddly, one of further caution. "Keep him long. Keep him long. He's gonna start coming in over the top. Stop him walking in with a straight one-two". If anyone thought that Joshua's camp had taken Ruiz lightly then surely these words of warning, after only one round, proved otherwise.

Round 2:

The second period was much like the first apart from a couple of quick flurries from the challenger early in the round. Ruiz let his fast hands go but Joshua managed to cover up and even hold his opponent at one point. Joshua was definitely heeding the advice of his trainer and trying to keep Ruiz at arms-length. Still, after 6 minutes of boxing, no significant punch had been landed.

Round 3:

> *"I think the fight is going toe-to-toe, two guys*
> *smashing each other's faces."*

Andy Ruiz' pre-fight prediction.

The same pattern appeared to be unfolding in the third round until Joshua connected with a straight right hand and, due to his momentum moving forward, suddenly found himself toe-to-toe with Ruiz. He could have clinched or stepped back into the long-range game, but instead chose to slug his way out of the close-up. Ruiz responded but Joshua got the better of the exchange. A stiff

199

right uppercut quickly followed by a left hook sent Ruiz down for the first time in his career. He got up at the count of 5. He looked more scared than dazed. As if he thought the referee Michael Griffin might stop the fight. Yet he did not seem hurt.

Anthony Joshua was known as a ferocious finisher and there were still two minutes left in the round. Even those who gave Ruiz a chance must have been thinking that there was no way he could survive those two minutes. Immediately they were ordered to fight by the referee, Joshua threw a hard right hand – his signature punch – which landed flush on the side of Ruiz's head. Sweat sprayed from the chubby kid's cheek. Ruiz not only took the punch well but came back, immediately firing his own.

When a boxer goes in for the finish the long-range game goes out of the window. A fighter needs to stand and plant his feet to let the big shots go. He needs to get close, and for Joshua that meant stepping inside Ruiz' firing range. As Joshua closed in looking to finish the fight Ruiz let his hands go firing in combinations. Both fighters were getting hit but not cleanly. Then suddenly a looping left hook from Ruiz caught Joshua on the temple. It shook Joshua all the way to his boots and through the canvas. His head seemed clear, but his legs were like Bambi on ice in the Disney cartoon. Ruiz immediately followed up with multiple punches mostly missing or hitting Joshua's guard. It seemed as though Joshua was about to go down slowly, but a right hand to the top of the head finally dropped him. Joshua was hurt and clearly dazed but got up at the count of 8. The round was still only at the half -way point. Now people were thinking; could Joshua survive one and a half minutes of Ruiz onslaught? Now it was Ruiz going in for the finish. With every assault Joshua looked extremely vulnerable and Ruiz could see it. Joshua was on very unsteady legs. Limbs which had not recovered from that big punch to his temple. His equilibrium was shot. Gone.

> *"This motherfucker came to fight tonight."*
>
> Mike Tyson's reaction to Ruiz flooring Joshua in the 3rd

With less than 30 seconds remaining a Ruiz onslaught almost forced Joshua through the ropes. The punches were not heavy –

mostly not connecting properly – almost pushing him down again. It was judged a knock down. Joshua's legs had deserted him. He just about managed to get up, again at the count of 8, but looking very wobbly. The referee asked Joshua to walk towards him, but the champion did not do as required. The referee would have been forgiven for calling the fight off at that moment. But he did not do so. Despite this Joshua gained a few extra seconds to recover and just as the two boxers were set to restart the bell rang. Joshua had been saved by the bell. Was the referee aware that the bell to end the round was only a few seconds away? It is unlikely in all the commotion and chaos that was the breath-taking third round.

While Joshua staggered back to his corner Ruiz did a little celebratory jig on the way back to his team. Even if he would not go on to win this fight Ruiz knew that he had just proven to everyone that he belonged at this level. He was silencing the doubters yet again.

Between rounds three and four 'AJ' was overheard asking his trainer Rob McCracken "What shot was it?". He was not aware which shot Ruiz had hurt him with. Did he mean the first right hand hook that took away his sense of balance or the one that turned out to be the last punch of the round and put him down for the 2nd time? He was clearly in desperate trouble.

> *"His equilibrium (pointing to the head). He's OK*
> *His body. Fucked up."*

Mike Tyson, on the punch that rocked Joshua.

Round 4:

The round began with an instant attack by Ruiz throwing several headshots. Then it calmed down. It seemed as though Ruiz was letting Joshua off the hook by not capitalising when the champion was clearly still on unsteady legs. Maybe the ferocity of the 3rd had taken its toll on Ruiz also. One thing is certain. Ruiz was a diligent fighter and very patient. He was sticking to the advice of his corner and biding his time. He could see that Joshua had not fully recovered but did not want to throw everything at him immediately. He set about walking him down and trying to break him down with head shots then body shots. Patience.

With just over two minutes of the round remaining Joshua caught Ruiz with a left hook similar to the punch that had floored the challenger in the third round. Ruiz swallowed it whole, shook his head and continued to stalk the bigger man. It was an ominous juncture in the fight. If Joshua had not feared defeat before that point, he must surely be worried now.

A little later with just under a minute and a half of the round remaining Joshua did the strangest of things. He stepped back and took a deep breath. Not just using his mouth but drawing his hands up over his chest just like a textbook breathing exercise. That was a poker "tell" if ever there was one. Ruiz stopped briefly and smiled as he watched Joshua trying to fill his lungs. Ruiz knew that Joshua was gassed out. At this stage in the fight the 'chubby kid' looked in a lot better shape than the chiselled, muscular Joshua.

Round 5:

A relatively quiet round with only a few exchanges. It looked to all observers as if Anthony Joshua was starting to emerge from the fog. Some mobility had returned, and he looked in a better place. Joshua was still trying to keep the smaller man off him, but Ruiz was persistent.

Ruiz was displaying remarkable ability to stick to his team's game plan. By this point Ruiz not only knew that Joshua could not hurt him, but that he (Ruiz), could hurt the bigger man. Patience.

During the interval McCracken continued drilling the message into Joshua. "Jab, jab, right hand." Plus; "When you catch him don't move in, don't look for power, look to box." Excellent advice from an experienced boxing professional. McCracken could see that Ruiz was not going to be knocked out. Joshua had to box at full reach if he was going to win this fight. More importantly McCracken could probably see what would happen if the two men went toe-to-toe and slugged it out.

Round 6:

This was a round of two halves. In the opening half things were looking up for Joshua as it looked like he was getting back into his sharpest work. Everything pointed to him clearing his head and starting to box throughout the latter half of the fight. He was certainly following the advice from his corner.

But then with just under a minute remaining Ruiz began to do the unthinkable. The shorter man with inferior reach was starting to outbox the British fighter. Ruiz was catching Joshua with long range jabs to the head and chest forcing the champion back. It was an ominous sign as the fight was only at the half-way point.

At the interval, having seemingly found his legs and gotten back into the fight, Joshua asked his trainer a very odd question "What shots will catch him?"

Trainer Robert McCracken replied with some bizarre advice. "Left and right. Left and right long then look for your shot on the side". Joshua then asked another strange question. "What shot should I watch out for?"

Judging by the way the fight was going, 'absolutely any shot that Ruiz throws' would have been the only worthwhile answer. But McCracken responded with "The jab and the right hand. Come on." What else could he say? The champion was clearly totally confused and in deep trouble. Meanwhile his corner was out of ideas and just like their fighter they were in survival mode.

Round 7:

> *"Anthony, don't underestimate this little fat boy.*
> *I'm coming for you."*

Andy Ruiz had warned Joshua several times.

Before the round Ruiz's trainer Manny Robles told him that Joshua was hurt and that now was the time to go to the head.

After only 30 seconds of the round Ruiz opened up with a ferocious two-fisted assault. Andy Ruiz could smell blood. He could sense victory. The attack lasted only a few seconds but ended with Joshua unable to stay upright. So many punches – twelve in all - most of them landing, in such a short burst is not very common in heavyweight boxing. Joshua had certainly never faced that kind of quick and sustained attack.

Thirty-five seconds into the round Joshua was down for the third time in the fight. He got up almost immediately while the referee was still waving Ruiz to a neutral corner. The referee gave Joshua every chance. Continuing the count while Joshua tried to look composed. Just before the referee allowed the fight to resume, Joshua looked over to Ruiz and smiled while raising his eyebrows. As if to say; 'I am still here. Do you think you got me?' Was it bluff or just the action of a confused fighter? What was going on in Joshua's mind? He must have been thinking; 'what can I do here? I am getting weaker, while he is getting stronger. I cannot stop his attacks.'

It was as if he knew what was coming. Anthony Joshua was in deep trouble. He knew the titles were slipping away and at this stage he also knew there was nothing he could do to stop it.

Ruiz went in for the finish. A little over one minute into the round, another quick flurry of two-fisted activity and Joshua went down on one knee in the centre of the ring. Rather than immediately trying to get up Joshua spat out his gumshield.

If anyone still doubted that this was Andy Ruiz' night or thought that Joshua may still rally again and fight to the end, then that one action surely signalled the end. Joshua's reign as heavyweight champion was over the second that he spat out his gumshield. It was the sign of a defeated man. At this stage Joshua was exhausted, he had no plan B and had run out of gas. He was being beaten up in front of his fans and he just wanted the nightmare to end.

Joshua did get up at the count of seven but walked over to his own corner away from the referee, leaving his gumshield in the centre of the ring for the referee to scoop up. He may have been trying to buy a few precious extra seconds, but the referee could see that there was no desire to continue. The body language said it all. The referee waved off the fight at one minute thirty seconds of round 7.

It wasn't supposed to happen, but it had. Andy Ruiz was the new heavyweight champion of the world. The images of the 'chubby kid' bouncing for joy in the centre of the ring with his arms held high beamed all around the world.

Aftermath

"I'm willing to die inside the ring to become the first
Mexican heavyweight champion of the world.
And that's what we're gonna do".

Andy Ruiz Jr.

Ruiz wanted the title so bad but was not prepared to put in the hard work to keep it. Even before the shock waves had settled there was talk of an immediate rematch.

Six months, six days after arguably the biggest shock in boxing history, Anthony Joshua regained all the belts he lost back in June of the same year. Joshua beat Andy Ruiz Jr. on points by a unanimous decision, winning almost every round according to the ringside judges. Nobody disputed the result. It was a clear victory and one that was wildly celebrated by Joshua's promotional team and by his fans in the media. The talk was of how Joshua had made this amazing comeback and "schooled" Ruiz over the 12 rounds. Joshua was hailed as an incredible athlete for being able to reverse the disappointment of 6 months earlier. If the words of Joshua's ever-growing team were to be believed this was one of the greatest boxing comebacks of all time. Joshua did indeed perform well on the night and thoroughly deserved his victory. But there was another side to the story.

At the rematch – held in Saudi Arabia - Andy Ruiz registered another huge shock before a punch was even thrown. He entered the ring looking even flabbier and heavier than he did for the first fight. Ruiz was nowhere near the man who had shocked the world the previous June. Everyone could see that the second Ruiz de-robed before the first bell. Those who had seen the weigh-in already knew it. Ruiz was over 15 pounds heavier than he was for the first fight and it was clear where all of those extra pounds had gone. At 283½ pounds (128.5kg) Ruiz was far heavier than he had been for all but his first two contests as a professional. Far heavier than what many considered his ideal fighting weight of around 250 to 255 pounds.

In contrast Joshua was a svelte 237 pounds (107.5kg), the lightest he had weighed since his early fights. While one fighter had trained hard in order to increase stamina and mobility, the other was obviously not going to be fit enough to impose himself on his opponent. Ruiz needed to be fast on his feet and have the stamina to maintain an aggressive onslaught. He did not have that level of fitness. Joshua on the other hand needed to be fast on his feet with the stamina to be able to hit and run for twelve rounds. It was immediately apparent by his lighter frame that this is what he had trained for.

Many people including some great boxers past and present were telling Joshua not to take an immediate rematch with Ruiz. There were cries of 'Ruiz is all wrong for Joshua' and 'the outcome will be the same'. Many suggested that Joshua should take another fight or two and regroup. Once again Joshua deserves a great deal of respect for doing what he wanted to do. He had clearly worked exceptionally hard training for the rematch to be able to box in a completely different manner than he was accustomed to. It was not Joshua's fault that Ruiz had not trained with the same dedication.

Joshua not only trained to fight differently; he also had demons to overcome. Psychologically, a rematch so soon after the loss and with no tune up fight(s) was a massive barrier and Joshua managed to overcome it.

Not only had Joshua regained the heavyweight titles in an immediate rematch; he did so only six months after losing the first fight. Joshua deserves recognition and respect for this feat. Joshua defied the odds in his rematch with Ruiz to join a small but elite list of fighters. Only four boxers have regained the heavyweight title in an immediate rematch: Floyd Patterson beating Ingemar Johansson in 1960, Muhammad Ali beating Leon Spinks in 1978, Lennox Lewis beating Hasim Rahman in 2001, and now Anthony Joshua beating Andy Ruiz in 2019.

Immediately after the fight Ruiz interrupted Joshua's ring interview to demand a third fight. Right at that moment a trilogy fight would have seemed the obvious thing for both fighters. However, in the post-fight press conference Ruiz admitted he ate too much, partied too hard, and basically did not take his first defence (the Joshua rematch) seriously. Such admissions did not go down well with neither boxing fans nor pundits. As a result many turned against Ruiz. He could have said, that Joshua simply ran away for 12 rounds fearing his power and kept his partying ways to himself. Maybe then he could have drummed up some interest in a trilogy fight. Instead, he was honest and that is not always the best policy in sports, especially boxing. In his particular case, it was even worse. After all the talk of representing his Mexican heritage and becoming the first ever Mexican heavyweight champion, Ruiz admitted being overweight, out of shape and too lazy to train. That was never going to go down well.

His trainer Robles revealed in interviews following the return fight that he tried everything he could to motivate Ruiz. All to no avail. Robles talked to Ruiz about leaving a legacy and being a role model to all the Mexican-American youth. That never worked. When reminders that he was representing the Mexican people was not enough motivation Robles tried the financial angle. Ruiz could make huge sums from only a few successful defences of the titles. That too was not enough. Ruiz seemed content that he had made enough money and would make even more in the rematch. Presumably he was looking no further than the investment he thought he needed for his (and his father's) construction company. We may never know for sure.

It seems unlikely that Ruiz will be able to maintain the kind of discipline he so clearly lacked after making history. How can he now, not only regain such dedication and discipline but sustain it for a year or more? For two training camps and in between fights. Because that is what he will need to do if he is to get the opportunity of that trilogy fight. Joshua's promoter Eddie Hearn clearly wants nothing to do with a fit and agile Ruiz. He has already said that he can have his third fight with Joshua if he gets a couple of wins against ranked fighters under his belt. What are the odds of that happening? Hearn appears convinced that it will never happen and judging by Ruiz' past it does look exceedingly unlikely. And that is a real shame for three good reasons.

One: Andy Ruiz can fight. He has good boxing skill and a tough chin. Ruiz deserves that third fight if only because there is unfinished business there for him after he clearly let himself and his countrymen down in the second fight. But only if he makes a genuine effort to get fit.

Two: Joshua will still have that nagging doubt that he cannot beat a fully fit Ruiz. He may not come out and admit it in public, but it will be secretly gnawing away at his pride. He did fantastically well in the return fight, but he knows he beat an unfit champion. He knows it was not the same fighter he met in New York city.

Third, and finally: Boxing fans deserve the trilogy. Great heavyweight trilogies do not come along that often and always generate huge interest (only one in the last 20 years; Tyson Fury vs Deontay Wilder). Joshua-Ruiz has the makings of a great trilogy and fight fans know all too well that there is unfinished business. It is currently even at one win apiece, but the first was a devastating KO win compared to a points victory in the second. A third fight is needed to decide who really is the best of these two massive heavyweights. Boxing fans deserve the answer to that question. But only if Ruiz intends to take a third fight seriously.

What everyone saw when the two fighters stepped into the ring for the rematch was that one had trained exceptionally well for a different style of fight while the other had seemingly done no training at all.

Most fighters would take a week or two off following such a famous victory. Especially those with young families. Then get back to the gym in training for the next fight. In Ruiz' case a first defence of his newly won titles, whether that was a Joshua rematch or any other opponent. In his position Ruiz would not even need to stay in his own gym. Given the newfound fame and TV chat show appearances Ruiz could easily train while moving around for a few weeks. Boxing gyms can be found in every town and city in the country. After all, what gym would not want the "Mexican Rocky" to use their facilities? Right? Actually, in this case, wrong. Andy Ruiz went on a two-month long hiatus. When he finally decided to return to training, he was not always there. Ruiz appeared on so many interviews on television and other platforms. Even appearing on Mike Tyson's YouTube channel. He could and should be allowed to do such work, albeit as an aside to the rigours of training. But what he shouldn't have done was neglect his training. Instead of fitting in the public appearances around his boxing workouts Ruiz was fitting the odd training session in between parties and stardom.

Andy Ruiz was not yet one year old in February 1990 when James "Buster" Douglas shocked the world in destroying Mike Tyson. But like everyone who knows anything about boxing he would have known all about the immediate downfall of Douglas. The squandering of his new-found glory is as infamous as his winning the titles was famous. Douglas failed to train properly for his first (and only) defence to Evander Holyfield. Losing his titles after gaining over 15 pounds in weight and reportedly ordering pizza to eat in the sauna when he should have been training. Incredibly Ruiz also came into his first defence (and Joshua rematch) some 15 pounds flabbier.

There is a great story in boxing circles which describes events at the weigh-in for the James "Buster" Douglas vs Evander Holyfield fight in Las Vegas in 1990. It is said that when Douglas stripped off to be weighed, people ran from the room into the casinos to bet on Holyfield. So evident was the lack of training on Douglas' part.

There are no casinos or gambling spots to run to in Saudi Arabia. But any non-Saudis present for the Joshua vs Ruiz 2 weigh-in would surely have been on the telephone to friends back home to make a bet on Joshua.

"Those who cannot remember the past
are condemned to repeat it."

Writer George Santayana, 1905
from his book 'The Life of Reason'

The slimmed down Anthony Joshua deserves congratulations for regaining the titles he lost six months earlier in New York. But Joshua's redemption was largely thanks to a fatter and slower Andy Ruiz who made it a lot easier than it should have been by forgetting (relatively) recent boxing history.

Any hopes of a trilogy fight between Joshua and Ruiz were further hampered in 2021. Since regaining the titles (at the time of writing) Joshua has fought twice. In his first defence 12 months later, Joshua beat Bulgarian Kubrat Pulev via ninth round knockout. Then on September 25th, 2021, Joshua lost all the belts again. It was a mandatory defence for the WBO belt although all belts were put on the line. This time the opponent was the former undisputed cruiserweight champion, the Ukrainian, Oleksandr Usyk.

The Ukrainian won via unanimous points decision. It was another shock although nothing on the scale of the Andy Ruiz upset. Usyk was in only his third heavyweight fight but had been a genuine star at cruiserweight as well as an outstanding amateur. Once again it was the physical differences between the two boxers that generated any level of shock in the result. Usyk is recognised as superior boxer compared to Joshua, but few expected the much larger Joshua to lose.

Joshua invoked the rematch clause and should have a second fight against Usyk. 'AJ' must now try to regain that focus, energy and determination he found in preparing for the rematch with Ruiz. It would be a truly incredible achievement if Joshua were to regain the titles again. At the time of writing the Joshua-Usyk rematch looks unlikely to take place as Usyk's his home country is involved in a conflict with Russia.

What happened to Andy Ruiz in the 6 months or so after the rematch is nothing short of a mystery. Many reporters have tried and failed to get that elusive interview. Ruiz's ex-trainer Manny Robles has himself been interviewed many times and even he did not know what the former champion had been up to or was doing.

Ruiz even split from the man who had guided him to that famous victory, his trainer Manny Robles. Fighters and trainers regularly part ways and for a number of reasons. What happened with Ruiz however was complete isolation. Nobody, not even Robles, saw or heard from Ruiz for many months after the Joshua rematch.

At the time of writing Ruiz had been working with a new trainer, Eddy Reynoso, who trains pound-for-pound king Saúl 'Canelo'

Álvarez. After 18 months of mostly self-imposed exile, Ruiz Jr. had shed nearly 30 pounds in weight to make his return to the ring against fellow Mexican-American, Chris 'The Nightmare' Areola on May 01, 2021.

Andy Ruiz won the fight via a unanimous points decision but not before being dropped – for only the second time in his career – in the second round. Ruiz recovered quickly and dominated the fight with his fast combinations.

Will this return victory be enough to keep Ruiz in the gym? Or will he see it as a lacklustre performance (relatively speaking) and once again withdraw into his shell? Ruiz soon picked up an injury which hampered any further training and potential fights through the end of 2021.

All boxing fans would surely like to see a fit – and relatively lighter – Andy Ruiz back in the heavyweight title contention. Only time will tell if he has the discipline and hunger to make it back to those dizzy heights of June 1st, 2019.

Was Andy Ruiz treated like a book judged by its cover?

His record spoke volumes and was there for everyone to see. The twenty-one KO wins – a knockout percentage of over 63% - was common knowledge in boxing circles and easy enough for the most casual of sports fans to find online.

Joshua had the Olympic gold medal, but Ruiz arguably had a better amateur record. Ruiz went into the fight with the same number of (pro) knockout wins as Joshua. Twenty-one apiece. Ruiz had had ten more fights overall but that does not diminish his knockout wins. Many of the knockout victims were handled with the same ruthless efficiency as many of Joshua's early finishes. There were similarities there at least.

There were some similarities between Jarrell Miller and Ruiz, their similar physical dimensions and their go forward stalking style of fighting. Ruiz however, had something in his arsenal that Miller did not. At least, that is, Miller had not displayed it in his key fights. Ruiz possessed great hand speed. Very fast for a heavyweight. When he let his hands go, Ruiz was able to fire off rapid two-fisted combinations. It is hard to prepare for that kind of speed if your sparring partners do not have it. You can replicate the size, even the power of a fighter like Ruiz, but it is highly unlikely that Joshua would have found anyone to spar with who possessed the speed of combinations that Ruiz would throw at him. Particularly at that short notice.

Joseph Parker was the only boxer to take Joshua the distance before the Joshua-Ruiz rematch. Parker has very similar physical attributes to Joshua when compared to Ruiz. Long 76" (193cm) reach advantage, 6' 4" (193cm) height advantage and a powerful looking frame. Yet Ruiz took Parker the distance. Ruiz also managed to ruffle a few of Parker's feathers in their 12-round tussle. The style of Ruiz worked well against the bigger man.

The Ruiz vs Parker fight should have been a blueprint for the Joshua vs Ruiz scrap. Had Joshua or his team really studied the Parker vs Ruiz fight? If they had it is hard to believe that they did not know what was coming.

The Joshua fight was very much a "Rocky" movie moment for Ruiz and boxing fans. The 'Mexican Rocky'. Many may not have viewed Andy Ruiz quite as Rocky Bilboa, but Joshua was certainly looked upon as an Apollo Creed like character. And the fight with a fairy-tale ending was in the Mecca of boxing, Madison Square Garden, New York City.

Ringside commentator Sugar Ray Leonard showed great respect for Ruiz's amazing upset victory with his comments after the fight:

> "This is a surprise to boxing fans and the world. You (Andy) are the epitome of don't judge a book by its cover. I am impressed. Ruiz fought like a big man and fought like Joshua should have. Andy, you proved all of us wrong, and that's why I love boxing."

In conclusion, it is difficult to change the way we see other people because vision is our primary sense. Humans are very visually biased creatures. It is easy to be fooled by what we see. What we see we tend to believe. We notice the biggest and most perfectly formed things and we think they are the best. We should really focus on the true value of everything we see. Focus on what lies beneath and the background story of what we see. Try to bring out the positives in anything that may not, at first, appear to be the biggest, the best or the flashiest. And we should never forget the most important lesson of all: **Don't judge a book by its cover!**

The Undercard...

If the result of the Joshua vs Ruiz fight went to plan and ended in a quick and easy victory for 'AJ' then the fans may have felt short changed. Perhaps promoter Hearn had this in mind when he stacked an undercard with some interesting encounters...

The promising British boxer, Josh Kelly faced off against the more experienced and perhaps unfortunately named Ray Robinson from Philadelphia in a welterweight contest. The Philly fighter clearly sees the irony and has been used to growing up with the pressure that name brings in boxing circles. His alias, 'The New' Ray Robinson, also shows that he has a sense of fun.

Kelly boxed in the 2016 Olympics and made his professional debut in April 2017. Within two years he had won nine fights with no defeats. Six of those wins he won by knockout.

The fight ended in a majority draw with Kelly getting the nod from one judge. It was a step up in class for Kelly of whom great things are expected. But his story is nothing compared to that of Robinson.

Robinson grew up in a world of domestic violence. His mother was a drug addict with seven kids to raise. Both Ray and his mother were beaten by his stepdad. Robinson was thrown down a flight of stairs at one time and his mother was shot at during his early childhood. Robinson entered a boxing gym at eight years of age and fell in love with the sport.

Then at the age of thirteen, while sparring, he suffered a freak accident when he slipped and injured his neck. Surgeons needed to graft part of his hip bone into his neck. The accident almost left him paralysed and Robinson thought that it may have been caused by being thrown down that staircase by his stepdad. Fortunately, he recovered and was able to return to boxing which he saw as his way out of poverty.

By 16 he was winning national tournaments, was given a college place and went from strength to strength. He was picked for the USA boxing team and as a result was getting paid to train. This was a dream come true for Robinson considering his poor background. In December 2006, age 20, Robinson made his professional debut and quickly racked up eleven wins in less than three years.

In December 2009 Robinson lost his unbeaten record in his 12th fight. A majority decision against Brad Solomon. In his next fight, seven months later, Robinson faced the highly rated, upcoming Shawn Porter over ten rounds. Robinson lost by unanimous decision even though he thought he had won the fight. It was a 2nd loss in succession and boxing politics being what it is probably meant it would now be even harder to get the big fights. Porter meanwhile would go on to fight for world titles and many top contenders.

Disillusioned after the points loss to Porter, Ray decided to give up boxing and spent the next 12 months taking regular jobs before a chance meeting with a local (Philadelphia) promoter brought him back to the sport. Robinson was asked to headline a local event in September 2011. He took the fight which he won by a seventh round TKO and began to rebuild his career.

In 2015 while preparing for his debut on HBO boxing, Robinson was involved in a car accident that (again) put him on the side lines, this time for a year and a half. Robinson returned to the ring in October 2016 and went on to win 4 fights. But having been unable to fight for over a year was going to further hamper any chance he had of getting a big career defining fight. In February 2018 Robinson lost for a third time. This was followed by a majority draw over 10 rounds just three months before facing Josh Kelly in New York. That first draw was against the much-fancied Lithuanian Egidijus Kavaliauskas who had an unbeaten 21-0 record.

'The New' Ray Robinson's story is a truly inspiring one. One of never giving up and always believing. While some fighters seem to have their career paths well defined others have to do it the hard way. Ray Robinson is definitely one of the latter. He may still get his chance as he is still at his peak. Meanwhile, Josh Kelly's progress in the division took a hit when he lost his unbeaten record via a sixth round TKO to David Avanesyan in in February 2021.

Former contender Chris Algieri squared off against another rising British star Tommy Coyle in a super lightweight bout. Algieri had a record of 23 wins and 3 losses. All of those losses were against top opposition and he had only been stopped once against top pound for pound contender Errol Spence Jr. His other two losses were against Amir Khan and Manny Pacquiao. Back in 2014 he had even taken a split decision victory against tough as steel Russian Ruslan Provodnikov. Algieri's three defeats were at welterweight and was never comfortable at the slightly bigger weight. Coyle had a similar record – on paper – but he hadn't fought at the same level as Algieri. Coyle had some success early in the second round but failed to capitalise on it and Algieri recovered and began to break Coyle down over the next few rounds. Just over one minute into round four Algieri caught Coyle with a left hook to the body which clearly hurt the British fighter. He followed it up with a few more and Coyle went down. Despite this setback Coyle showed great courage to rally back and make a real scrap of this bout. But bravery alone is not enough to win fights and the American's greater experience showed. When Coyle staggered back to his corner at the end of round number eight his trainer Jamie Moore did the right thing and stopped the fight.

Many spectators had still not taken their seats when Ireland's Katie Taylor met the Belgian Delphine Persoon for the undisputed female lightweight unification bout. Those absent spectators missed a thriller. If the main bout of the evening had gone according to plan with an easy win for Joshua, then this fight would have been the best on the card. A ferocious non-stop slugfest which many called the greatest women's fight they had ever seen. All belts were on the line. Taylor held the WBA, IBF and WBO titles while Persoon was the WBC champion.

Taylor, like Anthony Joshua, was a gold medal winner at the 2012 London Olympic games and had been fast tracked, going 13 fights unbeaten to take three belts. Persoon on the other hand had taken longer, with 44 fights to her name. The Belgian works as a railway policewoman and had been boxing professionally since 2009. She had also previously held the IBF lightweight title but was stripped of the belt for failing to make a defence.

Persoon hardly put a foot back as she relentlessly pursued Taylor. At the half-way point it looked like Persoon was winning the fight. Taylor then picked up the pace and looked to be getting the upper hand for a few rounds. However, Persoon never stopped pushing forward and although there were no knockdowns the last round could have easily been scored as a 10-8 to the Belgian.

It was a very close contest with many observers believing that Persoon had done enough to take all the belts. However, the judges gave it the Irish boxer by a majority decision. Two judges had Taylor ahead by just one round with the third scoring it a draw.

The rematch was arranged for August 22, 2020 in an event to be staged in the garden of Eddie Hearn's promotional headquarters. Although part of a pay-for-view TV broadcast the event took place with no audience due to restrictions on sporting crowds brought about by the coronavirus 'pandemic'. This time Katie Taylor left no doubt in anyone's mind who had won the fight. Persoon, as relentless as in the first fight had no answer to Taylor who boxed a clever fight. Unlike the first meeting Taylor did not get drawn into a slugfest and controlled the fight at her own pace.

The chief supporting bout was for the WBA world super-middleweight title. Callum Smith from Liverpool, England making his first defence of the title against Hassan N'Dam NJikam, a Cameroon born fighter boxing out of France.

Smith entered the bout with a perfect 25-0 record and was looking for a good performance in order to set up a huge match with one of boxing's biggest stars in Saúl 'Canelo' Alvarez. He certainly did not disappoint. N'Jikam, with a record of 37-3, went down in the first and second rounds thanks to solid left-hand lead shots from Smith. N'Jikam never looked in too much trouble but it only seemed a matter of time. In the third round with only 15 seconds remaining Smith threw an explosive right hand that flattened the challenger. Although he got up at the count of eight the referee correctly waved the fight off.

This was a confident show by Smith who showed greater counter punching for the first two knockdowns. Even more impressive was the one punch power he displayed. All three knockdowns were single punches. Following the fight Smith said he did not want to wait around for the Saúl 'Canelo' Álvarez fight but wanted to stay active. Wise words from an intelligent fighter. However, the showdown with Álvarez, did materialise 18 months later. The Mexican pound-for-pound number one taking Smith's belt on his way toward unifying the division.

APPENDICES

Some notes for those not too familiar with boxing…

Lineal Champion

The term 'lineal champion' denotes the man who beat the man who beat the man… When Joe Frazier met Mohammed Ali in "The Fight of the Century" in 1971, he was considered the world champion and held the WBC and WBA belts. But many people still considered Ali the true champion. He was in fact the lineal champion. Ali never lost the title in the ring as he was stripped of the title due to his political stance on the Vietnam war. When Frazier won the fight, he not only retained the WBC and WBA titles, but he also became the (new) lineal champion.

Sometimes the continuity of the lineal champion is broken. If a boxer retires and does not fight again there is no way anyone can beat them. For example, when Rocky Marciano retired undefeated his run as the lineal champion ended and a new one began.

Opinions differ as to the value of the lineal championship. Often the best in the division does not necessarily get the chance to meet the lineal champion in the ring. However, there are others who believe it is more important than the myriad of "world" titles currently being fought for.

Boxing's Weight Divisions Explained

Many readers may already be familiar with the weight classes and terminology, however, newcomers to the sport of boxing may find this section helpful. Since the early 1900s there were only 8 weight divisions (or classes). These are often referred to as the "traditional" or "classic" weight classes. The classic weight classes are:

Heavyweight	200+ lbs (+90.71 kg)
Light heavyweight	168–175 lbs (76.20 - 79.37 kg)
Middleweight	154–160 lbs (69.85 - 72.57 kg)

Welterweight	140–147 lbs (63.50 - 66.67 kg)
Lightweight	130–135 lbs (58.96 - 61.23 kg)
Featherweight	122–126 lbs (55.33 - 57.15 kg)
Bantamweight	115–118 lbs (52.16 - 53.52 kg)
Flyweight	108–112 lbs (48.98 - 50.80 kg)

Over time more weight divisions were introduced. These sat in between two of classic weight divisions so are sometimes referred to as the "tweener divisions". These newer divisions only started to gain recognition from the late 1950s but are now well established.

These inter-weight divisions are:

Cruiser, 175–200 lbs (79.37 - 90.71 kg), between light-heavy and heavyweight

Super-middleweight, 160–168 lbs (72.57 - 76.20 kg), between middleweight and light-heavyweight

Super-welterweight, 147–154 lbs (66.67 - 69.85 kg), between welterweight and middleweight

Super-lightweight, 135–140 lbs (61.23 - 63.50 kg), between lightweight and welterweight

Super-featherweight 126–130 lbs (57.15 - 58.96 kg), between featherweight and lightweight

Super-bantamweight 118–122 lbs (53.52 - 55.33 kg), between bantamweight and featherweight

Super-flyweight 112–115 lbs (50.80 - 52.16 kg), between flyweight and bantamweight

There are also two newer, lighter weight divisions. These are:

Light-flyweight 105–108 lbs (47.62 - 48.98 kg)

Straw-weight 105 lbs (47.62 kg)

These newer divisions are mostly named with either a "super", "light" or "junior" in front of their names. For example, in between lightweight and welterweight there is the super-lightweight division. This is also called light-welterweight or junior-welterweight. If the higher (classic) weight division is mentioned, then "junior" and "light" are directly interchangeable. If the lower (classic) weight class is used, then the word is preceded by "super".

Some weight classes only use one term. Super-middleweight can only use "super" as the weight above is called light-heavyweight. "Junior-light-heavyweight" or "light-light-heavyweight" do not make sense. For that reason, this text has tried to use "super" to describe the inter-weight classes, although there will be uses of the other two terms ("junior" and "light").

Boxing Acronyms

Acronym	Denotes...
IBF	International Boxing Federation (founded 1976)
WBA	World Boxing Association (founded 1921)
WBC	World Boxing Council (founded 1963)
WBO	World Boxing Organisation (founded 1988)
WBU	World Boxing Union (founded 1995 and not universally recognised)
MD	Majority Decision – 2 judges score for the same fighter, 3rd judge scores fight a draw
SD	Split Decision - Judges score fight 2 to 1 in favour of the winner
TKO	Technical Knockout
UD	Unanimous (points) Decision
IBO	International Boxing Organisation (founded 1988 and not universally recognised)

Printed in Great Britain
by Amazon